PANZER
COMMANDERS
OF THE
WESTERN FRONT

The Stackpole Military History Series

THE AMERICAN CIVIL WAR
Cavalry Raids of the Civil War
Ghost, Thunderbolt, and Wizard
Pickett's Charge
Witness to Gettysburg

WORLD WAR II
Armor Battles of the Waffen-SS, 1943–45
Army of the West
Australian Commandos
The B-24 in China
Backwater War
The Battle of Sicily
Beyond the Beachhead
The Brandenburger Commandos
The Brigade
Bringing the Thunder
Coast Watching in World War II
Colossal Cracks
A Dangerous Assignment
D-Day to Berlin
Dive Bomber!
A Drop Too Many
Eagles of the Third Reich
Exit Rommel
Fist from the Sky
Flying American Combat Aircraft of World War II
Forging the Thunderbolt
Fortress France
The German Defeat in the East, 1944–45
German Order of Battle, Vol. 1
German Order of Battle, Vol. 2
German Order of Battle, Vol. 3
The Germans in Normandy
Germany's Panzer Arm in World War II
GI Ingenuity
The Great Ships
Grenadiers
Infantry Aces
Iron Arm
Iron Knights
Kampfgruppe Peiper at the Battle of the Bulge
Kursk
Luftwaffe Aces
Massacre at Tobruk

Mechanized Juggernaut or Military Anachronism?
Messerschmitts over Sicily
Michael Wittmann, Vol. 1
Michael Wittmann, Vol. 2
Mountain Warriors
The Nazi Rocketeers
On the Canal
Operation Mercury
Packs On!
Panzer Aces
Panzer Aces II
Panzer Commanders of the Western Front
The Panzer Legions
Panzers in Winter
The Path to Blitzkrieg
Retreat to the Reich
Rommel's Desert Commanders
Rommel's Desert War
The Savage Sky
A Soldier in the Cockpit
Soviet Blitzkrieg
Stalin's Keys to Victory
Surviving Bataan and Beyond
T-34 in Action
Tigers in the Mud
The 12th SS, Vol. 1
The 12th SS, Vol. 2
The War against Rommel's Supply Lines
War in the Aegean

THE COLD WAR / VIETNAM
Cyclops in the Jungle
Flying American Combat Aircraft: The Cold War
Here There Are Tigers
Land with No Sun
Street without Joy
Through the Valley

WARS OF THE MIDDLE EAST
Never-Ending Conflict

GENERAL MILITARY HISTORY
Carriers in Combat
Desert Battles
Guerrilla Warfare

PANZER COMMANDERS OF THE WESTERN FRONT

German Tank Generals in World War II

Samuel W. Mitcham, Jr.

STACKPOLE
BOOKS

Published by
STACKPOLE BOOKS
5067 Ritter Road
Mechanicsburg, PA 17055
www.stackpolebooks.com

Cover photo from Robert J. Edwards Jr. and Michael H. Pruett, Field Uniforms of German Army Panzer Forces in World War II *(Winnipeg, Canada: J. J. Fedorowicz Publishing Inc., 1993).*

Cover design by Tracy Patterson

Printed in the United States of America

10 9 8 7 6 5 4 3 2 1

Library of Congress Cataloging-in-Publication Data

Mitcham, Samuel W.
  Panzer commanders of the Western Front : German tank generals in World War II / Samuel W. Mitcham, Jr.
       p. cm. — (Stackpole military history series)
  Includes bibliographical references and index.
  ISBN 978-0-8117-3507-0
  1. World War, 1939–1945—Tank warfare. 2. World War, 1939–1945—Campaigns—Western Front. 3. Generals—Germany—Biography. I. Title.
  D757.54.M57 2008
  940.54'13430922—dc22
  [B]
                                              2008003164

Contents

List of Maps vii

Introduction ix

Chapter 1   Baron Hans von Funck 1

Chapter 2   Baron Harald von Elverfeldt 59

Chapter 3   Erwin Jollasse 81

Chapter 4   Baron Heinrich von Luettwitz 113

Chapter 5   Fritz Bayerlein 153

Appendix A   Table of Comparative Ranks 195

Appendix B   German Staff Positions in World War II 197

Appendix C   Characteristics of Selected
World War II Tanks 199

Notes 201

Bibliography 241

Index 243

List of Maps

1.1   The Manstein Plan 10

1.2   The North African Theater of Operations 17

1.3   The Eastern Front 24

1.4   The Battles of Encirclement on the
Eastern Front, 1941 26

1.5   The Vyazma-Bryansk Encirclement, 1941 28

1.6   The Area of Operations of Army Group B, 1944 38

1.7   The Normandy Front, July 1, 1944 40

1.8   The Battle of Mortain, August 6–7, 1944 43

1.9   The Falaise Sector, August 7–11, 1944 44

1.10   The Falaise Pocket, August 13, 1944 48

1.11   The Allied Drive to the Seine 51

2.1   The Battle of Moscow, January 1–14, 1942 66

3.1   The Battle of Kiev, 1941 88

4.1   The Battle of Kursk, 1943 126

4.2   The Western Front 128

4.3   The Battle of Villers-Bocage 132

4.4   The Battle of the Ardennes,
December 26, 1944–January 16, 1945 149

5.1   The Second Battle of El Alamein,
October 23–24, 1942 161

5.2   The Battle of the Ruhr Pocket, 1945 187

Introduction

This book is largely, though not entirely, based on the papers of Friedrich von Stauffenberg, a man who became a close friend of mine, and focuses on the lives of five panzer generals who fought on the Western Front in 1944. The book is unique in that the stories of the five men covered here are not the standard-issue biographies of famous men, such as Erwin Rommel, the "Desert Fox," or Field Marshal Walter Model, "the Fuehrer's Fireman," or Heinz Guderian, the "Father of the Blitzkrieg"; rather, they are about individuals who are most obscure. Without men like them, however, Hitler could not have won his victories, because the *blitzkrieg* would not have worked. Today, more than sixty years after the war, it is becoming more and more rare to find important firsthand information and sources. I believe that this book will be considered an important firsthand work because it is based on the papers of an astute firsthand observer, and even the most knowledgeable World War II expert likely will learn things from it.

Werner Theodor Friedrich Hubert Maria Schenk, Graf von Stauffenberg, was born in Stuttgart in 1905, the son of a general staff officer. His father, Dr. Franz Wilhelm von Stauffenberg (1878–1950) served in various general staff positions during World War II and became a battalion commander. He was wounded and captured by the Americans in the battle of the Argonne Forest in 1918. He retired as a lieutenant colonel and later became chairman of the *Oberschwaebischen Elektrizitaetswerke*, the Upper Swabian Power Company. Friedrich's cousin was Col. Claus von Stauffenberg, who lost an arm and an eye while serving as chief of operations (Ia) of the 10th Panzer Division in Tunisia. Later, on July 20, 1944, Claus placed a bomb under Hitler's table and led the plot to overthrow the Nazi regime. Friedrich was severely injured in a bicycle accident when he was fourteen years old and thus was unable to go into the family profession, although he knew a great many members of the *Panzertruppen*.

Friedrich studied agriculture in Hungary and Southwest Africa (formerly German Southwest Africa and now Namibia) and received an advanced degree in Hungary. During the Nazi era, he worked for the *Reichskuratorium fuer Landwirtschaft* as an agricultural official. He married Christa Bauer during this period, but their marriage ended in divorce. In 1954, he married Erica Lassen of Hamburg. He had a daughter, apparently from the first marriage. He was reluctant to discuss this part of his life, so I never pressed the subject.

After World War II, Friedrich went into the banking business and worked for the deutsche Rentenbank. He lived in South America, where he came to know other German emigrants and helped them when he could. Later, he became an American citizen and a businessman in the Silver Springs, Maryland, near Washington, D.C. He wrote to me after one of my earlier books was published, and we developed a close personal friendship, had a lively correspondence, and talked often on the telephone. I was a professor at Henderson State University in Arkadelphia, Arkansas, at that time, and I visited him during my research trips to Washington. When I got a job offer from a large university, he advised me to stay at Henderson State. I certainly wish that I had listened to him.

In the mid-1980s, Friedrich attempted to write a book about the panzer officers. I tried to help him get it published, but without success. He knew so much, however, that it was incredible. During one of our conversations, I mentioned a theory I had about the battle of Sicily and expressed my decision to write a book about that campaign. Friedrich told me that he was a close friend of Gen. Hans Hube's former aide and even had part of the general's personnel file. I then invited him to coauthor the book with me. It was one of the best decisions I ever made. *The Battle of Sicily* was very successful. Unfortunately, Friedrich died in 1989, before the book was published.

Seeing that his illness would soon be fatal, Friedrich sent me his papers, two unpublished manuscripts, as well as the "201 Files," personal extracts of about fifty panzer officers. I used this material as a source for years. In 2006, Chris Evans, the history editor at Stackpole Books, noticed that I had cited the Stauffenberg Papers in one of my earlier books, which Stackpole was in the process of republishing as a paperback. Chris wanted to know whether I could write a book using the Stauffenberg Papers. I replied that a lot of information has come to light since Friedrich died, but yes, the papers could form the basis for a book, and I felt that I had become a good enough historian to fill in some of the blanks. (Friedrich, for example, lost contact with Gen. Erwin Jollasse and his family in 1945.) I went to work, and the result is what you now hold in your hand. It is up to the reader to determine how well I succeeded.

Incidentally, Stauffenberg's American friends called him Von.

In addition to Friedrich von Stauffenberg, I thank my wife, Donna, and my children, Lacy and Gavin, for their love and support. Thanks also to Melinda Matthews of the Interlibrary Loan Department at the University of Louisiana at Monroe for all of her help.

CHAPTER 1

Baron Hans von Funck

The family von Funck originated in East Prussia, probably as descendants of the Teutonic Knights who conquered the region in the twelfth century. Their earliest known ancestor flourished around the year 1355. The first *Freiherr* (Baron) von Funck was an official of the Prussian monarchy who died in 1643. One of Hans von Funck's later ancestors, Baron Carl von Funck, fought against Napoleon, rose to the rank of major general, and was killed in action during the battle of Leipzig in 1813.

Hans's father, Carl (1851–1913), was a Royal Prussian administrative official who ran a large rural district contiguous to his state near Aachen. He married Marie von Luetzow in 1887 and had two sons. Baron Albrecht von Funck, the older brother of the future panzer general, was born at Aachen on October 25, 1889. He entered the army in 1908, fought in the First World War, won the coveted *Erinritter* of the Order of St. John in 1917, and continued service under the *Reichswehr* through 1939, by which time he was a lieutenant colonel on the staff of the German ambassador to Belgrade. He later served as part of the occupation government in Yugoslavia, was captured by Tito's partisans at the end of the war, and died a colonel in a prison compound on October 17, 1945. He and his wife, *Freifrau* (Baroness) Lonnie von Gultlingen, had no children.

Baron Hans Emil Richard von Funck was born at the family estate on December 23, 1891, and grew to be a large, well-built youth. He was educated at the usual schools in nearby Elbing. His mother died in 1902, and his father subsequently remarried prior to his death in 1913.

Being orphaned at the age of twenty-three prompted Hans to volunteer for the army—he was urged on by his brother, already a *Leutnant* (second lieutenant), at the outbreak of World War I in August 1914 (see Appendix A for a Table of Comparative Ranks). On October 11, the younger Funck took the field with the 2nd Dragoon

Regiment, serving in one of the hard-pressed divisions facing the Russian onslaught in the east.

Tangentially involved in the victory of Tannenberg, Hans's regiment engaged in the pursuit of the retreating enemy, and he was awarded the Iron Cross, 2nd Class, in late 1914. On June 15, 1915, he was patented as a second lieutenant, retroactive to December 19, 1913, and continued as a platoon commander with the dragoons.

On April 12, 1916, he was appointed the ordnance (orderly) officer of his cavalry regiment, but his ability as an active commander led to his being transferred, as of May 10, to the acting command of the Machine Gun Section—a post he held until July 27, 1917, when he reluctantly accepted an appointment to equipment officer. Once again, however, his skill in active command resulted in his regimental commander returning him to field duty as a squadron leader on September 16, 1917.

The end of the war in November 1918 had little real effect on the status of units serving in the east, despite the Brest-Litovsk Treaty of earlier that year. White Russians, Poles, renegade Soviet bandits, and Ukrainian dissidents all squabbled along the German border, and the 2nd Dragoons was one of the few highly mobile forces available to oppose encroachments.

On February 15, 1919, Lieutenant Funck was again given command of the Machine Gun Squadron, which now included machine guns mounted on flatbed trucks and a few primitive armored cars. Thus, this early, Funck became a pioneer in mechanized forces. On April 1, 1923, he was promoted to *Oberleutnant* (first lieutenant) retroactive to April 1, 1914—thus guaranteeing his position in the 100,000-man *Reichswehr*, which was all Germany was allowed under the Treaty of Versailles.[1] Funck's promotion also confirmed his rank as machine-gun commander in the new 2nd Infantry Division, based at Stettin, Pomerania, on the mouth of the Oder.

On March 21, 1924, he took the standard requirement *Wehrkreis* examination for leadership ability, passing it with a better-than-average score. Funck's ability so impressed Lt. Gen. Erich von Tschischewitz, the commander at Stettin, that he secured for the lieutenant a slot in a course in senior leadership and tactics at the local war school from October 1, 1924, to September 30, 1925.[2]

Emerging with very high scores in his work, Funck was attached as an adjutant to General von Tschischewitz's 2nd Division staff, remaining in this capacity until the close of the general's period of command in September 1926. Interestingly enough, during this period, Capt. Heinz Guderian, who later became famous as the "Father of the Blitzkrieg," was acting as tactics instructor at the Stettin War School, having served under Tschischewitz when he was inspector of motor transport (1921–23). The general, if not a farseeing advocate of mechanization, certainly appreciated the use of vehicles in a modern army and did his best to promote the interests of both of these early proponents of armor.

In the fall of 1926, Tschischewitz left Stettin to assume command of *Gruppenkommando* (Army Group) 2 at Kassel; Captain Guderian and Oberleutnant von Funck returned to Berlin, where Funck was assigned a desk in the Motor Transport Branch of the *Reichswehrministerium* (Defense Ministry), a stint of duty that at least familiarized him with the ideas of the new motor branch. He became better acquainted with Guderian and one or two other young officers who later became important.

When the periodic rotation came up, on October 1, 1927, Funck was assigned to the 6th Cavalry Regiment, which was commanded by a Lieutenant Colonel Halm, a former inspector of motor transport. The lieutenant was given command of the motorized elements: the 1st Motorcycle Section, the 1st Signal Detachment, and the 1st Pioneer Company. On April 1, 1928, he was promoted to *Rittmeister* (captain of cavalry).

A month later, on May 1, the newly promoted captain was summoned to Berlin again, but this time by Maj. Gen. Edmund Wachenfeld,[3] the new chief of staff of Army Group 1, to supervise the organization of the motorized elements in the Berlin area—a task he performed assiduously until ordered to report again to the Defense Ministry on April 1, 1930.

Col. Oswald Lutz, the chief of staff to the inspector of motor transport, asked Major Guderian to take over a new mechanized battalion being formed in the Berlin area but needed a suitable replacement at the motorized arms carrier desk at the Inspectorate.[4] Guderian recommended Funck, who now reported to work with Guderian until Guderian left for his active assignment in February 1931. The *Rittmeister* labored at the arms desk duties until the fall of 1932, though in 1931 Lutz had become inspector of motor troops and Guderian became his chief of staff.

Meanwhile, Funck also had a personal life. It is not clear exactly what family relationships or outside circumstances played a part in the November 1915 marriage of the newly promoted Lt. Hans von Funck to Irmgard, daughter of Maj. Adolf von Kritter. The wedding was held in the Lutheran Church in Goettingen while the lieutenant was on leave in the Hessian city—none of which makes an explanation of subsequent events any easier.

The new Baroness von Funck remained in Goettingen, possibly because her stepmother-in-law was still in residence at the family estate at Aachen, or because she wanted to remain close to her own family. In any case, Hans tolerated the arrangement and apparently spent much of his leave with her in Hesse. On September 25, 1916, their first child, Hans Joachim Albrecht Wilhelm, was born at Goettingen, followed on July 17, 1918, by Ingeborg Ilse Emy Gerda Margarethe, and finally, on March 3, 1920, by Burkhard Karl Eberhard Joachim. But with Hans totally involved in his career, the marriage appears to have gone stale; by October 1932, the captain had acquired a small house at Neisse outside Berlin and had his elder son, age sixteen, with him and at school in the capital. Back on garrison duty at this time, Funck took command of the I Battalion of the 11th Cavalry Regiment (I/11th Cavalry), which was stationed near Berlin.

Again it fell to his duty to head up experimental mechanized units attached to the regiment—a task he had virtually accomplished by the summer of 1933. Meanwhile, the Weimar Republic had been replaced by the Third Reich under Chancellor Adolf Hitler. On July 1, 1933, a dazed Captain Funck was ordered to report again to the Reich Defense Ministry to take up the post of first adjutant to Gen. of Artillery Baron Werner von Fritsch, the newly appointed *Chef der Heeresleitung* (commander in chief of the army).[5]

Fritsch was not an innovative officer; an artilleryman but an enthusiastic horseman, he was cold, austere, and overly cautious. His adjutants nevertheless grew to admire and respect him, and Funck in particular enjoyed his daily walks with Fritsch through the Tiergarten, when the Prussian general was unusually urbane and cordial.

On August 1, 1934, shortly after Fritsch had officially become *Oberbefehlshaber des Heeres* (OB d H) and the first peacetime expansion of the new *Wehrmacht* (armed forces) was authorized, Funck was promoted to major (twenty-first in the day's seniority) and officially removed his cavalry yellow *Waffenfahrbe* (uniform markings) to replace it with the new *Panzertruppe* pink. Thus—a bit belatedly—he became only about the twenty-fifth officer to be gazetted to the mechanized troop command staff of the defense ministry.

In the spring of 1936, young Hans Joachim von Funck, now age nineteen and a half, had finished a standard curriculum and was posted to a military training academy at Dahlem. The second son, Burkhard, age sixteen, joined his father at Neisse to complete his schooling. Major Funck, meanwhile, accompanied Fritsch to the summer maneuvers of the 1st Panzer Division at Muenster and both were impressed.

On September 1, 1936, Funck was "nominated" (*ernennung*) to the rank of lieutenant colonel—a sort of brevet commission to cover him for a future rather important assignment. Fritsch, prompted by the war minister, Field Marshal Werner von Blomberg, was considering sending a team of experts into Spain, where Franco's troops were attacking the leftist government.[6]

Though Blomberg had already appointed Lt. Col. Hans Karl von Scheele as mission chief, Fritsch and Oswald Lutz of the Panzer Command realized this was the ideal training ground for the fledgling armored units.[7] They settled on Funck, Fritsch's representative, and Ritter Wilhelm von Thoma, Lutz's choice as a field commander, to go to Spain as separate but equal observers.[8] Hence, on September 16, after a ten-day intensive conference with Fritsch and Lutz, Lt. Col. (*ernennung*) Baron Hans von Funck was detached from regular duties and assigned on temporary basis to the war ministry and the Supreme Command of the *Luftwaffe* (OKL). On September 20, under the pseudonym of Capt. Wilhelm Strunk, he duly left Berlin by plane for the headquarters of the White Army of Seville. On September 28, the Army High Command listed Lieutenant Colonel Funck as being attached to the staff of *Wehrkreis IV* at Dresden—although he was nowhere near Dresden. In fact, on September 25, a Capt. W. Strunk checked in with Colonel Scheele at his headquarters at Seville; Thoma, meanwhile, began to assemble a tank force to aid the Republicans in their attack on Madrid.

On November 18, the German government determined to recognize the Republican government, which had now established itself at Burgos. With the hearty support of Fritsch and other prominent

members of the German High Command, Funck was officially transferred once more to the aegis of the High Command of the Army
(*Oberkommando des Heeres,* or OKH) dated November 30, 1936, and
was appointed military attaché to the Burgos government.

In December, the new soldier-diplomat was informed by his government that he was senior officer for all military personnel working
in Spain and was not actually subordinate to the recently appointed
Maj. Gen. Wilhelm Faupel, chargé d'affaires for Germany. This was
quite fortunate, as Faupel was intensely unpopular with the Spanish
authorities.[9]

Funck worked closely with both army colonels and the *Luftwaffe*
brass who had set up the famous Condor Legion to train their pilots
in warfare. He was somewhat critical of Franco in his reports to
Fritsch, believing that the "Crusade" idea of the Republican leader
was too idealistic to serve the purpose of a final defeat of the Loyalists
and Nationalists and their Russian advisers.

On March 1, 1937, he was promoted to full colonel, but the
simultaneous promotion of von Scheele prompted Fritsch to instruct
Viktor von Schwedler, the chief of the Army Personnel Office (*Heerespersonnelamt,* or HPA) to make Funck's promotion retroactive to February 1. The new colonel continued to conduct his observations
throughout the year, causing Ambassador Faupel and Foreign Office
Secretary of State Baron Ernst von Weiszaecker considerable annoyance. Fritsch, however, was fully satisfied with the status quo and,
being firmly entrenched as the third most powerful non-Nazi in the
defense hierarchy (Blomberg and Adm. Erich Raeder, commander in
chief of the navy, were more secure, supposedly, successfully pro-
tected his capable protégé. In December 1937, young Lt. Hans
Joachim von Funck was posted to Burgos as his father's adjutant—the
twenty-one-year-old's first active-duty assignment.

The Blomberg-Fritsch crisis took place in late January 1938, when
Blomberg was dismissed as war minister for marrying an alleged former prostitute, and Fritsch was relieved of his command on trumped-
up charges of homosexuality.[10] Colonel Funck's position was
destroyed as effectively as if he had been in Berlin and associated with
them. Heads from all ranks rolled, as Hitler, Goering, and Foreign
Minister Joachim von Ribbentrop—and their new military protégés,
the Keitel brothers and Gen. Walther von Brauchitsch, the new

commander in chief of the army—disposed of anyone who had the misfortune of offending them.[11]

Although Faupel had been recalled for his incapable conduct toward the Spanish leaders in August 1937, his successor, Eberhard von Stohrer—a career diplomat who was accustomed to the niceties of protocol—did not appreciate Funck's independent appointment. Col. Walther Warlimont, who had preceded Hans in Spain during the summer of 1936, had resented being supplanted and now, as a close associate of Alfred Jodl, the chief of operations of the Armed Forces High Command (*Oberkommando des Wehrmacht*, or OKW), was able to inveigh against him.[12]

First of all, in February, Colonel Funck was told emphatically that he was now under the orders of Ambassador Stohrer who consequently would restrict his activities—and his reports—to the Burgos area. The obedient colonel adapted at once, but he continued to voice his honest opinions about the Spanish Republican officials—which disturbed Stohrer, who had established a congenial relationship with Franco and his foreign minister, Ramón Serrano Súñer.

Stohrer wrote bitterly to Weiszaecker, who presented the problem to Maj. Gen. Bodewin Keitel. The major general had insinuated himself into the HPA when the efficient Schwedler had been switched to a field command. Keitel was aided in his efforts by the combination of circumstances surrounding Funck personally.[13]

Irmgard von Funck, back in Goettingen, had decided that her life was too restricted by an unloving husband, constantly away from her home, and had entered a plea for divorce with the local judiciary. Since a German military officer and aristocrat was involved, the Hessian court requested information from the HPA.

Divorce was very ill regarded by Hitler—although his tool, Brauchitsch, was in the process of obtaining one. Keitel, aware of Hitler's feelings, forwarded the information to von Brauchitsch, with a copy to Maj. Rudolf Schmundt, Hitler's adjutant.

Meanwhile, Funck, during his service in Berlin, had struck up an acquaintance with a lovely young woman of noble birth, the daughter of a retired cavalry captain whom he had known during the war. Baroness Maria von Mirbach was nearing thirty and was unmarried. Bright and intelligent, she had worked on a part-time basis with the War Ministry steno pool. Hence when, in June 1939, the colonel was recalled from Spain at the conclusion of the Civil War, he was taken to task about the divorce action and agreed not to stir up trouble—or publicity—by contesting it. He also quickly resumed his friendship with Maria von Mirbach. It is most probable that in July they agreed to marry—once the divorce became effective.

On August 1, 1939, Colonel Funck—now assigned to the Attaché Branch—was sent to take up a full-time military attaché post at Lisbon, Portugal. Previously Lt. Col. Hans-Joachim von Horn, from Paris, had doubled in brass as the military observer in Portugal; now, with the intense possibility of a war in the near future, it was felt that an experienced observer in the notoriously pro-British country was necessary.[14]

Funck reported to the German ambassador, the experienced Baron Oswald von Hoyningen-Huehne, in record time. The baron had known Funck during the early thirties and, being an ex-military man himself, was pleased to have a full-time experienced officer on his staff. Hence it was from Lisbon that Colonel Funck watched the outbreak of World War II and the monthlong *Wehrmacht blitzkrieg* over Poland. Being a fighting soldier first and foremost, Hans at once wrote to the HPA for a field assignment. Luckily, at that time, Guderian was begging for officers to staff the four light divisions that had proven so ineffective in Poland and were being converted into the 6th, 7th, 8th, and 9th Panzer Divisions.

On September 30, almost by return diplomatic pouch, came orders for Colonel Funck to report forthwith to the Wunsdorf Maneuver Area outside Berlin to take command, not of a new unit, but of the veteran 5th Panzer Regiment (*Wunsdorf*) of the 3rd Panzer Division. The colonel wasted no time in flying via Barcelona and Milan, over the Alps to Vienna, and then to the Berlin's Tempelhof Airfield—a trip that required three days because of the distance involved.

On October 5, Funck reported to divisional headquarters, where the operations officer, Major von dem Borne, informed him that the former divisional and regimental commanders, Lt. Gen. Baron Leo Geyr von Schweppenburg and Col. Karl Freiherr von Thungen, were absent, and the new divisional commander, Maj. Gen. Horst Stumpff, had not yet arrived. (See Appendix B for a list of German staff positions in World War II.) The colonel therefore left Berlin by car and arrived at the garrison of Wunsdorf, where he took up residence.

The following day, October 6, Hans conferred with his two battalion and six company commanders and made a leisurely tour of the installation, machine shops, motor pool, and barracks. Then he drove into Berlin again to visit his youngest son, Burkhard, at the military hospital. The boy had been severely injured during the Polish campaign, though Heinz Guderian erronously reported that he had been killed.[15]

Major General Stumpff arrived early on the morning of the seventh, from his interim command of the 10th Panzer Division. A veteran panzer officer who had served in the 3rd Panzer since its inception in late 1935, Stumpff had a reputation for bravery coupled with audacity.[16] He and Funck took to each other at once.

While the officers worked at integrating new equipment and training new personnel for the division, Colonel Funck was notified—sometime in late November, ostensibly—that his wife's divorce had been granted by the Hessian court and he was a free man once again. During the Christmas season, he proposed marriage to Maria von Mirbach, and she accepted.

On February 2, 1940, at the garrison church at Berlin-Wunsdorf, Hans and Maria were married, with Major General Stumpff as his officer's best man. None of the Funck children attended the ceremony, but this was because Hans Joachim was still stationed in Lisbon, on the staff of Colonel Esebeck, the new military attaché, and Burkhard remained hospitalized. Ingeborg was with her mother in Goettingen.

On March 1, 1940, the 3rd (Berlin) Panzer Division stood to and began its move to the eastern banks of the Rhine, preparatory for its employment in the forthcoming attack on the Western Allies. It was deployed opposite the Dutch-Belgian frontier and attached to Gen. of Cavalry Erich Hoepner's XVI Motorized Korps.[17] During the last week of March and all of April, the regiments of the 3rd were exercised in the open ground on the west bank of the Rhine north of Aachen and readied for their assault aimed at Hannut in Belgium.

Map 1.1 shows the German plan for the conquest of France and the Low Countries. It was called the Manstein Plan because it was originated by Lt. Gen. Erich von Manstein.) In Phase 1, Army Group B under Fedor von Bock would attack into the Netherlands and Belgium. In Phase 2, the Allies would react by rushing their best forces—

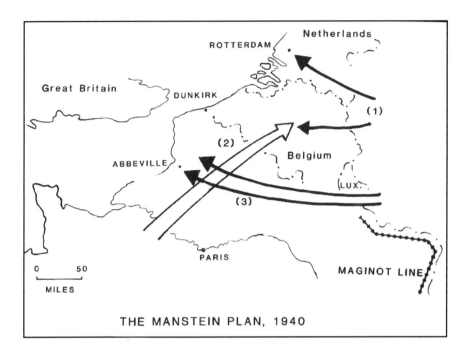

THE MANSTEIN PLAN, 1940

including almost all of their armor—into Belgium, especially along the Dyle River. Then in Phase 3, Army Group B, with seven of Germany's ten panzer divisions, would cut them off by driving through the Ardennes to the sea. The plan worked exactly as Manstein had envisioned it. Funck and the 3rd Panzer Division were part of Rundstedt's Army Group A, shown as (3) on Map 1.1.

May 11, 1940, dawned clear. After a sharp artillery bombardment, the two panzer regiments of the 3rd lunged into enemy territory against minor and disorganized Belgian resistance. It was not until the late morning of the twelfth that the 3rd Panzer, having crossed the Meuse north of Maastricht, ran into elements of the French Cavalry Corps of Gen. Rene Prioux and a sharp skirmish began, in which the defenders were largely successful.

Overnight, Colonel Funck and his officers brought up their heavier tanks, and Stumpff and his artillery regiment commander, Colonel Foerster, worked on deploying the guns. When the morning of the twelfth dawned, the German panzers renewed the attack against the formidable but ineptly handled French forces. One historian quoted a German officer as observing "their lack of maneuverability and the fact that they fight singly and in loose formation, not all together under one command. They cannot take advantage of strength and numbers."[18]

This battle, called either Merdorp or Hannut according to the historian consulted, was the first tank battle of the Second World War, and only the second in history (the first was at Cambrai in 1918). The French lost about fifty tanks and fell back unceremoniously to the rear of their infantry along the Dyle River.

Hoepner ordered his two divisions to advance in pursuit as soon as they were able to reorganize. German losses probably almost equaled those of the French, chiefly in the PzKw I tanks, which were already obsolete as early as the Polish campaign. (See Appendix C for characteristics of selected World War II tanks.) Funck's regiment had suffered only minor losses, some of which were salvageable, and he pushed ahead through the night, accompanied by Maj. Baron Irnfried von Wechmar's reconnaissance battalion.

In the early hours of May 13, the colonel, riding with Wechmar's van, secured an unopposed crossing of the Dyle and set up a strong bridgehead, into which, during the course of the day, poured the motorcycle battalion, a mobile artillery battery, and the 3rd Motorized Infantry Regiment of Col. Ulrich Kleemann. This timely move went a long way toward convincing the Allied commanders that they should pull back from the Dyle to the Escaut—as they did beginning late on the fourteenth.

Hoepner cautiously followed up the Anglo-French retirement on the fifteenth, advancing his mechanized infantry southwestward and allowing his panzer regiments considerable freedom of movement. Funck's compact units, with Wechmar's battalion in support, broke out of the bridgehead and barreled toward Gembloux. A dispatch rider from army group headquarters caught up with the colonel toward evening and presented him with his clasp to the Iron Cross, Second Class, for the battle of the twelfth.

When they reached the Gembloux Gap on the sixteenth, and it was evident that the Anglo-French were in general retreat toward more favorable defensive positions, Hoepner ordered his various battle groups to rendezvous to the east of Mons. He correctly expected that orders would soon be forthcoming to aim south, rather than west—and leave to the infantry corps the hard slogging with the entrenched enemy armies.

On May 18, indeed, the XVI Corps received just such an order, and Colonel Funck was awarded the Panzer Battle Badge in Silver—the award given for armored engagements on three separate days, in this case, May 11, 12, and 13. The *Oberst*, however, determined to secure Mons before altering his line of advance; the 5th Panzer Regiment, with the recon battalion, took the Belgian city on the nineteenth.

This was the last real action of this phase of the campaign. The division now advanced from May 19 to 23, raced almost unopposed via Charleroi and Maubeuge, passed by the XV Corps, and reached the town of Doullens, where it was halted by the famous Fuehrer Order of May 24, which allowed the British and much of the French Army to escape during the "Miracle of Dunkirk." Renewed action after a two-day delay saw Colonel Funck's battle group again in a sharp series of actions around Lille, where the French Seventh Army was destroyed. Funck's men took the fortified town of Nourrent-Fontes on May 28. That evening he received the clasp to his Iron Cross, First Class.

On May 29, the XVI Panzer Corps was ordered out of the line and sent to a regrouping area on the Somme to receive replacement equipment and personnel. At the same time, the corps found it had been put under control of General Kleist's *Panzergruppenkommandostab* for operations against France. On June 3, the 3rd Panzer moved up to the Somme opposite Peronne in preparation for the storm crossing, which was ordered for the fifth.

Although Ewald von Kleist had been in control of the crossing of the Meuse around Sedan back in May, he seemed not to have learned the proper way of launching a river assault.[19] Then, too, the French—dug in here in defense of their home country—were resolved to stand and die if need be.

Kleist pushed the infantry regiments across on June 5 and established a pair of small bridgeheads, one at Amiens, the other at Peronne. Despite the protests of Hoepner and his division commanders, Kleist ordered the tanks into the confined area to overwhelm the stubborn infantry defenders. What Kleist did not take into consideration, however, was that behind the infantry, the French had massed hundreds of their 75-millimeter guns. The result was that the panzers were fish in a barrel in the confined space of the bridgehead. By the evening of June 7, one of Kleist's two corps (it does not seem to have been Hoepner's) was missing 65 percent of its tank strength.

Angry recriminations echoed back up the command ladder all the way to Col. Gen. Fedor von Bock, the army group commander, who now intervened to save the frustrated armor.[20] Sending regular infantry into the embattled bridgeheads, Bock ordered the panzers back to the north bank of the Somme and directed them to proceed upriver to the area commanded by Field Marshal Gerd von Rundstedt, where Guderian's new panzer group was to try a crossing at Rethel and Chateau-Porcien.

Again the infantry went in to seize a bridgehead, but it was held up near Chateau-Porcien by the fanatical French resistance. This time, however, Guderian was on the scene. During the night of June 9/10, he got his armor across the river and attacked at dawn, completely disrupting the French defenders. The artillery here was overrun before it could zero in on the massed panzers.

Colonel Funck's 5th Panzer Regiment debouched beyond Rethel late on June 9, on the heels of Guderian's armor, which wheeled to the east. There then began an almost unimpeded race to the south, as the four panzer divisions of Kleist's group dashed toward the Mediterranean. The 3rd Panzer took Dijon on June 16, while Funck, with Wechmar's reconnaissance battalion, pressed on ahead to seize Lyons on June 20, thus bringing his division's part of the campaign to an end. The French government in Bordeaux sued for peace a day or two later.

General Stumpff's division spent the end of June and most of July as the occupying force in and around Lyons, guarding against the possibility of a renewed effort by the French to continue the war. The units received new equipment and new personnel, to be incorporated into the division, which enjoyed the quiet of a peacetime garrison.

Satisfied that peace was secure, OKH ordered the 3rd Panzer Division back to Berlin, where it was to be reorganized in accordance with Hitler's ideas about expanding the number of panzer divisions by halving the number of tanks in each division. The 3rd did not complete the journey by train until mid-August, and at once Stumpff, Fritz Kuehn (the 3rd Panzer Brigade commander), and Colonels Funck and Gabler of the panzer regiments joined in protests with the other panzer commanders to prevent the proposed halving of their divisions' strengths, but to no avail.

In September, General Stumpff took an extended leave to settle some affairs at home. Maj. Gen. Friedrich "Fritz" Kuehn acted as temporary division commander,[21] and Col. Adolf Gabler, the senior regimental commander, acted as brigade commander, though Funck's commission was senior to Gabler's (1937 versus 1939), because Gabler had been with the division two weeks longer.

With Stumpff's return in early October, a whole series of changes took place: Kuehn was given command of the newly operational 15th Panzer Division at Kaiserslautern, while Colonel Gabler was detailed to the Panzer Troops Training Center at Linz, Austria. Funck was tentatively designated to assume command of the 3rd Panzer Brigade, although it was already very likely that this headquarters would be disbanded under the new "watering-down" process the Fuehrer was insisting upon.

Meanwhile, the baron requested a brief leave, commencing on October 15. With his wife, he proceeded to Halberstadt, where his father-in-law had found him a pleasant estate just outside the town of Blankenburg. Funck was delighted with this lovely house in the Harz and purchased it, establishing Maria there until he could arrange for a house near Berlin. On November 1, he returned to duty at Wunsdorf. The reorganization of the 3rd Panzer Division had been going apace during his absence; the 5th Panzer Regiment and the 3rd Reconnaissance Battalion under Col. Johannes Streich and Lt. Col. Baron von Wechmar, had already been detached and sent to Krampnitz for assignment to another unit. One battalion of the artillery regiment and the antitank gun battalion had also been unceremoniously snatched away.

Funck's brigade headquarters was a skeleton: besides the colonel, only Maj. Wolf Hausser, his staff officer, and Lt. Georg von Zydow, his adjutant, were attached. No longer a part of the 3rd Panzer, but not assigned elsewhere, the three officers passed a fortnight in games of chess and poker.

The letter Funck wrote to the *Panzertruppen* Inspectorate on November 2, however, had a belated effect. Guderian was in Berlin and at loose ends, intent upon trying to avert the further diminution of his panzers. He used his considerable influence to have the former 3rd Brigade Headquarters sent to Krampnitz, to take over the training of what was being called the 5th Light Division—mostly the units of the old 3rd Panzer. To Funck, who had served with Wechmar, Maj. Wilhelm Lorenz and Lt. Col. Julius von Bernuth in France, this was an ideal assignment.[22] Though as yet without sufficient infantry or artillery, the hybrid unit was used to serving together, and it was put through training exercises throughout December.

Meanwhile, events were taking place in distant North Africa that were going to profoundly affect not only Funck, but many of his associates and friends as well. Following their deliberately fortuitous attack on France in June 1940, the Italians were anxious to show off their military muscle in an overwhelming attack on the small but elite British forces based in Egypt. Following an unopposed march to Sidi Barrani inside that frontier, however, the huge Italian Tenth Army was counterattacked and completely routed during November and December 1940 by the gallant British.

Mussolini now decided to ask for German help, although he had previously turned down an offer of troops by Hitler. In November, Ritter Wilhelm von Thoma, the erstwhile German panzer commander in Spain and an outspoken critic of Italian delusions of grandeur, had visited the shattered Italian forces in Libya and returned to Berlin with proposals of a massive armored reinforcement: four panzer divisions to replace the incapable Fascist divisions.

But the Fuehrer was already planning his Russian campaign and refused to consider such an allocation of force, and the Italian High Command was insulted and infuriated by the very idea of letting the Germans get such a massive aggregation of troops into their African "empire." The officers of Hitler's staff admonished Thoma most severely for such a proposal and posted him unceremoniously to a field command in Poland.[23]

A second opinion was needed, Hitler felt; Thoma's caustic comment that "one British soldier is as good as twelve Italians" could not be true! He inquired among his flunkies for another officer to send to Libya, one acquainted with the Italians and their methods of warfare, and also one with enough diplomacy to avoid offending the Commando Supremo or its representatives in Tripoli. Meanwhile, however, the Italians were suffering disaster after disaster: the British terrier was routing the Italian ox and was snapping at its heels as it fled toward Tripoli.

At the Army Personnel Office (*Heerespersonnelamt*, or HPA) on the Bendlerstrasse, the inept Bodewin Keitel desperately consulted with panzer officers on his staff or awaiting postings; Funck's name came up almost at once. Besides his familiarity with the Italian Army, gained in Spain, he also had a trained force of tankers and motorized infantry that could be utilized promptly.

Bodewin Keitel relayed this news to his brother, OKW commander in chief Field Marshal Wilhelm Keitel, and also reminded him of Funck's earlier run-ins with the High Command and his unfortunate divorce.[24] They decided to overlook these problems for the time being; otherwise, Colonel Funck filled their needs more than adequately.

On January 1, 1941, Funck received his promotion to major general and simultaneously was ordered to fly forthwith via Rome and Sicily to Tripoli. Meanwhile, elements of the 5th Light were loaded aboard Junker and Heinkel transports and sent off behind him.

The new general arrived at Tripoli on January 5, conferred with the distraught Italian civil and military officials there, and then made a quick tour of the uncertain Italian positions. He was engaged in this when Bardia fell to British and Australian forces that were simultaneously besieging Tobruk (see Map 1.2). On the ninth, Funck was recalled to Berlin to make his report—one he had already decided upon, given what he knew of the condition of his "brigade" and what he had seen of the Italians' demoralization.

Despite the urgency of his recall, Funck had a Fiesler Storch observation aircraft fly and Lieutenant Zydow into the besieged port of Tobruk on January 17 so that he could see the situation of that fortress firsthand. The next day, he flew back to Tripoli, where he warned the Italians that their garrison would probably surrender within a couple of days. (Tobruk capitulated on January 22.) He then took off for Sicily and from thence flew to Rome, where, on the twenty-second, he conferred with the German military attaché, Lt. Gen. Enno von Rintelen, and the Italian commanders.

Funck was officially named commander of the 5th Light Division on January 29. Meanwhile, the division's equipment was already being transferred south to Naples and Taranto for expedited shipment to Libya, while the personnel were being flown over the Alps to the various aerodomes in southern Italy. Funck checked in with Major Hausser and Lieutenant Colonel Wechmar and gave them his impressions of the Libyan debacle before again taking off to make his report to Berlin.

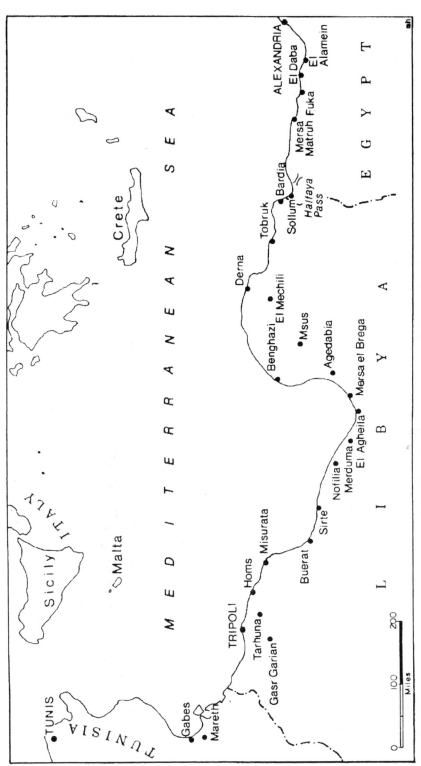

The North African Theater of Operations

In his best uniform and with his decorations, Funck reported to the Fuehrer's officers in the Reich chancellory on January 25. After delivering his preliminary observations to General Jodl, he was instructed to wait until Hitler was free, so that he could make whatever recommendations he felt the situation called for.

Shortly after 2 P.M., von Funck, an erect six-foot-two example of a Prussian soldier, followed by Zydow with a map and note case, was ushered into the Fuehrer's presence. At full attention, he delivered his report, to this effect: The Italians were totally demoralized and could not be expected to pull their own chestnuts out of the North African fire. The officers were not emotionally or intellectually capable of a strong defense, much less any concerted offense, and the soldiers were untrained and lacked enthusiasm, discipline, and motivation.

As to German assistance, Funck went on imperturbably, the 5th Light was totally inadequate to stem the current tide, even if it was augmented by more infantry and artillery—which it must have in any case. Only a full corps—at least three divisions—could possibly put a brake on the Italian debacle. If this was not immediately available, perhaps the Italians could support the 5th Light with at least three of their "showpiece" divisions, currently cooling their heels in Rome. With these committed, under an overall German field commander, and with air and augmented artillery support, the British could be stopped somewhere near Sirte, thus saving Tripoli at least.

Hitler listened with growing annoyance: this was Thoma all over again. He now broke in to observe—quite correctly—that "the madness of the whole affair is that while the Italians bleat about lack of material, they are too proud to ask for either German arms or soldiers! Il Duce might go along if our boys were in Italian uniforms and ate linguine!"

He then asked Funck his opinion of the British, which the baron gave succinctly: "The British can take all of Libya if their supplies hold out. The Italians alone will be unable to stop them."

"But is not that the case exactly?" Hitler asked. "By now the English must have outrun their supplies and surely be ready for a defeat?"

"Not by the Italians," the general replied. "Nor will the 5th Light be sufficient to do more than delay them. At least one more German division must be sent across, if there is enough time. Meanwhile, I would insist upon the Italians themselves rushing those three divisions to Libya."

"But you say the Italians cannot stop the British!"

"With the disorganized and untrained rabble now in Libya, no! The three Italian divisions in Rome are better quality—in training and in equipment. Under a German commander, and laced with German units, the British should be held short of Tripoli. Later, when more German forces arrive, they can be forced back."

"We will consider your recommendations," Hitler said, closing the interview.

Funck returned to Wunsdorf to await developments, but he was resolved on one thing: if given command of the German forces in Cyrenaica, he would have to have unlimited authority over both German and Italian forces. This proviso was communicated to General Jodl on January 29 and then relayed to Hitler—who immediately lost his temper.

According to an aide present at the time, who communicated this to Zydow, Hitler is supposed to have shouted: "Independent command?! Nonsense! He is an arrogant one, that Funck. The other day—all the time he was giving his report—he was looking down his long aristocratic nose at me—me, his commander in chief!!"

Heartened by this reaction, Keitel took the opportunity to bring up all the old skeletons: Funck's close association with the late General von Fritsch, his high-handed management of the Spanish assignment, and finally, his divorce. This was enough for Hitler; learning that Col. Johannes Streich was already in Tripoli, he ordered him promoted to major general and given command of the 5th Light Division, replacing Funck.[25]

Jodl demurred here—not out of any fondness for the baron, but because of the purely military aspects that Funck had pointed out. Streich was too junior and inexperienced to command an Allied army; the Italians would hardly obey him. Hence a corps command would have to be set up with an officer of suitable rank and experience in charge.

Hitler agreed at once and chose the man for the job: Lt. Gen. Erwin Rommel of the 7th Panzer Division.[26] On February 6, Rommel left Gera in Thuringia for Berlin to confer with Hitler, and, thanks to the efforts of some of his friends at the HPA, Funck received orders to go to Gera to take over command of the 7th Panzer—a fortuitous exchange for the baron, who had not been particularly sanguine about the African expedition.

On February 7, Funck and his aide reached Gera and were introduced to the crack panzer division that had made so much history in France during May and June 1940. Only recently returned from the French Channel coast, where it had been slated for participation in the proposed invasion of England, the 7th had been reinforced up to full strength and its tanks were almost all the powerful Mark III and IV panzers—the best Germany then possessed.

From his new operations officer (Ia), Maj. Lothar Berger, Funck received the divisional order of battle, and met his officers, all future stars of the panzer service:

> *Schuetzen Brigade 7* (7th Rifle Brigade), commanded by Col. Baron Hans von Boineburg-Lengsfeld
>
> *Schuetzen Regiment 6* (of two battalions), commanded by Lt. Col. Hans Junck
>
> *Schuetzen Regiment 7* (of two battalions), commanded by Lt. Col. Rudolf von Paris
>
> *Kradschutz Battalion 7* (7th Motorcycle Battalion), commanded by Major Friedrich von Steinkeller
>
> 25th Panzer Regiment, commanded by veteran Col. Karl Rothenburg
>
> 1st Panzer Battalion, commanded by Maj. Adalbert Schulz
>
> 2nd Panzer Battalion, commanded by Maj. Franz von Lindenau
>
> *Aufklaerung Abteilung 7* (7th Reconnaissance Battalion), commanded by Rittmeister Hans von Luck
>
> *Artillerie Regiment 78* (78th Panzer Artillery Regiment), three artillery battalions under Lt. Col. Gottfried Froelich
>
> *Panzer Jaeger Abteilung 42* (42nd Anti-Tank Battalion), commanded by Lt. Col. Johannes Mickl and later Maj. Gerhard von Eskefort.[27]

The reconnaissance and motorcycle battalions were merged on May 1, 1941; Steinkeller became the commander, and Luck was named Funck's adjutant. Rommel requested that Mickl and Luck be transferred to Africa. Funck did not care for Mickl, so he sent the colonel to Africa right away, but he fought to retain Luck. Rommel, however, had considerably more influence at Fuehrer Headquarters than Funck. As a result, Hans von Luck was sent to Africa in January 1942.[28] In the meantime, the 37th Panzer Reconnaissance Battalion was added to the table of organization of the 7th Panzer Division in the fall of 1941, and Luck was named its commander. Maj. Gerhard von Enkefort succeeded Mickl as commander of the 42nd Anti-Tank Battalion in the spring of 1941.

The peaceful job of training ended in mid-April, with orders for the division to move eastward into Poland, where it was to come under the command of Gen. Rudolf Schmidt's XXXIX Panzer Corps, of the 3rd Panzer Group, led by Col. Gen. Hermann Hoth. Their task would be a drive into central Russia, to the north of Brest-Litovsk.[29]

Major General Freiherr von Funck had by now thoroughly familiarized himself with his command—and his men. Though Rommel had been respected by the soldiers, he had not been all that likable; Funck, on the other hand, was popular, and his appearance at bivouac or sentry post was viewed with considerable pleasure, although he expected—and got—efficient and disciplined obedience.

During the ensuing campaign, one young *Feldwebel* (sergeant) from Mainz received word of his mother's serious illness. Though he was engaged in heavy fighting and had intense responsibility for the division, Funck heard of the problem via the usual grapevine. He had pulled the sergeant out of the battle and put aboard a supply truck bound for a rail junction, with a leave pass signed by the general himself.

Another incident involved a new lieutenant, recently graduated from a leadership school and a devout National Socialist, who was assigned a platoon in the motorized infantry. The youngster proved to be a martinet, who strove to terrorize his men and force them into feats of sheer stupidity—apparently to acquire for himself a reputation for bravery. His company commander attempted, with as much tact as possible, to restrain the Nazi but to no avail. The platoon sergeant, also trying to save lives and mellow the foolhardy young officer, was soon up for court-martial, brought by the arrogant youth for failure to "obey a superior officer."

When the case arrived at divisional headquarters, Funck read the charges and then visited the sergeant in his detention cell. According to the sources, the general drove to the sector of the front where the lieutenant's command was located and visited with the soldiers of the platoon—unbeknownst to the sleeping commander.

The lieutenant had ordered a full-scale assault on a Soviet position on a hill overlooking German lines. There was no real reason for any such assault, as the spring thaw was still immobilizing both armies and the hill was no great threat to the German forces. Furthermore, a frontal assault against plunging fire would be costly, even if successful.

Funck was carrying a rifle when dawn broke and the lieutenant came out of his bunker to give orders for the platoon to attack. The youngster was stunned to see his general standing with the soldiers. Funck smiled at him cheerfully and said: "If you feel this attack is of such great importance for the future of the Wehrmacht, lieutenant, it would be amiss of me to let you do it alone. I value the chance to accomplish so worthwhile a mission. Surely you will not deny me the opportunity."

Needless to say, the attack was abruptly canceled. The lieutenant was later killed in action after having maintained a very low profile. The sergeant was exonerated of charges and transferred to another unit. His story became general knowledge throughout the division, and veterans were telling the incident as late as 1944, when Hasso von Manteuffel was commanding the 7th.

On June 22, 1941, the whole might of the previously invincible *Wehrmacht*, including Funck's 7th Panzer, struck a surprised Russian nation, and the Germans rapidly made penetrations in many sectors. Funck's forces crossed the Soviet frontier in tandem with the 20th Panzer, led by his old commander and friend Gen. Horst Stumpff. Behind, to clean up, was the 20th Motorized Infantry Division under Maj. Gen. Hans Zorn.[30] On the very first day, the panzers bypassed Grodno and rushed eastward toward the Niemen. On the twenty-fourth, the baron, leading with Steinkeller's recon battalion, entered Vilna on the Vileiku River, having secured the Niemen crossings in a blaze of speed.

Hoth now aimed northeast, across the Dnieper-Dvina land bridge toward the main Soviet depots of Vitebsk and Polotsk on the Dvina River. Orders from OKH prevented this sensible if daring maneuver, however, and instead shunted XXXIX Panzer Corps southeast to establish contact with Guderian behind Soviet forces in the Minsk-Bialystok encirclement. But like Guderian, Hoth was clever about "misunderstanding" orders, so the 7th and 20th Panzers more or less continued their eastern advance. Funck reached the Beresina River at Borissov on July 3–4.

During the next few days, all the armor and infantry were involved in repelling desperate attempts by the Soviet forces to break out of their trap, but of the enemy was contained, despite the Russians' best efforts. The 7th pushed forward toward the headwaters of the Dvina, and on July 9, Steinkeller's motorcyclists captured a Soviet antiaircraft officer who was carrying orders for Soviet reinforcements being detrained around Vitebsk.

While sending these on to Schmidt and Hoth, Funck and Stumpff rushed straight to the railroad and decimated the surprised and disorganized Soviet rifle divisions. On July 10, Stumpff's 20th Panzer took Vitebsk (see Map 1.3). Rudolf Schmidt's XXXIX Corps was now directed southward, along the east bank of the Dvina, to outflank Smolensk, which Guderian's troops captured on July 16; however, Russian assaults on the 20th Motorized and 7th Panzer Divisions at Lesko and along the Demidovo Highway effectively stalled the drive for one or two days.

A brisk tank battle erupted along the Moscow Highway west of occupied Yartsevo as Soviet general Eremenko attempted to blunt the German advance. Funck was up with his panzers throughout the engagement of July 17–18, and the 7th was responsible for the destruction of forty-two Russian tanks and numerous other vehicles, though with some losses to the Germans. Colonel Paris of the 7th Infantry was killed on July 18; the veteran Col. Karl Rothenberg of the 25th Panzer Regiment was seriously wounded on June 27 and later died in the hospital at Brest-Litovsk on June 29; Hans Junck of the 6th Regiment was wounded on July 21 during a sharp breakout attempt. Thus Funck was forced to restaff his three major units. Meanwhile, he was awarded the Knight's Cross of the Iron Cross for the battle of July 17.

While the major focus of the campaign began to swing toward the south, with Guderian at the Yelnia Salient during late July and early August, the weary troops of Hoth's group hung grimly to their precarious positions east of Smolensk, with part of their forces containing a major Soviet encirclement just to the north of that burned-out city. These fifteen Soviet divisions did not finally surrender until

August 5, when it was reported that 309,000 prisoners, more than 3,000 tanks, and a similar number of guns had fallen into German hands. (Map 1.4 shows this battle of encirclement and the other major battles of encirclement on the Eastern Front in 1941.) So generally satisfied was the High Command that it suggested that Hoth's group should be moved northward to support the assault on Leningrad. In fact, however, the LVII Panzer Corps and part of XXXIX Corps were moved to attack Russian forces around Velikye Luki. Funck's division—which had suffered so badly—was put into reserve at Opochka, where it received some badly needed rest and reinforcement. But this was short-lived. The Soviet attacks around Velikye Luki soon grew so serious that the 7th Panzer had to be committed on the southernmost German flank.

On August 20, the division crossed the Loiana to Frol and smashed a Russian division at Makovia, thus throwing the Soviet offensive off center. Hoth, with his main group and large masses of infantry, now launched a counterattack, which captured Velikye Luki on August 22–26, along with 34,000 prisoners.

A further drive eastward captured Toropetz on August 29, whereupon the weak hinge between Army Groups North and Center was satisfactorily shored up, and the hard-pressed panzer units were again allowed a breather, pending the great push on Moscow—now too long delayed. Funck's 7th Panzer was now subordinated to the LVI Panzer Corps of Gen. of Panzer Troops Erich von Manstein, who was soon succeeded by Gen. of Panzer Troops Ferdinand Schaal, along with the 6th Panzer Division of Lt. Gen. Franz Landgraf and the 14th Motorized Infantry Division of Maj. Gen. Friedrich Fuerst.[31] Only the last was south of Velikye Luki; Schaal was at Bobruisk and the 6th Panzer was still operating near Leningrad.

September was relatively quiet for the most part. The Soviets were working feverishly to fortify their positions, and the Germans worked equally hard to bring up ammunition and supplies to make their proposed offensive invincible. General Schaal visited the headquarters of the 7th on September 25 with the news that Landgraf's division had sustained serious injuries in a Soviet attack on September 12, south of Leningrad, but was now being refitted at Dangavpils and should join the corps in a few days. Funck, meanwhile, again had new officers: Col. Eduard Hauser now commanded the 25th Panzer.[32] The new

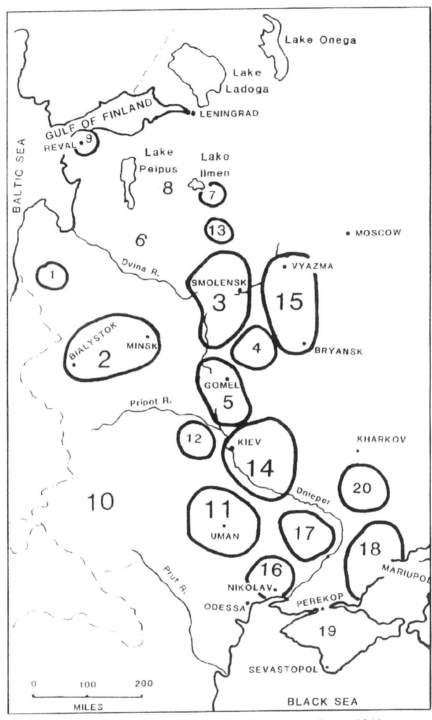

The Battles of Encirclement on the Eastern Front, 1941

chiefs of Infantry Regiments 6 and 7 were Col. Hasso von Manteuffel and Col. Gunther Lungershausen. Gottfried Froehlich still commanded the 78th Panzer Artillery, and Major Steinkeller headed up the reconnaissance battalion. All in all, it was a stellar cast of commanders—a fact the rank and file of the division fully appreciated, with morale being sky high.

The final drive commenced on September 30, as three full panzer armies surged from their assembly areas along the Velikye Luki-Yartsevo-Roslavl-Glukhov line. General Funck was in the northernmost assault, aimed at Byeli and Kholm, to the north and east of Vyazma.

On the first day of October, Steinkeller's recon battalion foiled an attempt by the Soviets to run "mine dogs" beneath his armored cars. These animals, with armed antitank mines mounted upon their backs, had been trained to run under moving armored vehicles, looking for food. They later did do some damage to another panzer division farther south. Meanwhile, the broken ground and marshy region around Byeli, bordering the sluggish Vop River, seriously hampered the movement of the tanks; Hoth therefore combined the 25th and 11th Panzer Regiments as Brigade Koll and pushed it rapidly behind the engineers, who laid a solid roadbed up to the Vop itself.

In a sharp engagement supported by dismounted infantry, the division routed the Russians from their offensive positions and then reunited for a drive to the Dnieper at Kholm. Funck's mixed-arms battle groups closely pursued the Russians until they crossed the Dnieper on October 6. On the seventh, Manteuffel's battle group seized a crossing of the Vyazma-Moscow Highway, well behind the former city, and the following day, Steinkeller's armored cars joined with the advance units of 10th Panzer Division of Hoepner's panzer group, sealing off fifty-five Russian divisions in the Vyazma Pocket. Meanwhile, another large pocket was formed at Bryansk by Weichs's 2nd Army and Guderian's 2nd Panzer Army (Map 1.5).

On October 10, the 7th Panzer received its first unit commendation from OKH and the commander in chief of the army, Field Marshal Brauchitsch, as quoted by Paul Carell: "I express my special commendation to the splendid 7th Panzer Division, which by its swift advance to Vyazma, has, for the third time in this campaign, made a major contribution to the encirclement of the enemy."

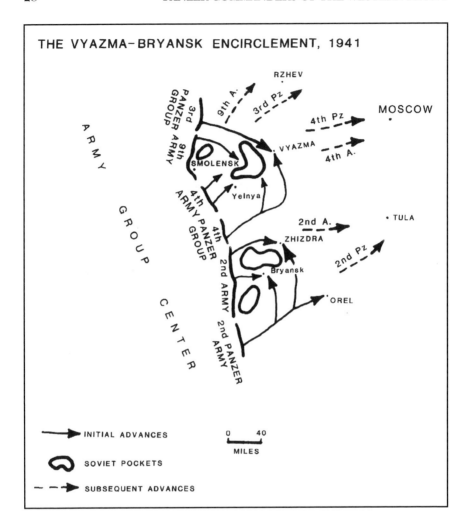

THE VYAZMA–BRYANSK ENCIRCLEMENT, 1941

Pushing quickly behind the panzer units, infantry began to forge a solid wall around the desperately struggling Russians; some did in fact manage to break out and escape eastward, but for the most part, the German lines held. On October 17–18, the Soviet remnants surrendered in burning Vyazma. The numbers of prisoners vary in different sources, but it seems that close to 650,000 men (four armies) were captured around Vyazma, and about 50,000 more (one army) surrendered in Bryansk.

The panzer troops who had begun the battle, though, were by now already engaged in a second potentially greater one. Hoepner's group had not paused even to secure the encirclement. It had sped northeast toward Mtsensk and Kaluga but was soon slowed to a snail's pace by the beginning of the *rasputitsa*, the fall rain. Colonel General Hoth had been sent south to the Ukraine for an army command in early October; Georg-Hans Reinhardt of the XXXXI Panzer Corps had succeeded him in command of 3rd Panzer Group.[33]

Funck's division dragged its laborious way northeastward, in tandem with the 6th Panzer Division (now under Maj. Gen. Erhard Raus), hampered by the gelatinous mud, steady rain, and stiffening Soviet resistance. Nevertheless, the panzer troops captured Klin on November 24 and secured Rogachevo later in the day.

Without proper winter clothing or equipment, the divisions pushed on through waist-deep snow, over treacherously icy roads, in unbearable cold. The seam between the two defending Soviet armies was burst open, and Funck assigned all his best and most mobile units to the command of the dashing young Col. Baron Hasso von Manteuffel for a lightning assault into the rear of the stunned Russians.[34] The battle group commander more than justified his appointment: he took the Moskva-Volga Canal Bridge by a coup de main, seized the pivotal town of Yakhroma along with its vital power station, and consolidated the bridgehead.

Funck directed the pressure of new units to the important lodgment north of Moscow, pushing Steinkeller and a battalion of Lungershausen's infantry through Solnechegorsk and bringing the township of Iskra, about four miles south along the canal, under attack on November 26. But two powerful fresh Soviet units, backed by T-34 tanks and batteries of Katyusha rocket launchers, began a furious counterattack on November 27, and the ill-supplied German forces were soon reduced to desperate straits.

The temperature dropped to eight below zero during the afternoon and twenty below at night. Oil and grease froze in automatic weapons, vehicles, and artillery, but the men—with no warm clothing or boots—suffered the worst. Funck radioed the distant supply base at Smolensk, which told him that as soon as conditions permitted, some gear would be sent up to Solnechegorsk for distribution—probably a matter of a week.

As it was, on November 29, Manteuffel was forced to evacuate his Vakhroma bridgehead and rejoin the main body on the western bank of the canal. A stint of better weather on November 30 and December 1 did allow a convoy from Smolensk to reach Sol-nechegorsk—carrying one coat per platoon for the division. The German infantrymen, however, had not waited. They had taken the fine fleece-lined greatcoats, insulated caps and gloves, and soft felt and lamb boots from dead Russians.

Men of the 5th Company, 7th Panzer Grenadier Regiment arrived at General Funck's headquarters late on the thirtieth with a gift—a beautiful sealskin coat with fur collar and hood taken from a captured Soviet colonel. The general thanked them profusely.

On December 5, the Russians counterattacked. Corps headquarters at Klin came under serious attack almost at once; farther south, two infantry divisions were heavily engaged and driven back in some disorder. Northward, Soviet tank forces cut off the main supply route for the corps and captured two of its fortified posts, Spas Zaulok and Yamolga. Funck responded immediately to the problem when advised of it: every rolling tank of the panzer regiment, led by Lt. Col. Horst Ohrloff, one of the division's finest tankmen, rushed to smash a Soviet force at Bolshoy Schapovo. The battle of Klin had begun.

Throughout the next week, the 7th and all the other units under Schaal's corps headquarters and Reinhardt's army exceeded their capabilities in a series of combats, retreats, enflankments and counterattacks. Col. Eduard Hauser became the hero of the German resistance; he was one of the last defenders to evacuate burning Klin late on December 16.

Despite every effort the Russians had expended, the components of 3rd Panzer Group were able to extricate themselves from their deadly positions and fall back to the semiprepared Lana (River) Line, between Starytsa and Volokolamsk. The positions held through the turn of the year, despite renewed Soviet assaults.

Funck's severely mauled division continued to hold a purely defensive position during the freezing months of January and February 1942. Meanwhile, Russian counterpressure built up drastically, and in the last week of February, it forced a further German retirement—this time all the way back to the Dvina before Vitebsk, trying to hold positions from Velizh through Demidov to Dukhovschina. Funck's forces fought fiercely in and around Demidov in mid-March but were driven out of the city by overwhelming Soviet pressure.

The forces of the 3rd Panzer Army, as the 3rd Panzer Group was redesignated on January 1, 1942, were almost spent by now, so heavily had they been engaged since the previous November, and it was amazing that they were able to hold the new line at all. Luckily for them, when the spring thaw set in in mid-April, it halted almost all hostilities in the area.

Orders now arrived for the remnants of the 7th Panzer Division to pull out of the line and entrain from Smolensk for a journey to France, leaving the surviving equipment of the division behind, to be divided among the units still on the battle line. Funck, with Lt. Col. Lothar Berger, Lieutenant Zydow, and the senior officers of the division—Colonel Hauser, Colonel Manteuffel, Colonel Steinkeller (now commanding the 7th Rifle Regiment), and Colonel Froehlich, the veteran artillery commander—supervised the 8,500 weary officers and men aboard the fleet of trains.

On May 11, 1942, Hans von Funck established his divisional head-quarters at Chalons-sur-Marne in France to begin the laborious task of rebuilding. He had, however, stopped off briefly in Berlin to visit a former subordinate, Col. Wolfgang Thomale, now awaiting reassign-ment. Thomale had served on the staff of the Panzer Inspectorate and had been able to put in a few words with that organization.[35] As a result, during the last week in May, 35 of the sturdy Panzerkampfwa-gen III Ausf. J (medium tanks) and 30 new Panzerkampfwagen IV Ausf. G (equipped with 75-millimeter guns) were given to the 25th Panzer Regiment—65 of a hoped-for 160 total. During the same period, 40 new junior officers and 800 men were assimilated into the understrength companies.

Throughout the pleasant days of summer, the division grew stronger and better trained, as its veteran officers worked diligently to restore it to its previous crack status. General Funck, however, was careful about morale, sending all the veterans of the deadly winter battles on rotating home leaves.

On August 15, 1942, Funck was awarded the *Ostmedaille* for service in Russia; on the twentieth, his three colonels—Hauser, Froehlich, and Manteuffel—received theirs. Funck was promoted to lieutenant general on September 1.

Powerful Anglo-American forces invaded the French African pos-sessions on Sunday, November 8, whereupon Vichy France broke off all relations with the United States. The next day, the 7th Panzer was ordered to take part in the German contingency plan *Anton*: the occupation of the rest of France. On the eleventh, Funck led his division in an unopposed race southward to secure Marseilles, which the troops accomplished with smooth efficiency by late in the evening.

The division remained in the vicinity of Marseilles for the rest of the year, continuing its buildup and training. Then in January 1943, it was ordered back into Germany, to its garrison headquarters at Gera, where it was to pick up some brand new equipment, chiefly a powerful battalion of 88-millimeter antiaircraft guns, which were extremely useful in antitank warfare as well.

By now, Funck was dealing with new subordinate officers—new in their commands, but veterans of the division. Col. Wolfgang Glaesemer now commanded the 6th Rifle Regiment, Lt. Col. Max Lemcke headed up 7th Rifle Regiment, and the dashing Lt. Col. Adalbert Schulz, called "Panzer" for his élan as a tankman, led the 25th Panzer Regiment. Glaesemer and Lemcke wore the Knight's Cross, and Panzer Schulz also had the Oak Leaves.[36] The veteran Colonel Froehlich—by now a close friend of Funck's—had been awarded the Knight's Cross as well. Of all the divisions in the panzer arm of the *Wehrmacht*, the 7th had—and kept—a reputation for retaining its officers. Captains of 1940 were colonels and generals by 1945.

During February 1943, the division was moved eastward, via Krakow and Kiev, to the southern sector of the Eastern Front, where, since the debacle of Stalingrad and the evacuation of the Caucasus, the German armies were being harried by huge Soviet concentrations of infantry and tanks. The 7th, together with the 11th Panzer and the 333rd Infantry, all rushed to Russia at this time, were placed under Gen. Siegfried Henrici's XXXX Panzer Corps headquarters and pushed from Zaphorozhe east to intercept a major Russian drive through Stalino. On February 14–15 the corps reached Slaveyansk—and was bypassed by a Russian armored corps.

Instead of a disaster for the Germans, this was a stroke of luck. Hermann Balck's 11th Panzer Division struck south and west to Krasnoarmeysk.[37] Meanwhile, Funck, carrying along a regiment of Maj. Gen. Wilhelm Kuenze's 333rd, swung north and west into the same area, thereby cutting off the Russians.

Funck led his rapid units over frost-hardened roads. Bypass the resisting strongpoints and leave them to the infantry, he ordered. On

February 23, Funck's units encircled the rail junction of Barvenkovo, and by the twenty-seventh, they had cut the Izyum-Slavyansk highway in three places and reached the Donetz—sealing the fate of General Popov's Armored Corps and endangering the flank of Kharitonov's 6th Soviet Army.

The first ten days of March saw the utter destruction of both Soviet forces: 23,000 died, but only 9,000 were taken prisoner. The haul in tanks, trucks, and guns was immense. The Russians had been effectively halted in their rush—and the spring thaws came early, bringing both armies to besodden halts on their forward lines. After this battle, the 7th Panzer Division was attached to the III Panzer Corps.

Funck's crack division had sustained minimal losses in personnel, but the battle damage to the equipment, in addition to normal wear and tear, was far larger than the general liked, and he and his maintenance personnel were glad of the weather-necessitated lull in order to do a thorough overhaul on the rolling stock. In mid-April, he sent Lieutenant Zydow to the quartermaster general of Army Group Don at Kharkov with a list of needed equipment, most notably tanks. The division should have fielded at least 160 tanks but had actually gone into action with only 95, of which 12 had become total losses and 20 others were obsolete.

So depleted were all the panzer divisions on the southern sector of the Eastern Front that the quartermaster merely filed the 7th's requisition. But a change in command in Feburary 1943 resulted in a surprising change in status. Col. Gen. Heinz Guderian had been appointed inspector general of panzer troops with exceptional and broad-ranging powers, and one of his first moves was to begin to supply the newest available tanks to the divisions of Army Group Don and its subordinate Army Detachment Kempf. Col. Wolfgang Thomale, a veteran of the 7th Panzer, became Guderian's chief of staff, and he particularly listened to the appeals of his old commander and friend. In preparation for the upcoming Operation *Zitadelle*, trainloads of the new Porsche Panzer tank began unloading at the Kharkov rail yards; Colonel Schulz supervised the move of forty of them to the 7th's cantonments southeast of Belgorod.

After the war, Gen. of Panzer Troops Hermann Breith wrote a detailed account of the III Panzer Corps operations in the Kursk offensive of July 5–13, 1943, for the U.S. Military Historical Commission. His account, written from firsthand experience, varies considerably from that of Paul Carell in his excellent *Scorched Earth*. Breith emphasizes the skill and efficiency of the 7th Panzer, which made the deepest inroads into the Soviet lines. He does not name any names, but he puts both the 6th and 19th Panzer Divisions in supporting and exploiting roles for the greater part of the battle. Carell, however, relying on after-the-war reminiscences, goes so far as to put Manteuffel as the divisional commander on July 8—an error of some magnitude for a usually accurate chronicler. His subsequent detailed description of the exploits of the 6th Panzer Division, though accurate enough, more or less gives the impression that this division accomplished all the major successes of the III Panzer Corps.

In any case, when the battle was called off on July 15–16, the 7th Panzer was an almost burned-out force; its losses in men and materiel were high. Colonel Manteuffel's rifle brigade was down to three-battalion strength. Panzer Schulz's regiment could field a bare fifteen tanks. General Funck had suffered a couple of flesh wounds during the course of the battle, but beyond a night in a dressing station, he remained in charge, although in poor health. The division, however, was not allowed a rest. Still under the III Panzer Corps, it was committed to the defense of Kharkov when the heavy Soviet counteroffensive smashed forward in early August. Funck, though by now much more ill, was tireless in his efforts to accomplish the impossible. On August 16, in defense near Akhtyrka on the road to Kharkov, the general passed out from exhaustion.

Lieutenant Zydow notified Colonel Glaesemer, the closest senior officer, to take temporary command, and he put Funck aboard a plane en route to the hospital at Kiev. Here, on August 16, the doctors declared him unfit for frontline duty and ordered him back to Germany for a rest. Meanwhile, Maj. Gen. Hasso von Manteuffel, of the 7th Rifle Brigade, was ordered to assume command of the 7th Panzer, taking over from Glaesemer at noon on the eighteenth.

Funck reached his home at Wunsdorf on the nineteenth and at once reported to the Berlin hospital, where he was again denied any field duty but was able to secure a certificate for restricted service at home. The next day, he reported to Guderian's headquarters and was put on Fuehrer Reserve, at the disposal of the Panzer Inspectorate.

On August 22, Guderian presented Funck with the Oak Leaves to his Knight's Cross for his exploits at Kharkov and Kursk. The general also received, belatedly, his German Cross in Gold, which had actually been awarded him as far back as March 14, 1943, for his skillful command of the Izyum encirclement of the month before.

During the next two months, the lieutenant general was assigned a desk at the Inspectorate headquarters in the old location on the Bendlerstrasse. His wealth of expertise on the recent operations in Russia was put to good use in lectures to the younger officer candidates and discussions of the design of tanks and self-propelled guns, some of which had proved so ineffective at Kursk.

In late November, Hans von Funck secured a clean bill of health from the Medical Board to resume active duty and at once began to petition to return to field duty. He was ordered again to the Eastern Front, to the northernmost sector of the 3rd Panzer Army's front around Vitebsk. On December 4, 1943, Gen. of Infantry Johannes Friessner, commander of the XXIII Corps, had gone on a long delayed rest leave, and Funck was asked to substitute for him.[38] This assignment to a stagnated infantry unit deployed in slit trenches, bunkers, and strongpoints centered around the town of Usuyaty, to the north of Vitebsk, was undoubtedly a waste of good armored leadership. The area remained quiet for the couple of weeks during which Funck was present—though he doubtless would have risen to the occasion had it offered itself.

Friessner resumed command on December 20, and Funck returned to Wunsdorf for the dismal Christmas season, made a bit more pleasant in that his eldest son, Hans Joachim, was home on leave. Nevertheless, the general was back at the Army Personnel Office on January 2, 1944, requesting a new assignment at the front. Such was not to be forthcoming, however; the Panzer Inspectorate again claimed him for a few fact-finding missions to the front, which at least allowed him to keep in contact with his luckier friends (if one can consider them so).

On February 15, however, Funck was attached to the staff of Lt. Gen. Nikolaus von Vormann, commanding officer of the XXXXVII Panzer Corps, which was attempting to break open the Korsum (Cherkassy) pocket.[39] By February 18, the survivors of the two infantry corps had managed to cross the Gniloy Tikish River and rejoin the German front, which in turn began to fall back westward under massive Soviet sledgehammer blows.

Both Vormann and Funck were promoted to general of panzer troops on February 28. Vormann was recalled to army group headquarters, and Funck succeeded him as commander of the XXXXVII Panzer Corps.

General Funck's hope of seeing active service died aborning, however. The three divisions that had hitherto been corps fighting forces were assigned to other nearby corps (III, XXIV, XXXXVI, and XXXXVIII), and the headquarters was recalled to Orgeyev on the lower Dniester, near the Romanian border, to supervise a few miscellaneous formations as a defensive force. The arrival of some regular infantry units in early April ended this assignment, and corps staff was sent first to Kishinew and then to Bacau in Romania.

On May 12, 1944, orders arrived from Berlin for the officers of the corps headquarters to take airplanes immediately for Normandy, in France, as a sort of intermediate headquarters for the several panzer divisions being rebuilt there. The several officers flew via Vienna and Strasbourg to an advanced airbase near Chartres, where the interim headquarters was established.

General Funck straightway drove north to La Roche–Guyon to pay his requests to *Generalfeldmarschall* (Field Marshal) Erwin Rommel, with whom, many months before, he had virtually exchanged commands. The meeting took place on May 26 and was cordial but not friendly; Funck was annoyed that his headquarters was not to have any field units attached to it, but was to act strictly as a training and liaison staff.

On May 20, Gen. of Panzer Troops Baron Leo Geyr von Schweppenburg, commanding officer of Panzer Group West and the overall panzer commander, albeit with little more responsibility than Funck, had visited Chartres from his own headquarters at Paris.[40] He proceeded to explain the conflicting and even overlapping areas of command in France, whereby the several panzer divisions were scattered from Brussels to the Mediterranean and were chiefly at the disposal of Hitler, who alone could give the order for their movement.

Funck was scarely heartened by these two interviews: He had been assured by the officers in Berlin that his assignment to the west was because he was considered an expert in armored warfare and that he would be given a free hand in making dispositions to counter the expected Allied invasion. Now, he discovered, he was only a supernumerary—outranked by two well-known and very senior panzer generals, both with superlative records. Nevertheless, he began to familiarize himself with the officers of his new staff, so as to establish a good working arrangement should the headquarters be activated for combat duty. His chief of staff was Col. Walther Reinhardt, a general staff officer and veteran of the Eastern Front, where he had served as operations officer and then chief of staff of the corps since 1942.

The XXXXVII's new operations officer (Ia) was also of the General Staff: Lieutenant Colonel Herschel, a long-time servant in the *Panzertruppen.* Captain Zydow was still the adjutant and only long-standing associate of the general. *Arko 113,* the corps artillery senior staff, was directed by Col. Gunther Zugehor, a Knight's Cross bearer, while a battalion of Ukrainian volunteers attached as outriders and headquarters guards, *Ostbattaillon 447,* was commanded by a reserve captain who spoke fluent Russian, Count Jurgen von Rittberg. *Nachrichtenabteilung 447,* the corps signals battalion, was in the hands of Maj. Richwein Froehlich, the younger brother of von Funck's old artillery commander. The supply unit, *Nachschubwesen Abteilung 447,* was the province of Maj. Heinrich Baehr.

The landing by the formidable Allied armies on the beaches of the Cotentin between the Orne River and Cherbourg (see Map 1.6) on June 6, 1944, was a success, due in large part to the total confusion among the senior German commanders. Panzer units were committed late and piecemeal; Allied air supremacy further disrupted the desperate efforts to contain the invaders. Geyr von Schweppenburg at once rushed his panzer group headquarters to Chateau le Caine, near Thury-Harcourt on the Caen River, so as to better coordinate his forces. He simultaneously directed Funck to bring his headquarters forward, hoping it could take over a couple of divisions. The move was hampered—as was everything else—by the cloud of Allied attack planes that hit anything that moved. Maj. Hugo Burgsthaler, the Ia of Panzer Group West, reached Vimont with Geyr's operations staff on June 7, but the general did not get there until June 8.

On June 9, guided by radio direction finders, four squadrons of rocket-firing Typhoons—forty aircraft in all—blasted Geyr's tactical headquarters. They were immediately followed by seventy-one Mitchell B-25 medium bombers, which carpet bombed it with 476

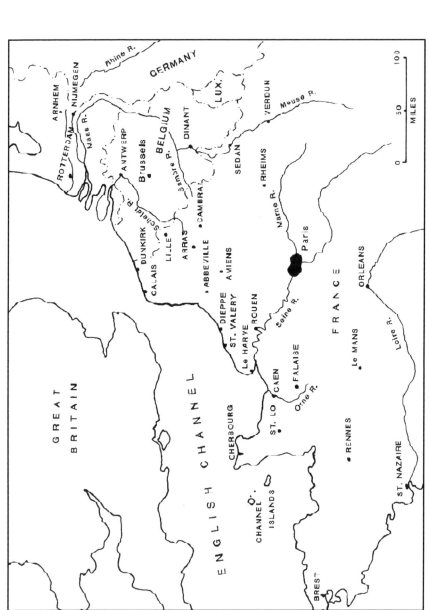

The Area of Operations of Army Group B, 1944

500-pound bombs. The general, though badly shaken, was only slightly wounded, but his headquarters was smashed, his staff company was slaughtered, and his entire operations staff was wiped out, including Major Burgsthaler. Maj. Gen. Ritter und Elder Sigismund-Hellmut von Dawans, the chief of staff of Panzer Group West, was among the dead. Geyr was soon able to return to duty, but his command apparatus was shattered, and his surviving staff members were understandably demoralized. Panzer Group West had to be withdrawn from the battle and was sent back to Paris to rebuild and reorganize.[41]

General Funck immediately put his own staff at Geyr's disposal. The XXXXVII Panzer Corps was activated—at a newer, safer headquarters in a concrete-reinforced cellar on the outskirts of St. Martin des Besaces. From here, it supervised the battles in defense of Villers-Bocage from June 11 to 14.

All in all, the entire front was under terrible Allied pressure and it was something of a credit to Funck that the formidable enemy was beaten back in this battle—not that he got any recognition for it at Fuehrer Headquarters. The alternating pressure by American, Canadian, and British forces all along the bulging, buckling front thoroughly disoriented the German commanders, who were slowly pushed back to the south. Map 1.7 shows the situation on July 1, 1944.

On June 30–July 1, Geyr von Schweppenburg was summarily relieved of his command over what was left of Panzer Group West by a Fuehrer Order.[42] Gen. of Panzer Troops Hans Eberbach arrived from the southern sector of the Russian Front on July 2 to take over the command. Though doubtless Eberbach was a very senior general, it was a personal affront to Funck. Nevertheless, both men acted together in a friendly and efficient manner.

During July, the situation grew worse as the Allied forces pushed further and further into the country. Under Eberbach, Funck's corps headquarters commanded two infantry divisions, as well as the 116th Panzer Division under Lt. Gen. Count Gerhard von Schwerin. Field Marshal Guenther von Kluge had replaced Gerd von Rundstedt as commander in chief of the Western Front on July 1.[43] On July 17, Erwin Rommel was severely wounded by a fighter bomber attack on his staff car and was sent home more dead than alive.

Losses among the men mounted steadily; the equipment suffered even worse, and thanks to the Allied air supremacy, little if any

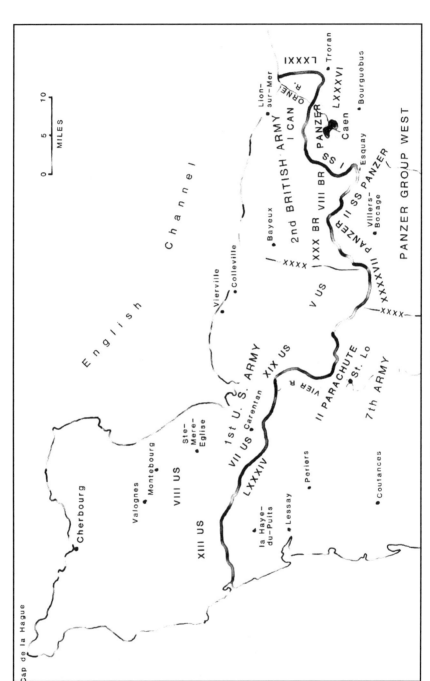

The Normandy Front, July 1, 1944

replacement materiel could be brought up. Even food and precious fuel were in short supply. Despite all of this, the Supreme Command—namely Hitler—expected nothing less than miracles from its field commanders: ground was to be held, no matter what; moreover, counterattacks were to be launched, whether they were possible or not. Thus on August 2, orders from *SS Oberstgruppenfuehrer* (SS Col. Gen.) Paul Hausser, the commander of the 7th Army, reached Funck: the Fuehrer had demanded an attack by every available panzer unit against the Allied forces at Mortain and Avranches. The XXXXVII Panzer headquarters would coordinate the blow, which must begin by August 8.

"My God!" the general shouted at Colonel Reinhardt. "What are they thinking of? August 8th—five days? The Jabos [Allied fighter bombers] will smash every vehicle we possess! We can't group up because of those airborne devils and if we don't group, we can't attack!"

"General Hausser agrees," Reinhardt replied, offering another piece of paper. "He advocates an immediate attack with everything we can scrape together—at dawn tomorrow, the 3rd."

OKW, however, refused that sensible suggestion; Hitler wanted the time to mass every piece of offensive equipment available—to be ready by August 10. By then, he is supposed to have observed, large numbers of American forces would have gone through the gap in the German lines and would thus be cut off by the counterattack.

General Funck appealed to Hausser, who then got hold of Kluge. Perhaps the attack could be scheduled for August 6, at dawn? Kluge forwarded the request to Fuehrer Headquarters at Rastenburg, East Prussia. No, OKW retorted, angrily. The attack must wait until August 8, not a day earlier. Meanwhile, collect every tank, gun, armored car—everything and anything! Hausser relayed this to Funck, who at once agreed with him that such a concentration would be sure to attract every Allied attack airplane in the area. Then Kluge sent a final order: they were to attack at once—by 2200 hours (10 P.M.) of August 6—and feed in everything they could lay their hands on.

This was what the general wanted. Orders were dispatched to the units involved: Lt. Gen. Baron Heinrich von Luettwitz's 2nd Panzer Division, Count Schwerin's badly understrength 116th Panzer Division, the few remnants of Fritz Bayerlein's Panzer Lehr Division, SS Theodor Wisch's 1st SS Panzer Division "*Leibstandarte* Adolf Hitler,"

SS Lt. Gen. Heinz Lammerding's 2nd SS Panzer Division "*Das Reich*," and the hastily brought-up battle group of the 17th SS Panzer Grenadier Division "*Goetz von Berlichingen*" under *SS Standartenfuehrer* (SS Col.) Eduard Diesenhofer. None of these men had any idea that the British Ultra code breakers had gotten wind of the plan and informed Gen. Omar N. Bradley, the commander of the U.S. 12th Army Group, who was already pouring reinforcements into the sector. Funck's attack was doomed before it began.

At 10 P.M., the right-wing forces lunged forward and, under the cover of darkness and later heavy overcast, made excellent progress. On the left, however, Schwerin was out of touch with his scattered units, and only a mixed battle group of motorcycles, half-track infantry, and three tanks got under way. Map 1.8 shows the battle of Mortain.

"Where is Wisch?" Schwerin's operations officer, Major Holtermann, telephoned Reinhardt. "He is supposed to be here to back us up!"

Some time later, Reinhardt found out what had happened to the tanks of the *Leibstandarte*: traveling along a two-mile stretch of sunken road, the column was halted by the purely fortuitous crash of an Allied night fighter on the lead tank. The whole cursing parade had to laboriously back up more than a mile to take another road.

"Schwerin has utterly fouled us up!" Funck growled at Hausser over the phone. "My right wing will be held up until after dawn!"

Still, Funck and Hausser were relatively well satisfied with the pace of the advance. Dove, Mesnil Dove, and Mesnil Addele all fell, and Avranches was less than ten miles distant. When the *Leibstandarte* and the 116th got under way, they overran St. Barthelmy before the tanks encountered units of an American armored division on the main Avranches road and a draw battle began.

The *Das Reich* division smashed the U.S. 30th Infantry Division at Mortain; *SS Gruppenfuehrer* Lammerding was, however, seriously wounded in the action, and command devolved on *SS Standartenfuehrer* Otto Baum, a much-decorated panzer officer. The survivors of the *Goetz von Berlichingen* division moved up in support of the *Das Reich* tanks.

By 9 A.M. on August 7, however, the heavy mists lifted and the sun shone in a clear sky—which was soon full of Allied warplanes. The attack was effectively stalled, and German losses mounted under the

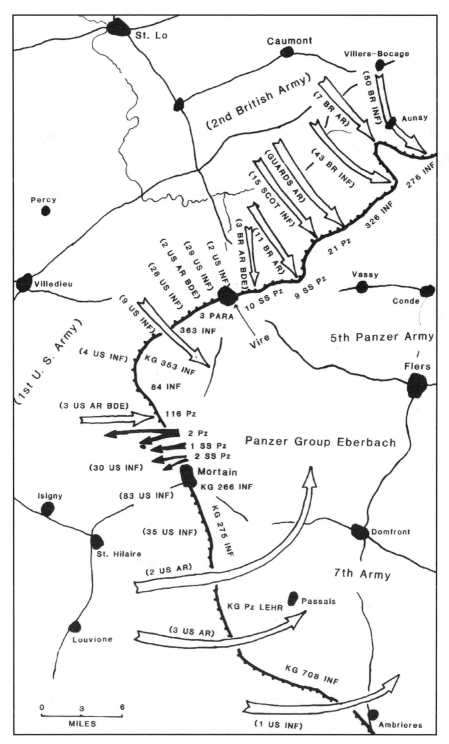

The Battle of Mortain, August 6–7, 1944

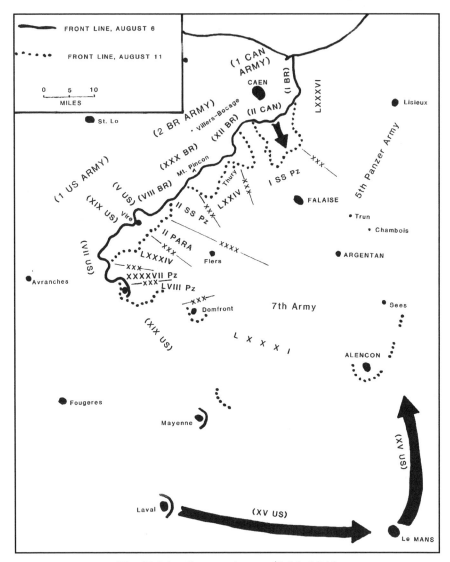

The Falaise Sector, August 7–11, 1944

aerial assaults. Promised *Luftwaffe* support ordered by Hitler had been met by the Allied air forces over the German bases, and not a single German plane managed to reach the Avranches front. The German ground forces, which had been assured of a 300-plane strike force, blamed the airmen bitterly for leaving them defenseless.

By nightfall on August 7, Funck was on record at Kluge's headquarters near Paris as advocating a withdrawal to his starting line. His unit commanders had all reported in—with most pessimistic statements. The 116th was still engaged to the west of Gathemo. The 2nd Panzer had just lost Mesnil-Adelee, which it had captured only that morning. *Leibstandarte* was under powerful assault about five miles east of Juvigny, and though Baum's panzers of *Das Reich* were still fighting in Mortain, his flank on Hill 314 was being decimated. *Standartenfuehrer* Diesenhofer's battle group had been driven out of Barenton by a U.S. heavy-weapons battalion.

U.S. air figures for the day wildly overstated their success. They reported 81 tanks totally destroyed, 54 seriously damaged, and another 26 hit. Considering that Funck had disposed of only 120 tanks total for his attack and on August 9 could still list 50 in service, the U.S. aviators' reports must be viewed as somewhat exaggerated.

Meanwhile, to the south, the U.S. XV Corps of Patton's 3rd Army captured Le Mans on August 8 and turned north, beginning an operation aimed at the encirclement of the 5th Panzer and 7th Armies in the Falaise-Argentan area (Map 1.9).

On August 8, Gen. Hans Eberbach was ordered to turn over command of his 5th Panzer Army (formerly Panzer Group West) to *SS Obergruppenfuehrer* Sepp Dietrich (formerly commander of the I SS Panzer Corps) and take command of a nebulous force to be styled *Panzergruppe* Eberbach. In 1946, General Eberbach did a special study for the U.S. Historical Division related to his various commands on the Western Front between July and September 1944, and a quote from one of his essays is very pertinent here:

> The attack on Avranches, according to an order from Hitler, will be repeated. With an emergency staff, I have to take over command of the panzer divisions provided for this attack, and will be subordinate to the C-in-C of the Seventh Army, SS General Hausser.
>
> I again immediately put forth, that I consider the attack as hopeless and my assignment to this post would therefore be very unpleasant to me. It did not help; the order was maintained. I had to go to the Seventh Army on the same day (August 9).
>
> The Seventh Army was obviously not very pleased with my turning up there. The insertion of my staff between the Army staff and the Corps (XXXXVII) Staff was unnecessary and

meant, in the prevailing situation, a very unpleasant length-
ening of the command channel.[44]

Funck also was obviously displeased, not so much at being under
Eberbach, whom he respected, but at the obvious slap at him for his
failure to succeed in his attack—an attack no other general could
have carried out any more successfully. Meanwhile, circumstances
were playing hob with the XXXXVII's staff: Colonel Reinhardt had
been posted to the command of one of the 116th Panzer Division's
panzer grenadier regiments, and Col. Georg von der Marwitz, from
Russia, was brought in on August 8 to succeed him.

On August 10, under heavy Allied pressure, the headquarters
evacuated St. Martin for Briouze. Funck and Zydow, in their car,
made the trip of fourteen miles in just under nine hours. The cars of
Marwitz and Herschel were not as fast or fortunate; both were hit by
fighter-bomber attacks, in which the former was severely wounded
and the latter killed.

Funck was at once assigned an officer from the army group staff
as his operations officer—Maj. Artur von Eckesparre, who had once
been Rommel's chief supply officer and now also had to temporarily
double in brass as corps chief of staff. On August 12, under intense
Allied attack, the headquarters evacuated Briouze under cover of
darkness and took over a ruined farmhouse at Vieux Ponts, a hamlet
of some strategic value.

On August 12, the remnant of Col. Max Sperling's 9th Panzer
Division—a battalion of grenadiers, a battalion of self-propelled guns,
and five tanks—falling back from Alençon, came under Funck's command and was posted in the wooded region between Joue and Ranes.
Funck sent orders to Schwerin to establish a command perimeter at
Sees, while the *Leibstandarte* was to move down from Fromentel to support the battered 9th. Here General Eberbach joined him, and both
were pinned down by a massive air-ground attack. Word arrived that
the battle group of the 116th at Sees had been virtually destroyed.

During the night of August 12–13, both generals moved to
Cheneuville, twenty-four miles west of Argentan—a move that took
nearly six hours because of the traffic congestion on the roads. Nevertheless, during the thirteenth and fourteenth, the scattered elements of the 116th and 2nd Panzer, and the *Leibstandarte*, moved up

into the area around Argentan but were driven back by fierce Allied attacks that threatened to seize the city itself.

Funck and Eberbach, joined on the fourteenth by *SS Gruppen-fuehrer* (SS Lt. Gen.) Willi Bittrich of the II SS Panzer Corps, were able to stabilize a new defensive line along the Orne River, from Le Ferte Meis through Ecouche to Fromentel, but by the morning of the fifteenth, it was undeniable that any chance for a renewed attack was hopeless; even maintaining a defense was now out of the question, for the 5th Panzer and 7th Armies were in danger of being encircled in the Argentan-Falaise area (Map 1.10). Nevertheless, army group passed along the latest Fuehrer Order, dated August 13. It insisted blithely on the attack "past Alençon westward." Funck privately informed Eberbach that his divisions were incapable of any such flight of fancy; *Leibstandarte* possessed only thirty battle-worthy tanks, while the 2nd Panzer could field twenty-five and the 116th only fifteen. As for the 9th Panzer, Colonel Sperling commanded the equivalent of a company, with no tanks or guns left in running order. His battle group was merged with the 2nd Panzer Division for tactical purposes.

On August 15, while Eberbach was conferring with Schwerin near Pommeinville, near Argentan, von Funck at Cheneuville received an order from Army Group B to report to the town of Necy for a senior general's conference with Field Marshal Kluge. He went, only to find Hausser, Eberbach, and Dietrich—but no Kluge. After a three-hour wait, the generals returned to their commands and the continued disasters on all sectors.

Kluge turned up late that evening, after a harrowing series of escapes from fighter-bomber attacks on his car; he was nervous and far more aware of the real state of affairs than ever before. He had, he told Funck, already suffered a serious accident in Russia as a result of a Soviet air attack on his command vehicle and had spent several months in the hospital. The Americans were far more dangerous, he felt.

The general sympathized but was adamant in his opinion that only an evacuation of the Falaise "finger" could save the two armies almost encircled within it. The field marshal promised to pass on all the recommendations to OKW in Berlin—for all the good it would do.

On the sixteenth and seventeenth, further losses were sustained, and the generals of the armies gave orders for all supply service and rear area troops to move as rapidly as possible via Trun and

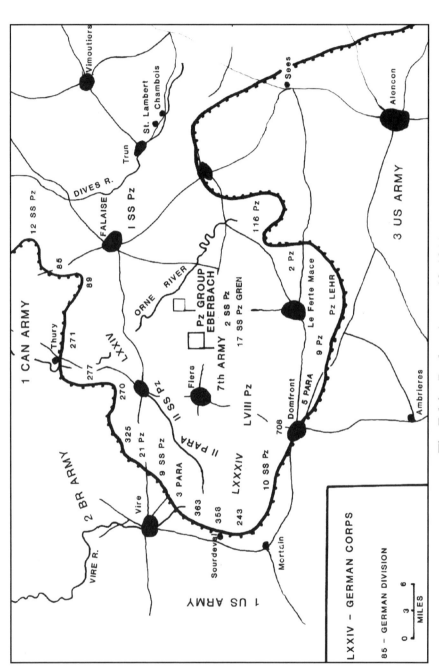

The Falaise Pocket, August 13, 1944

LXXIV – GERMAN CORPS

85 – GERMAN DIVISION

0   3   6
MILES

Chambois to the relative safety of Lisieux and Vimoutiers. Falaise fell on the seventeenth, and Army Group B ordered the II SS Panzer Corps out to a reserve position, but this was canceled when the defenses southwest of Falaise collapsed and Allied troops threatened Trun.

During the same period, the 116th Panzer's much battered companies were routed out of their positions east of Argentan, allowing a Canadian column to reach and capture Le Bourg St. Leonard. Allied artillery was now within close range of Chambois. Funck, who had left Vieux Ponts on the seventeenth, and reestablished a headquarters outside Chambois, now had to move again, this time to the vicinity of Aubrey.

On August 18, Field Marshal Walther Model, who had just replaced Kluge, conferred with the senior generals outside the pocket and gave the order for the withdrawal. The next four days were terrible ones; although a small gap in the Allied lines was held open, the U.S. and Canadian forces dominated the area with artillery fire and aircraft attacks.

Thanks to a lack of supplies, practically all the guns, tanks, and trucks of the XXXXVII Corps—what remained of them—had to be abandoned. Funck and his staff officers joined General Luettwitz and his surviving officers with a group of three armored cars, preceded and followed by King Tiger tanks, for the final breakout at night on August 21.

The convoy of vehicles, covered with riding troopers, surged to safety and eventually reached the Seine. Luettwitz was mildly wounded in the attack on the hills, but after a brief pause at a field hospital, he reported back to duty. General Funck established his new headquarters at Metz in Alsace on August 25. Here he, Eckesparre, and Zydow were joined by a sad Lt. Col. Guenther von Kluge, recently the chief of staff to Eberbach (until August 21) and lately returned from identifying the body of his father, Field Marshal Kluge, who had committed suicide near Dombasle at noon on August 18.[45]

The unfortunate young man was quickly put to work to take his mind off the problem, and there was work aplenty. Under the corps were the remnants of four panzer divisions, which had been bled white in the recent campaign. These were the 2nd under the ailing Lt. Gen. Baron von Luettwitz, the 9th of Colonel Sperling, the 116th of Lt. Gen. Count von Schwerin, and the Panzer Lehr Division (130th) under Lt. Gen. Fritz Bayerlein.

Funck made a circuit of the four headquarters between August 28 and September 4—his last official act as a field commander. His report was gloomy. Despite everything the field police could do—the weeding out of refugees, soldiers caught in roadblocks behind the Seine, and those returning from leave and wound recovery—the divisions were in dire straits. The 2nd Panzer Division was down to twenty-seven tanks (most of them recent replacements), twelve pieces of artillery, and 1,600 men. Luettwitz's wound required him to report to a hosptial in Germany on September 1, and Col. Gustav von Nostitz-Wallwitz, erstwhile chief of staff of the LVII Panzer Corps in France, was named acting commander.[46] The division was to man positions along the West Wall covering Aachen.

The 9th Panzer Division, to which the one-armed Maj. Gen. Gerhard Mueller was assigned on September 2, still had no tanks, but it had commandeered two batteries of 105-millimeter self-propelled guns and its grenadier strength rose from 140 in mid-August to 1,700 by September 2. Many of its new men were veterans.

The 116th Panzer Division, still commanded by Schwerin, had emerged in much better shape than almost any other formation that had escaped from the pocket. In passing through Verdun, a trainload of new Tiger tanks had been appropriated—thus saving them from capture by the pursuing U.S. 3rd Army, which took the town on September 1. Hence the 16th Panzer Regiment had forty runners, and the division had a full regiment of artillery and 3,400 grenadiers—a size so comfortable that on September 6, the 116th was sent to defend the city of Aachen, which was threatened by the U.S. 1st Army.

Panzer Lehr was the worst off; it had withstood the Allies almost from the very beginning of the Normandy campaign. Bayerlein reported eleven tanks serviceable, no artillery, and less than 500 men, chiefly men returning from leave. Subsequently, the Panzer Lehr Division was ordered back to Frankfurt for a major refitting.

On September 4, Gen. of Panzer Troops Baron Hans von Funck, back at his Metz headquarters, received a cold order from the Supreme Command: he was to relinquish command of the XXXXVII Panzer Corps Headquarters forthwith and report to Wiesbaden, the command center of *Wehrkreis XII*, for possible reassignment. No explanation was given.

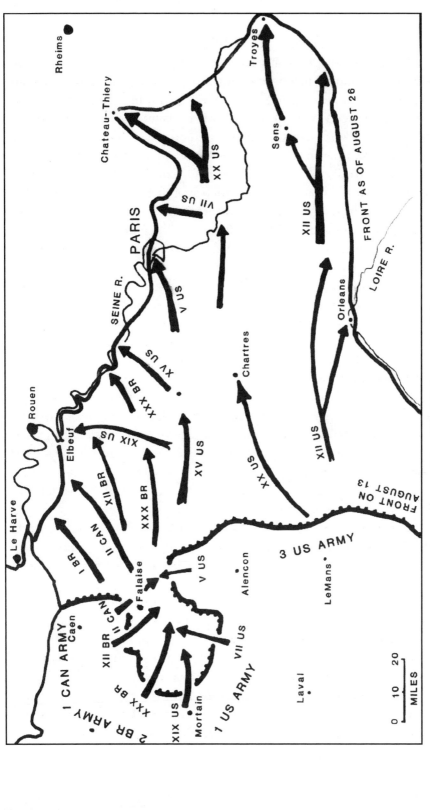

The Allied Drive to the Seine

Funck called together his staff to say his farewells and welcome Luettwitz, who was returning from the hospital to take over the corps. Kluge, Eckesparre, Froehlich, and Zuegelhor were effusive in their assurances of their appreciation in serving with him; much of the sadness experienced by comrades-in-arms was ameliorated by the fact that Luettwitz was a popular officer and an old friend.

On September 6, General Funck checked in with Gen. of Infantry Walther Schroth, the *Wehrkreis* commander, who was also serving on the so-called Court of Honor, which was dishonorably discharging officers involved in the July 20 assassination attempt against Adolf Hitler. Schroth was an old-line officer who had a deep sense of honor, and over dinner, he lamented the unpleasant duty he had been roped into.[47]

Two days later, General Schroth's car went out of control on a rain-slick highway and crashed in flaming ruins. The general died in the explosion. Lt. Gen. Kurt von Berg, an artilleryman unfit for further active service, was promptly appointed as acting *Wehrkreis* commander.[48] Funck, who had seniority, was of course at once aware that his career was over—for some reason he was "out to pasture."

The general obtained permission to travel to Berlin, although travel was severely restricted as a result of the confusion of the time and as well as Hitler's draconian measures to keep close tabs on anyone who was *Wehrmacht* and an aristocrat. Funck found his wife still living in Wunsdorf, despite his many suggestions that she move down into the Harz, where there were fewer air raids and less danger of imminent Soviet invasion.

On September 20, he sent in his card to the Panzer Inspectorate on the Bendlerstrasse, where Lt. Gen. Adolf von Schell, a member of the staff, met with him.[49] Many years before, the two had been acquainted while serving in the capital. Funck had then been Fritsch's adjutant, while Schell had been attached to the Armor Development Branch of the High Command. The inspector was therefore most cordial, but he had to admit that his hands were tied. Somebody—someone with considerable power—had decided that Funck was no longer persona grata to the army.

The baron was not daunted. He knew of no reason for such animosity. His career had hardly been spectacular enough to make him any enemies. Patiently, working through Schell, he arranged for an appointment with the chief of the general staff, Col. Gen. Heinz Guderian.

On October 1, he was received by Lt. Gen. Walter Wenck, the deputy chief of the General Staff. Wenck was another panzer veteran who had served in many staff assignments, as well as some hectic Russian field duty, and he had been chief of staff of the 1st Panzer Army while von Funck's 7th Panzer had been attached to it.[50]

Wenck was equally friendly—but equally pessimistic with regard to any future employment for the general. He conveyed to Funck a message of apology from Colonel General Guderian, who would be unable to see him personally but suggested that he return to Wiesbaden and enjoy a period of leisure. Meanwhile, Guderian would investigate the matter and see what he could do.

Funck returned to Wunsdorf where he made arrangements for the disposal of his house. Then, with papers issued by the Panzer Inspectorate, where Wolfgang Thomale was still chief of staff, he and his wife, Maria, traveled to the small Harz Mountain resort town of Blankenburg, some miles to the west of Quedlinburg and almost due north of the famous Klyffhauser Mountain, the legendary burial place of Frederick Barbarossa. There he reopened the long-locked door of the pretty residence on the town's outskirts—a safe enough place, he then thought, from both the Allied air forces and the Russians. He was half right.

In mid-October, Funck again reported to the *Wehrkreis* headquarters at Wiesbaden, only to find that no news of any sort had been forthcoming. With the now imminent threat of Allied forces reaching the Rhine, the *Wehrkreis* was in considerable confusion. Enemy aircraft lashed the cities day and night. General Berg, on his own initiative, assigned Funck to the post of commander of *Ersatz* (Reserve) Panzer Headquarters XII, which was involved in the training and resupply of armored forces in the field—notably the 15th and 36th Panzer Grenadier Divisions, both operating across the Rhine and in the Saar region. Funck also set about forming a reserve panzer brigade at the Oberuersel Maneuver Grounds. In late November and early December, this brigade was incorporated into the 11th and 9th Panzer Divisions.

At the advent of January 1945, with the Ardennes Offensive already a losing proposition and enemy forces close to the Rhine's west bank along a broad front, General Funck was summoned to Berlin. His fond hope of being employed again was effectively dashed in a short, frigid interview with Gen. of Infantry Wilhelm Burgdorf, the National Socialist officer appointment chief, who also served as chief of the Army Personnel Office and Hitler's special adviser on military affairs.[51]

Funck was to be retired, albeit with a full pension and the right to wear his uniform. No reason was given. Burgdorf was brief and brusque. He gave no answers and showed Funck out after just a few moments. Angry, the general drove at once to the battered *Bendlerstrasse* offices of the Panzer Inspectorate.

General Schell, whose health had been impaired ever since his terrible ordeal as commander of the 25th Panzer Division in the battle of Fastov in late 1943, was now retired. A neat panzer major agreed to try to solicit for Funck an appointment with General Thomale. The following morning, an aide delivered a note to the bachelor officers quarters at Wunsdorf, where Funck was staying. In the message, Thomale apologized for not being able to see his old friend, but suggested he call upon General Wenck at Zossen. There he might be able to obtain some sort of answers to his questions.

Funck waited three days before Wenck had a free hour—and then it was at an underground officers' club in the Zossen Military Complex. The staff general at once informed Funck that the interview was informal and off the record. Keitel and Jodl, he said, had never forgiven the panzer officer for his 1939 faux pas—both military and private. They had fanned Hitler's own antipathy toward the tall general, acquired at the January 1941 briefing on Libya. Efforts had been made to tie Funck into the military's conspiracy against the Fuehrer, but nothing even remotely incriminating had been turned up, which even further exasperated Keitel, who kept saying that Funck had been an intimate of Col. Gen. Erich Hoepner, one of the principal conspirators.[52] Yet no evidence could be produced that linked them in any way but at the most distant professional level. But Funck was an aristocrat, he had embarrassed the chief of OKW by his divorce, he had further refused to communicate through proper channels when in Spain, and last but not least, he had shown his sneering disregard of his Fuehrer. The final blow to his career had been his refusal to obey the orders he had received at Argentan to cut off the American forces by recapturing Alençon.

General Wenck spread his hands wide in a helpless gesture. He, Thomale, and Guderian had done everything in their power to have these foolish prejudices discarded. Guderian had even presented the Fuehrer with a number of favorable, even commendatory, statements from officers who had commanded or served with Funck in Russia and France. Regrettably, four of these commendations had emanated from Hoepner, Guenther von Kluge, Erwin Rommel and Rudolf Schmidt—the first three alleged conspirators, the last a vituperative critic of Hitler.[53]

The recommendations of Walter Model, Sepp Dietrich, Paul Hausser and Hasso von Manteuffel—all well regarded by the pro-Nazi generals—were thus set unceremoniously aside by the Fuehrer and his cronies. All Guderian had been able to salvage was Funck's good-conduct record, his full pension, and his right to wear his uniform with decorations.

As of February 25, 1945, Gen. of Panzer Troops Hans Emil Richard Funck would be *Entlassen; ausser Dienst*—retired.

Funck sadly returned to Wiesbaden and took his leave of his fellow officers. Captain Zydow had asked for permission to remain his aide. Guderian, through General Thomale, had him therefore assigned as *zu Verfugung* (at disposal) of *Wehrkreis XI*, where the town of Blankenburg was located. On February 25, the two officers arrived at the pleasant house in the Harz—and that might have been the end of the story.

In late April, however, war came even this far from the borders of beleaguered Germany. The German 11th Army—a shadow formation at best—established its headquarters at Blankenburg on April 21, but, on April 23, the U.S. 9th Infantry Division swept into the town and captured Gen. of Artillery Walther Lucht and his entire staff. General Funck was also taken prisoner, but as a retired personage, he was allowed to reside at home under house arrest. In fact, several fields adjoining the estate were turned into impromptu POW compounds and began to fill rapidly with captured or surrendered German soldiers.

In May, the capitulation at Rheims was signed, effectively ending hostilities, and an uneasy peace settled on the Anhalt countryside. Funck had been given to understand that the U.S.-Soviet zones of occupation would be divided by the River Elbe. He was later to be astounded when, for no particular reason, U.S.-Russian bigwigs playing with grease pencils on their huge scale maps arbitrarily decided that the River Mulde would constitute a frontier, thus enclosing all Amhalt within the Eastern Zone.

The Soviet authorities moved into the area before the month of June was out and began an immediate roundup of all National Socialist and *Wehrmacht* people they could get a line on. General Funck was loaded aboard a truck without more than a small suitcase and was borne away toward Russia. Maria von Funck was several months pregnant, and the Soviet authorities did not disturb her. Instead, pro-Soviet Germans were induced to begin to set up a people's government, and by the end of July, most Soviet troops had been pulled back toward their own borders.

Captain Zydow had been interned by the U.S. forces in May and was released from the POW camp in mid-July. In civilian clothes, he succeeded in reaching Blankenburg, to find Maria alone except for an old servant. He took up residence there, posing as a relative of the family. The new German authorities paid no attention, beyond issuing appropriate rationing documents and People's Republic identification.

On August 8, 1945, Arndt Werner Karl Stefan Goetz Burkhard von Funck was born at the estate, aided by an elderly doctor and the old servant. When the mother and infant were well enough, Zydow began to arrange to leave the Eastern Zone as soon as possible. Meanwhile, through various channels, he instituted a discreet inquiry into the whereabouts of the general.

Funck, with other senior German officers rounded up by the Soviet occupation authorities, was arraigned before a Soviet military court, which was enforcing a law promulgated by the Supreme Soviet *Politburo* in 1943: any German officer who served against the armies of the U.S.S.R. above the rank of colonel was an enemy of the people of the Soviet state and an obstructionist. The minimum sentence was ten years in one of the gulags.

It is not recorded where the unfortunate general was incarcerated, but he did indeed suffer the callous and often vicious treatment accorded to the "Fascist Imperialist war criminals" for a full ten years, being released in 1955 in the general amnesty declared by the new Soviet premier, Nikita Khrushchev. Age fifty-four when he began his imprisonment, Funck was a weak, white-haired sixty-four-year-old when he was eventually repatriated to the West German Republic.

Meanwhile, Zydow had succeeded in securing a passage visa for Maria and her young son. One of Funck's older sons had been of considerable assistance in this enterprise and had even managed to secure for her a small house at Viersen, a junction city not far from Duesseldorf. Zydow left them here in late 1945, prior to leaving Germany for life in South America, where he was an import-export official in the early 1950s, with offices at Buenos Aires and Montevideo.

The subsequent life of the Funcks is therefore conjectural. The general died on February 14, 1979, at the ripe old age of eighty-eight. His eldest son, Hans Joachim, had become a businessman at München-Gladbach after the war, but Burkhard entered the *Bundeswehr* when it was formed in the late 1950s, finally retiring as an *Oberst im Generalstabes* (colonel of the general staff) before 1981. The young Arndt is currently with the *Bundeswehr*. As of 1981, General Funck's ex-wife, Irmgard, his daughter, Ingeborg, and his widow, Maria, were all still alive.

CHAPTER 2

Baron Harald von Elverfeldt

On February 6, 1900, Baron Harald Gustav Max von Elverfeldt was born at Hildesheim, the family's principal residence. The Elverfeldts are a very old, predominantly Catholic family resident in and around Cologne, descending from Hermann von Heppendorf, a knight in the service of the prince archbishop of Cologne. Harald's father, Maj. Ferdinand Johann Georg von Elverfeldt, was attached to the Imperial Embassy at St. Petersburg shortly after the twentieth century began. Harald spent several years there, acquiring an excellent mastery of the Russian language. Maria, his mother, died in 1911 when he was still in school, and father and son returned to Germany soon after.

Ferdinand took over a regiment at the outbreak of the World War I but was soon posted back to the greater general staff. Harald eagerly sought admission to the army but was too young to succeed through the first three years of the war. On March 25, 1918, however, only a few weeks past his eighteenth birthday, Harald secured his patent as a *Faehnrich* (senior officer cadet) in the 1st Guards Regiment of Foot. He was rushed through an officer training course and took the field with a *Stosstrupp* (storm battalion) on May 10, 1918. Almost at once he was wounded in action, awarded the Iron Cross, Second Class, and invalided back to Berlin. The war ended soon after, the empire fell, and the kaiser abdicated. Harald, meanwhile, joined the *Freikorps* and fought the Bolsheviks in the Baltic States.[1]

Harald's father, now a lieutenant colonel, resigned his commission and retired to Hildesheim immediately after the armistice, but he had put in a good word for his son with friends, who were now charged with organizing the 100,000-man *Reichswehr*. As a result, on November 24, 1919, Harald, at age nineteen, was commissioned as a reserve second lieutenant with a Weimar patent and was allowed to attend clandestine officer training courses being held in and around

Cologne. In 1921, he sadly laid his father to rest in the family cemetery at Hildesheim, and then was almost immediately put on active duty and attached to a *Reichswehr* regiment (the 9th Infantry) in the capital, as ordnance (orderly) officer to the colonel commanding.

Harald von Elverfeldt's reserve commission was confirmed on June 10, 1922, retroactive to April 1, 1919, and he took command of one of the regiment's companies, now stationed at Potsdam. During this period, he made the acquaintance of a lovely young lady, also residing in Berlin.

Baroness Elizabeth von Berg had been born in 1902. Her father was the recently promoted Maj. Gen. Baron Gustav von Berg, and her mother had been Stephanie Schaffhausen, from another prominent military family. On April 6, 1923 (his military record gives the date as March 12), Harald and Elizabeth were married at the garrison church at Potsdam in the presence of numerous prominent soldiers, including at least four generals. Their first child, a daughter named Sigrid Maria, was born on March 30, 1924.

In December 1924, the twenty-four-year-old Harald was named battalion adjutant, a post he held for the next ten months, before being posted away from Berlin on October 1, 1925, to the Army Officers' Technical Training School IV at Dresden. He remained here until his matriculation on February 20, 1926, during which time he had been promoted to first lieutenant. He was assigned to the 11th Infantry Regiment, stationed near Dresden, as a battalion adjutant, and served in this post until October 10, 1927, when he was again sent to a special *Lehrgang* (training course), this time in the fundamentals of motorization (*Motorisien Wesens*)—a highly technical schooling from which he graduated on March 31, 1928. He then resumed his adjutancy to the battalion at Dresden.

On January 18, 1929, his second child, a daughter named Mechtilde Stephanie, was born in the Dresden hospital. In early May, he took a week-long course in the history of infantry—a code name for a special general staff advanced course. He was then relieved of his post in Dresden and ordered to Muenster, in *Wehrkreis VI* (VI Military District), whose commander was Lt. Gen. Emil Fleck, a close friend of his now-retired father-in-law.[2]

Harald left his regimental staff duties on October 1, 1931, to become the aide to General Fleck, who guided him through the final examinations for the general staff, the so-called *Wehrkreisprufung.* He graduated on March 13, 1932. When General Fleck left Muenster for a posting in Berlin on December 31, he took Harald with him.

Fleck was promoted to full general and retired on March 1, 1933, but he arranged for Elverfeldt to be posted to the staff of the city commandant of Berlin, under whom he was promoted to captain on September 1. While in this posting, Harald became very friendly with many staff officers in the city and attracted the attention of the chief of the *Truppenamt* of the *Reichswehrministerium* (the chief of the clandestine general staff), Gen. of Artillery Ludwig Beck, who had succeeded Lt. Gen. Wilhelm Adam in October 1933.[3] Hence on May 1, 1934, Elverfeldt was appointed to the Intelligence Bureau (T-3) of the *Truppenamt* (Troop Office). In October 1935, he was transferred to the Training Branch (*Oberquartiermeister II*, or O Qu II), headed by Maj. Gen. Rudolf Schmidt. By early the next year, he was acting as Schmidt's chief of staff.

Harald's next promotion—to major—went into effect on March 1, 1937. In October, Schmidt took over command of the 1st Panzer Division and was replaced by Lt. Gen. Franz Halder, who did not wish to retain the major as chief of staff.[4] Twelve days later, Elverfeldt took over his first field command, as a company commander in the 33rd Infantry Regiment of the 28th Infantry Division, stationed near Breslau.

For a little more than a year, the major struggled in this unfamiliar assignment; his expertise was officially listed as of the panzer forces, and the 28th was devoid of any mechanized units. Also, as a major, he was much too senior for a mere company command. Heinz Guderian, who had given up a field command for a staff assignment, managed to solve Harald's problem and arranged for Elverfeldt to be named Ia (operations officer cum chief of staff) of the hybrid 3rd Light Division, posted at Cottbus for mobilization.

Maj. Gen. Adolf Kuntzen, who had formerly headed up the Armor Branch at HPA until this time, had taken over the command of the abnormally formed unit and developed a close attachment to his new staff officer.[5] Together they led the division into Poland and saw their worst fears realized: the division proved to be a failure, with insufficient armor, unwieldy infantry and cavalry formations, and artillery of uneven quality. On being recalled to Germany in October, the officers were pleased at the chance to convert it into a panzer division, the 8th. Elverfeldt was rewarded with the clasp to his Iron Cross, Second Class, on September 20, as the division disengaged, and the Iron Cross, First Class, on October 8, 1939. He was promoted to lieutenant colonel on November 1.

Until January 1940, Harald worked shoulder to shoulder with Kuntzen in whipping the reorganizing and expanding division into shape. In fact, he was so assiduous at his job as to attract favorable attention from several senior officers—not the least of whom was Gen. of Infantry Hermann Hoth, commander of the XV Motorized Corps, which had directed both the 2nd and 3rd Light Divisions in Poland and was still in operational control of the 8th Panzer. Hoth's capable chief of staff, Johann Joachim "Hajo" Stever, was also impressed.[6] The corps' operations officer, Lt. Col. Count Karl Theodor von Sponeck, was due to be rotated to a field command.[7] Hoth and Stever got the ear of the HPA Armor chief, and on February 5, 1940, Elverfeldt moved into the more commodius command facilities of the XV Motorized Corps at Jena. Meanwhile, Stever was promoted and given command of the 4th Panzer Division, despite his uncertain health. Elverfeldt thus had to familiarize himself with his new, more arduous and complicated duties virtually on his own. The appointment of Col. Julius von Bernuth as corps chief of staff came as a pleasant relief to Elverfeldt.[8] He had worked with von Bernuth in 1935–36 in the *Reichswehr* Ministry.

The opening of the French campaign in May 1940 called for all the skill and effort of both staff officers. Hoth was always at the front, checking with his two divisional commanders—Maj. Gen. Erwin Rommel of the 7th Panzer and Lt. Gen. Max von Hartlieb of the 5th Panzer—or their subordinate units. The headquarters had its hands full with information control and dissemination of orders and situation reports. From the beginning to the end of the German drive to the English Channel, XV Corps made no mistakes and achieved its every objective. This fact proved the expertise of both staff officers. Colonel Bernuth was subsequently awarded the Knight's Cross, while Elverfeldt received two OKH commendations, both personally signed by Franz Halder, the chief of the general staff.

For the final strike across the Somme into the interior of France, the corps was entrusted with the attack to capture Cherbourg, Lorient, and Sainte Nazaire. Hoth continued his perambulations among the front runners of his galloping divisions, and between them, Bernuth and Elverfeldt kept the mobile corps headquarters functioning at top efficiency, even to the point of introducing a radio-mounted armored car into their general's caravan.

The final collapse of France in late June brought the most resounding victory of the German Army to a conclusion. Hoth was promoted to the rank of colonel general on July 19, 1940, and the corps headquarters returned to Jena. On November 3, it was redesignated the 3rd Panzer Group, an intermediate status between corps and army level.

In mid-February 1941, both Bernuth and Elverfeldt were again up for transfer—much to Hoth's disgust. Baron Harald von Elverfeldt was directed to Insterburg in East Prussia, where the LVI Motorized Corps was being set up under the command of Gen. of Infantry Fritz Erich von Manstein.[9] Elverfeldt was posted as corps chief of staff and found himself serving another infantry soldier with revolutionary ideas.

The staff pulled itself together in short order so as to be ready for the assignment of divisions to be employed in the forthcoming invasion of the Soviet Union. Maj. Erich Detleffson was assigned as Ia (operations),[10] Col. Guido von Kessel was named Ic (intelligence), Maj. Eugen Kleinschmidt was appointed quartermaster, and Rittmeister (captain of cavalry) Hello Kohler became signals officer. To assist him, Elverfeldt secured the services of Maj. Horst Niemann, a capable young officer from the general staff.

In his excellent postwar memoir of the Russian campaign, Manstein has quite a few things to say of his staff:

> Our tactical Headquarters lived almost the whole time in tents and the two command vehicles. . . . We always used to pitch our little camp in a wood or a copse near the main axis of advance—if possible by a lake or stream so that we could take a quick plunge before breakfast. . . . It was indispensible that the corps Q [Quartermaster] branch should usually remain stationary for several days at a time in order to keep the flow of supplies moving. The Commanding General and his operations branch, on the other hand, had to move their

tactical headquarters once or even twice a day if they were to keep in touch with the mechanized divisions. This called for a high degree of mobility on the part of the headquarters. . . .

While the chief of staff naturally had to stay behind the command post to deal with the work and telephone calls, I spent the days, and often part of the nights, out on the road. . . . Such flexible leadership on my part was, of course, possible only because I was able to take a wireless vehicle along with me on these trips under our excellent signals officer, Kohler.[11]

Thus the corps performed for the first three and a half months of the Russian campaign, achieving excellent success as long as it was allowed to use its own discretion. Later, shunted into swamplands and compelled into poor areas of operations, Manstein protested against such a waste of mobility several times. His chief of staff, who handled much of the business end of the corps, made careful notes of all these facts. Indeed, on several occasions, Manstein assigned him to combined arms units going into action, thus giving the staff officer some practical field experience.

On the evening of September 12, Manstein was notified that he was to take over command of the 11th Army in the Crimea and took leave of his staff early on the thirteenth. His encomium to Elverfeldt in his memoir says he was "a cool, high minded and never failing counsellor."[12] He also mentioned the staff most favorably. Indeed, Elverfeldt and his officers had the command to themselves for ten days from September 13 to 23, 1941. Thus on September 16, when the LVI Motorized Corps was transferred to Panzer Group 3 (under Colonel General Hoth) and committed to an attack on Demyansk, the lieutenant colonel held a close rein on the 6th and 7th Panzer Divisions, which formed the corps' fighting strength.

Lt. Gen. Ferdinand Schaal, who had briefly commanded the Afrika Korps until dysentery had forced him home to recover, had been selected by OKH as corps commander, but the lingering effects of his illness prevented his leaving Germany for the front until September 23. He arrived at the LVI's headquarters early the next day. Elverfeldt briefed him quickly of the developments here on the northern flank of Army Group Center.

While the battle for Kiev raged on in the southern sector of the Eastern Front, the units to the north held their ground and marked time. Schaal, in the usual panzer tradition, made the rounds of his unit headquarters, meeting his officers and studying the terrain. Headquarters had moved up to Jarsevo, close to the front lines. On September 29, Elverfeldt relayed the deadline to General Schaal: jump-off was set for dawn the following day.

The LVI Corps smashed through the surprised Soviet picket lines north and south of the Smolensk-Moscow highway and in six days had reached a point where the troops could seize the undamaged Dnieper bridges at Kholm. Crossing the river, they sped north—well behind the important Soviet headquarters city of Vyazma. Two days later, the 6th Panzer Division, supported by elements of Hans Funck's 7th Panzer, made junction at Vyazma with Maj. Gen. Wolfgang Fischer's 10th Panzer, which was advancing from the south.[13] Six Soviet armies with fifty-five divisions were encircled.

Hereafter, the shorter distances—from Yartsevo and Roslavl—enabled the slogging infantry to arrive in time to prevent the Soviets from being able to break out, thus freeing the panzer forces for assaults eastward toward Gzatsch and Moshaisk. Schaal continued his close contact with his racing forces until the onset of the *rasputitsa* (the fall rains) slowed everything to a crawl.

Snow and then subzero temperatures finally halted all German advances by early December. By now, the headquarters of the LVI Motorized was at the town of Bolskoi-Shehapovo, north of Moscow, near the Moscow-Volga Canal, while the subordinate units held more forward positions. The Soviet counterattack struck on December 6. By the seventh, the staff and headquarters personnel were hard put to defend themselves, carbines in hand. Reinforcements arrived and helped them hold off the Soviets, but Schaal removed the headquarters to the larger and more defensible city of Klin (see Map 2.1). Herein were waged the desperate battles of December 1941, when Elverfeldt on many occasions was required to command mixed army battle groups in repelling fierce hordes of Soviet troops, which at times almost cut off the citadel. When at length the corps headquarters was authorized to evacuate the town (December 13–14), it was all the officers—field and staff—could do to restrain a panic among the cold,

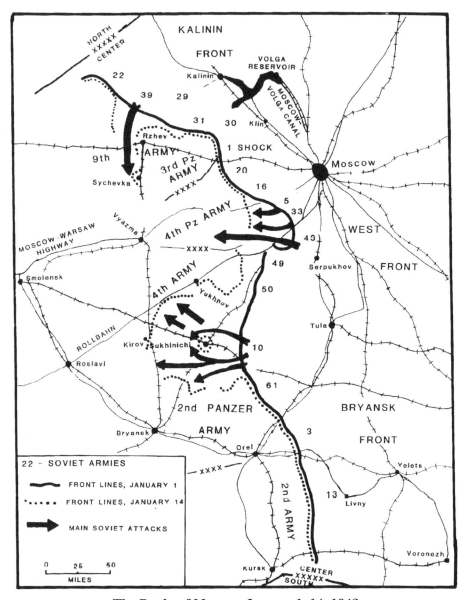

The Battle of Moscow, January 1–14, 1942

hungry, and demoralized troops. They did succeed, and the corps took up new defensive positions on the Lama, some fifty-six miles back.

Additional retreats took place during January and into February 1942, all the way back to a line from Lake Volga to Rzhev to Gzhatsk, but only after severe losses had been inflicted on the German units as a result of Hitler's refusal to allow an orderly retreat, as his generals wished. Nevertheless, by March, when the early spring thaw stopped further movements, the LVI Corps, now officially a panzer corps, was well dug in above Rzhev in good defensive posture.

On March 1, Elverfeldt was promoted to full colonel, and on the twentieth, he received the German Cross in Gold from General Schaal for his many contributions to the orderly operations of the corps. Regrettably, however, now it became the chore of the LVI's headquarters to head up antipartisan operations in the Spas-Demensk and Kirov areas of the front. Large areas behind the German front—one centered around Dorogobuzh, southwest of Vyazma, the other between Roslavl and Spas-Demensk, held huge guerrilla concentrations.

Elverfeldt was somewhat out of his element in this type of action but soon adapted to what was, after all, only a variation in normal combat. He was chiefly responsible for the planning of several major anti-partisan operations, notably Operation *Eisvogel* (Kingfisher) in September 1942 and Operation *Ziguenerbaron* (Robber Baron) from May 16 to June 6, 1943. Robber Baron, conducted in the Bryansk area, was the largest, and resulted in the killing of some 1,500 partisans.

Meanwhile, Elverfeldt received his *Ostmedaille* on August 5, 1942, and replaced Col. Hans Krebs as chief of staff to Col. Gen. Walter Model's 9th Army on January 20, 1943.[14] He supervised the last stages of Operation *Bueffel II* (Buffalo II), during which the 9th Army and the northern wing of the 2nd Panzer Army dropped back from Kirov to a prepared defensive line along the Desna from Bryansk to Doro-gobusch, thus firming up the linkage with the 4th Army and freeing up several German divisions for the Kursk offensive. For his part in this operation, Colonel Elverfeldt received a commendation from Field Marshal Guenther von Kluge, along with Maj. Gen. Hans Roet-tiger, chief of staff of the 4th Army, and Maj. Gen. Eberhard von Kurowski, chief of staff of the 2nd Panzer Army.

In July 1943, the great German assault, known as Operation *Citadelle*, was launched in the vicinity of Kursk. It failed. Soviet counterattacks at Orel forced the 9th Army back toward the so-called Hagen Line and the chief of staff was involved in the hastily organized defense in front of Bryansk. Meanwhile, on August 1, 1943, Elverfeldt's former commander, General Schaal, who had been somewhat ill over a period of several months, was forced to hand over his command to infantry Lt. Gen. Friedrich Hossbach. Schaal returned to Germany, where he was given command of *Wehrkreis* Bohemia and Moravia.[15]

Model and Elverfeldt, by dint of hard work, succeeded in stabilizing the front, largely because Model was given temporary command over both the 2nd Army and 2nd Panzer Army, as well as his own 9th. Thus the three badly mangled formations cooperated in holding at least a tenuous continuing front.

On September 1, Elverfeldt was given a rank commensurate with his prestigious post—that of major general—and received his new insignia from Model. But the nervous anxiety and exhausting hours of living on the knife's edge finally took their toll on the new general, and he was forced to take a rest leave in Germany beginning in late September 1943. While recovering his health, Elverfeldt spent much of his time with his family outside Cologne. He was attached as Fuehrer Reserve officer to the Armor Bureau (P-3) of the Army Personnel Office (HPA), now headed by Hitler's personal adjutant, Lt. Gen. Rudolf Schmundt.[16] The baron's reputation as a brilliant chief of staff, and as a capable field commander when necessity required it, had placed his name high on the list of future appointments. On October 31, Maj. Gen. Wolfdietrich Ritter von Xylander, the overworked chief of staff of Col. Gen. Erwin Jaenicke's 17th Army in the Crimea, was sent on a recuperatory leave.[17] Schmundt required Elverfeldt to act as the chief in the now relatively quiet sector. The baron acceded to the order; the Crimea indeed was a most pleasant place to work during the winter of 1943–44.

Xylander returned to duty on February 15, 1944, and Harald returned to Germany, much refreshed and eager for reassignment to a battle area. At this point in the war, however, every senior formation had a chief of staff who could not be displaced, and as a result,

Schmundt assigned Elverfeldt to the instruction staff of the Training School for Higher Leadership Candidates.

The general fumed at being given such a passive post, but he applied his considerable expertise to the assignment, while in both east and west the German Army was dealt hammer blows by the overpowering forces of the Grand Alliance. Nevertheless, with biweekly persistence, Elverfeldt submitted requests for reassignment to the HPA.

Schmundt was blinded and mortally wounded during the July 20, 1944, attempt on Hitler's life (he died in October). He was replaced by the inept Lt. Gen. Wilhelm Burgdorf, who reacted to the deluge of requests for transfer by Elverfeldt by adamantly refusing to consider any such thing—and so informed Harald. Normally, a good general staff officer who was so perfectly trained, he never would have considered going outside of the proper channels, but faced with Burgdorf's intractability, Elverfeldt immediately wrote to his former commanders, requesting their aid.

By now, the late summer and early fall of 1944, Schaal had been arrested, Hoth was in Fuehrer Reserve, and Kuntzen was unemployed following the disasters in France, for which he was held partially responsible. All three promised to give of their good offices but doubted it would do much good. As Schaal pointed out, members of the general staff were now persona non grata at Fuehrer Headquarters, because many of them had been involved in the abortive assassination attempt of July 20. At this point, however, Walter Model was able to secure a command for his former chief of staff. On September 20, Harald was ordered at all speed to the Western Front, where he took over command of the remnants of the 9th Panzer Division the next day. This was to tax his skill and ingenuity to the utmost.

The 9th Panzer had been all but destroyed in the Falaise-Argentan battles of August 1944, losing two commanders in succession to wounds. Pulled back behind the Siegfried Line in early September, it had received little new equipment but an influx of raw recruits, who had been massacred in successive attacks on U.S. positions around Aachen on September 11 to 14.

Reinforced by miscellaneous personnel scraped up from all over and given ten obsolete tanks from a defunct brigade, the 9th again suffered grievous losses in a day of battle on September 15. On the sixteenth, Gen. of Panzer Troops Erich Brandenburger, commander of the 7th Army, visited its headquarters and summarily sacked its commander, Maj. Gen. Gerhard Mueller, and its operations officer, Lt. Col. Wilhelm Friedel.[18] Command thus devolved on a reserve lieutenant colonel with minimal experience—hence Model's expeditious order for Elverfeldt to get up to the front.

The general arrived just in time to oversee the withdrawal of the division to a rearward position, where it was to be extensively refitted and reequipped. Here he took a survey of the unit and found that it had been bled white. He reported the following disastrous facts:

HQ, 9th Panzer: normal complement, 14 tanks; present, 5 tanks

33rd Panzer Regiment: normal complement, 800 men, 120 tanks; present, 150 men, 1 tank

9th Panzer Reconnaissance Unit: normal complement, 640 men; present, 50 men

10th Panzer Grenadier Regiment: normal complement, 1,100 men; present, 216 men

11th Panzer Grenadier Regiment: normal complement, 1,099 men; present, 246 men

102nd Panzer Artillery Regiment: normal complement, 1,055 men, 86 guns; present, 600 men, 20 guns

287th Flak Unit: normal complement, 780 men, 24 guns; present, 430 men, 10 guns

81st Panzer Signal, 86th Panzer Engineer, and 50th Anti-Tank Battalions: normal complement, 850 men; present, 234 men

Major General Elverfeldt submitted these figures to the army and army group with recommendations that the unit not be committed to further fighting without substantial rest and rehabilitation. Model snapped back with an order for the unit to move north to the threatened Arnhem area. Luckily for the weary 9th, this battle had been virtually concluded by the time it arrived, and Elverfeldt was directed to report to the headquarters of the XXXXVII Panzer Corps (under Lt. Gen., later Gen. of Panzer Troops, Heinrich von Luettwitz), which was to the rear of the left wing of the 1st Parachute Army. The 9th relocated around the township of Bracelen, west of the Ruhr River.

During the first three weeks of October, reinforcements and new equipment were hurried into the area. Many of new arrivals were veterans, returning from wounded leave. Thus by October 20, the newly arrived Ia, Major Linden, could state in his situation report to the divisional commander that the division's strength was 11,000 men, with 22 Panther tanks, 30 105-millimeter and 150-millimeter howitzers, plus 178 armored vehicles of various types (including two batteries of self-propelled guns) and 240 softskin vehicles.

Elverfeldt was rightly proud of his work and that of his junior officers. The division was once again a viable fighting force. When it was ordered back into action, Elverfeldt and his men were well pleased with the chance to reclaim the 9th's reputation as a crack fighting force. From the U.S. Army's official history of the Siegfried Line campaign, it is possible to elicit evidence that indeed the 9th did achieve that part of its objective. To begin with, the history explains:

> The attack was to strike sparely manned positions of the 7th U.S. Armored Division along the Deurne Canal and the Noorder Canal deep within the Peel Marshes west of Venlo. The center of the thrust was to be the town of Meijel, near the junction of the two canals. Only a limited objective was assigned: to carve a quadrilateral bulge into the Allied lines six miles deep encompassing about 45 square miles. The deepest point of the penetration was to be at Asten, northwest of Meijel alongside the Bois le Rue Canal.[19]

General Luettwitz was supposed to direct the assault with his XXXXVII Panzer Corps Headquarters, under the supervision of Field Marshal Walter Model, commander in chief of Army Group B. Over both was Field Marshal Gerd von Rundstedt, the OB West, who was to have the calmest head as the days went by.[20]

Bad weather during several days of mid-October held up the beginnings of the attack, but at last, at dawn on the twenty-seventh, massed artillery from the corps park and from the 9th and 15th Panzer Grenadier Divisions, supervised by the able Col. Ewald Kraus, the commander of the 9th Panzer Artillery Regiment, laid down a forty-minute barrage on the marshes, catching the U.S. forces by complete surprise. Elverfeldt commanded the tanks and grenadiers in their two-pronged attack. He had studied the inhospitable terrain firsthand during the preceding three days, at considerable risk, and employed similar methods to those used by Manstein's LVI Panzer Corps in northern Russia in terrain unsuitable for armor.

The U.S. historian made this singular statement, which was not far off the mark: "Although no relationship between this attack and the enemy's December counteroffensive in the Ardennes could be claimed, the former when subjected to hindsight looked in many respects like a small scale dress rehearsal for the Ardennes."[21]

Elverfeldt, up with his tank regiment, launched two reinforced battalions in a two-pronged attack at Meijel, which was only lightly held by a cavalry troop of the 7th Armored. Forced from their positions, the cavalrymen rallied and, reinforced by a second troop, attempted a counterattack, which was thrown back with losses.

Simultaneously, Reserve Col. Johannes Reich led a tank company, backed by self-propelled guns and a grenadier battalion, in a surge along the Meijel-Deurne highway from Heitrak. Crossing the Deurne Canal, he routed another cavalry troop and established a secure bridgehead. Reinforcements of tanks from the 7th Armored's Combat Command R contained a further drive but could not close off a second highway leading northwest from Meijel to Asten.

To the southwest, a third attack—by a panzer grenadier regiment of the 15th Panzer Grenadier Division (under the divisional artillery commander, Col. Hans Joachim Deckert[22])—forced a limited withdrawal of another 7th Cavalry troop near Nederweert, but the arrival of substantial reinforcements from Combat Command A managed to stabilize the position by nightfall on the twenty-seventh. Here the German attack had to do without armor, while the Americans utilized a full battalion of Shermans.

The U.S. commanders, hastily reinforced by some British forces, now prepared a counterattack against Meijel along the only two highways, Luettwitz, acting on Elverfeldt's recommendations, committed the rest of the 15th Panzer Grenadier Division to the positions attained at Heitrak, while the 9th Recon Battalion pushed farther west from Meijel toward Asten. The Allied attack thus made little or no headway.

Meanwhile, Elverfeldt had concentrated the 9th's panzers and grenadiers to the center and south of the zone of penetration, near

Nederweert and aimed at Asten. Slight progress was registered during the twenty-eighth and overnight.

Early on the twenty-ninth, having successfully probed for weak spots, the general renewed his all-out attack. Combat Command R was driven pell-mell backward halfway to Asten and only massed Allied artillery fire prevented a still deeper penetration. Simultaneous armor and self-propelled gun assaults northwest from Heitrak toward Deurne threw back Combat Command B, which strove to make a stand at the key road junction of Liesel but was again driven back.

Elverfeldt and Luettwitz, up with the foremost troops, as they tried to be as much of the time as possible, were well pleased with their limited success. Both, however, were quick to realize that little more could be safely accomplished, with more and more reinforcements being rushed to the area by the Allied commander, Gen. Bernard Montgomery. But their view was not shared by the exuberant Model, who as early as midday on the 28th had requested the use of the 116th Panzer and a Volks artillery brigade to force an even deeper penetration. The fact that neither of these units was readily available, coupled with the stiffening American resistance, already evident as early as noon on the twenty-ninth, caused OB West to veto this idea. Maj. Gen. Bodo Zimmermann, the Ic (intelligence officer) of the Western staff, further noted that a continued commitment of the 9th Panzer and 15th Panzer Grenadier would doubtless result in losses of men and materiel that could not be made up within the immediate future.[23]

Elverfeldt, touring his forward positions late on the twenty-ninth, was forced to concur. Thirty of his precious Panther tanks had already been irretrievably lost, and his killed and wounded were in excess of the acceptable rate for the accomplishments achieved. He reported this to Luettwitz, who, with Rundstedt's authorization, ordered the disengagement of the 15th Panzer Grenadier on the thirtieth.

Volksgrenadier units were put into the Needervert and Leisel sectors to hold, if possible, the gains achieved, but Elverfeldt secured Rundstedt's permission to remain along the Deurne Canal for a day or two longer as a reserve. In fact, the Allied forces—with Montgomery's usual methodicalness—merely began to gather during October 31 and November 1, without making any appreciable advances.

The German higher commands made a few adjustments to the battle order in this area, inserting *Gruppe von Manteuffel* (5th Panzer Army) as the immediate superior headquarters over the XXXXVII

Panzer and, during the first week of November, the 9th Panzer was successfully withdrawn and placed in reserve. Later, on November 12, a special order from Hitler instructed Rundstedt that under no circumstances were the divisions of the XXXXVII Panzer Corps to be employed in the line—not even if they lost some ground.

The reason for this, of which Elverfeldt and most other generals were unaware, was the Fuehrer's preoccupation with the great Ardennes offensive, which was already well along in the planning stages. As it was, however, the 9th Panzer would have to be used to shore up the front.

In his bivouac on the east bank of the Ruhr, Elverfeldt took stock of his strength in equipment after the four-day battle: 28 Panthers and 14 Panzer Mark IVs, 30 assault guns, 42 105-millimeter and 155-millimeter howitzers, and 204 other vehicles, including self-propelled guns and half-tracks. In men, the division still controlled more than 10,000 soldiers.

The scene of action shifted somewhat by mid-November as American forces began a serious drive for the Roer, committing the U.S. XIX and VII Corps from the Wourichen-Wurselen area in a drive north and east. By November 17, the two infantry divisions holding around Loverich, Puffendorf, and Setterich—the 183rd and 246th *Volksgrenadier*—were decimated and Elverfeldt was ordered to hit the spearheads of the U.S. 2nd Armored Division at Puffendorf.

On November 16, Elverfeldt moved his units up to their jumping-off positions and arranged his favorite three-prong mixed-arms attack, with aid from the 506th Heavy Panzer Battalion. The general debouched from Annenweiler and struck combat units of the American armor at Immendorf and Puffendorf. The U.S. historian testified to the skill and power of the several battles that raged all along the front in rain and mud, which gave the Germans a slight advantage.

After dawn on the seventeenth, the tanks of the 506th Panzer Battalion crashed into assembling U.S. armor at Gereonweiter and Prummern. The second column—most of the 10th Panzer Grenadier Regiment, with half a dozen supporting tanks—attacked a U.S. assembly area at Immendorf. The general led the main counterattack at Puffendorf, with twenty-eight Tiger tanks and the heavy-weapons battalion of the 11th Panzer Grenadier Regiment.

The benefit of surprise served well at first, but the American forces were on the ground in large numbers, and though Elverfeldt's attack drove his enemy back some distance, neither of the other attacks achieved any major penetration. Losses on both sides were fairly heavy. The Americans lost ten medium and six light tanks, while the 9th Panzer lost eleven Panthers. Nevertheless, by employing his grenadiers during the night of November 17–18, and with support from the 15th Panzer Grenadier Division on the eighteenth, Elverfeldt stalemated the 2nd Armored, which had to regroup and could not launch its renewed attacks until November 20. Then the U.S. attack gained some ground, threatening the Puffendorf-Gareontweiler highway by seizing a ridge adjoining it. Elverfeldt, coordinating the counterstrike by grenadiers of both divisions and bringing up both artillery regiments, hit back ferociously on the twenty-first. After dusk, three companies of the 11th Panzer Grenadier Regiment annihilated two platoons of the 2nd Armored and almost destroyed a relieving company, before a tank-supported American counterattack retook the hill position.

The next morning, the 9th Panzer reported 1,100 casualties killed, wounded, or missing in the six-day battle. It had lost a total of eighty-six tanks, thirty of which were salvaged and returned to service. During the same period, the U.S. Army's official history listed 1,300 casualties, plus seventy-six tanks, of which forty were salvageable. It also claimed 2,385 POWs for the entire month, mostly from the decimated infantry divisions.

On November 23, units of the 10th SS Panzer Division began to arrive in this sector to relieve the 9th Panzer, which was now ordered back into the Ardennes for a quick refit before the onset of the top-secret counteroffensive ordered by Hitler. Elverfeldt remained on the scene until the last of his forces had been relieved, and thus was involved in a relieving effort with a battle group (*Kampfgruppe*) of a company of Panthers, a grenadier battalion, and two platoons of the 506th Panzer Battalion between November 29 and December 1, which drove an American contingent out of the town of Lindern.

Although the general tried many different attacks and managed to completely surround the U.S. troops for some time, American aircraft and tanks were able to supply and reinforce their little pocket. On December 2, Elverfeldt was ordered to leave the defenses to the

10th SS and bring his survivors straightway back to the gathering area of the rest of the division.

By December 5, Elverfeldt was at his division headquarters at Daun, well to the rear of the forces being massed for the attack on the U.S. positions in eastern Belgium, and was annoyed to find that he and his men were to be kept as OKW reserve, meaning they might not even get into action at all.

Following a short but massive barrage, hundreds of thousands of German troops and hundreds of panzers crashed into the sparsely held enemy front on December 16. Elverfeldt spent his time up at the forward headquarters of Field Marshal Model, listening to the reports of initial successes. But as the days went on, it became increasingly obvious that the attack was being stalled in many places, and Allied reinforcements were being rushed up to further slow the German armored prongs.

At long last, on December 23, orders finally came from Fuehrer Headquarters to commit the 9th Panzer and 15th Panzer Grenadier Divisions in the area of General Luettwitz's XXXXVII Panzer Corps around Bastogne and the Ourthe River. Elverfeldt rushed back to Daun, saw that his units topped off their fuel tanks, and ordered a straight route march by night to the front.

A bit of confusion occurred the next day, when Hitler suddenly decided to commit the 9th on the flank between the XXXXVII Corps and 7th Army, but it did not cause any serious delay, as Model and Manteuffel (commander of the 5th Panzer Army) had already decided that that particular move was unneccessary. They assigned a position closer to the center of action for Elverfeldt. Early on Christmas morning, therefore, the general deployed his units between the Panzer Lehr and the 2nd Panzer Divisions, between Humain and Foy Notre Dame, a cutoff advance point of one of the 2nd Panzer's battle groups. Maj. Gen. Meinrad von Lauchert, the commander of the 2nd, wanted to launch a full-scale relief operation, so Elverfeldt assigned a *Kampfgruppe* of his 11th Panzer Grenadier Regiment with panzer and artillery support to the area around Humainville, thus freeing the units of the 2nd Panzer.[24]

Elverfeldt could now deploy some ninety Panther and Tiger tanks, plus thirty-five self-propelled guns, but the artillery regiment was held up en route by enemy air attacks and could not rejoin the main column for some time. On the evening of the twenty-fifth, General Luettwitz gave the 9th its orders: debouch out of Humainville and secure the hamlet of Buissonville. This could be carried out only by a limited force, however, since the bulk of the division was out of fuel and had to hold the flank post of Rochefort.

Under such a handicap—and Elverfeldt made a point of getting this across to both Luettwitz and Manteuffel—the limited strike at Buissonville was doomed to an early failure, as the Americans were holding the village in considerable force. Not only was the 9th's battle group forced back, but the U.S. artillery now began to bombard Humainville. Elverfeldt then redeployed his division in the vicinity of the little Lesse River north to Remaigne, with its center holding at Humainville. Here it was subjected to artillery and air attack for three days. Elverfeldt's command vehicle was hit by a bomb fragment around noon on December 28, and the general received a fairly incapacitating wound.

Rushed back to Cologne for treatment, he was temporarily replaced by Maj. Gen. Friedrich Wilhelm von Mellenthin, another former staff officer.[25] Mellenthin recounted: "On the 29th set off for the 9th Panzer Division, which was in the wooded hills northwest of Houffalize; the ice bound roads glittered in the sunshine and I witnessed the uninterrupted air attacks on our traffic routes and supply dumps. Not a single German plane was in the air, innumerable vehicles were shot up and their blackened wrecks littered the roads."[26]

In the official HPA record for Harald von Elverfeldt's service in the army, there is no mention of either his wound or his absence from command. In fact, the record states that he moved from m.F.b. (*mit der Fuhrung bei,* meaning acting commander) to KDR (*Kommandeur,* or commander) as of January 1, 1945. But Elverfeldt's adjutant, then Capt. Erich Sigler, who was a refugee in Paraguay in 1952–54, attested to he fighter-bomber attack that resulted in the general's hospitalization in Cologne, and Major General Mellenthin described his assumption of temporary command over the 9th Panzer in his excellent biographical study, *Panzer Battles.*

Even Mellenthin is vague on how long the baron was actually absent on wounded leave, however, and Sigler was posted to the staff of General Luettwitz on either December 31, 1944, or January 1, 1945, so he was also uncertain of the timing. Ostensibly, Elverfeldt was well enough to return to duty by February 28, although he may well have returned to divisional headquarters earlier.[27]

By the end of February, little was left of the once proud division that had acted as a rear guard for the enforced withdrawal from the Ardennes. On the twenty-eighth, it was again committed to action, this time under the LXXXI Corps headquarters of Gen. of Infantry Friedrich Koechling, but on March 1, Koechling virtually exchanged commands with Lt. Gen. Fritz Bayerlein, a veteran panzer commander, and with the forward elements of the 11th Panzer Division, the 9th moved up to its rallying point of the Eleft River north of Juelich.[28]

Elverfeldt found his strength down to twenty-nine tanks, twenty of them new Tigers, and sixteen self-propelled guns, with his two regiments down to two battalion strength. Only his artillery, which had fallen hopelessly behind during the last two months of to-ing and fro-ing, had caught up with the division and was at almost full strength. Having crossed the Eleft and taken position behind the antitank emplacements of infantry, Elverfeldt's weakened force engaged in several sharp counterattacks against U.S. armored thrusts during the entire day of March 2, but with negligible results.

The next day, powerful armored and infantry forces of the American army once more attacked around Stommelen and along the Aachen-Cologne highway, driving the 9th Panzer away to its south, splitting it from the ad hoc *Korps Bayerlein*, which now scrambled to escape across the Rhine at Worringen. Elverfeldt found himself once again under the LXXXI Corps on the outer perimeter of the Rhine, with two or three damaged bridges leading back over it into Cologne.

On March 3 and 4, the "seemingly ineradicable 9th Panzer" fought U.S. Maj. Gen. Maurice Rose's 3rd Armored Division, inflicting severe losses on it, but at serious harm to itself. On the 6th, just after daylight, the U.S. forces broke into the suburbs of Cologne, and the grenadiers of the 9th began a dogged struggle through the ruins, with Elverfeldt and his officers armed and fighting in the front lines. The U.S. Army's official history then sums it up succinctly: "Almost all resistance by the 9th Panzer Division collapsed a short while later [on the afternoon of March 6], when the division commander, General-major Harald Freiherr von Elverfeldt, was killed."[29]

The general's staff was fortunate enough to get his body safely out of the city, and Elverfeldt was buried with full military honors at the

Hildesheim Cemetery, among his ancestors, on March 11. As a final gesture to his bravery, on March 23, 1945, the Reich awarded his widow his posthumous Oak Leaves to the Knight's Cross. His posthumous promotion to lieutenant general was authorized by HPA effective March 1, 1945, so that the pension for his survivors would be larger.[30] His service record, however, includes the award but not the promotion.

Summarizing the life of Baron Harald von Elverfeldt and his abilities presents no few problems, since none of the firsthand German authors even mention him. From the available sources and the awards given him during his years of service, however, it is obvious that as both a senior staff officer and field commander, he was capable and brave, earning respect from such disparate officers as the sagacious Ferdinand Schaal, the conservative Adolf Kuntzen, and the innovative, explosive Walter Model. Even as a staff officer, Elverfeldt on occasion took over field commands, which he executed with considerable skill—enough to prompt several commendations from his commanders. His plans for antipartisan operations under the 9th Army were masterpieces of detail and were carried out with some success by the forces employed.

All in all, Elverfeldt deserves much better from military history than he has heretofore been accorded.

CHAPTER 3

Erwin Jollasse

O^f all the panzer divisional commanders on the Western Front during the period of the Allied invasion, Erwin Jollasse is perhaps the least known today. In all the various histories written in three countries—Great Britain, the United States, and West Germany—his name rarely appears. The 9th Panzer Division, which he commanded, on the other hand, is mentioned consistently, usually in the context of its superhuman efforts in battle, which resulted in its almost total destruction.

From mid-August 1944 on, the 9th Panzer's successive commanders—Max Sperling and Gerhard Muller—figure at least in the U.S. official histories. Jollasse is completely overlooked, even by this exhaustive work. He finished the war in Czechoslovakia and was able to surrender to American forces at Ising, near Travenstein in Upper Bavaria, on June 8, 1945, and he subsequently gave a deposition to the U.S. Army Historical Commission on the activities of the 9th Panzer in France during the summer of 1944.[1]

Erwin Jollasse was born in Hamburg on December 8, 1892, the son of architect Johannes Jollasse and his wife, Martilla, nee Biernatzki. Of Lutheran upbringing, the young fellow entered in the standard schools of the time, graduating in 1910 with particular skill in chemistry and an excellent working knowledge of both French and English.

For some reason, although there seems to have been no history of military service in the family, Erwin decided to enter the Imperial Army and managed to secure an appointment as a *Fahnenjunker* (officer-cadet) on October 3, 1911. He was patented as a *Leutnant* (second lieutenant) on June 6, 1913, retroactive to June 16, 1911.

At the outbreak of the First World War, he took over a platoon in one of the companies of the 25th *Reichsjaeger* Regiment on August 2, 1914, and on August 27, he assumed command of the company.

Seeing service in the advance on the Marne, he received the Iron Cross, Second Class, in October and became battalion adjutant on November 2. Jollasse continued in service on the Western Front until his knowledge of chemistry was discovered by the High Command; then on December 20, 1915, he became the gas warfare officer on the staff of the 15th Reichsjaeger Division. On August 18, 1916, he was patented *Oberleutnant* (first lieutenant).

In 1917, in response to a call for volunteers for the new air service, Jollasse reported to the Aerial Reconnaissance School West on May 8. After graduation as a pilot observer in September, he was appointed commander of the reconnaissance wing of the 8th Field Artillery Regiment on October 10. In this assignment, he was twice forced down, the second time rather badly wounded. Awarded the Iron Cross, First Class, on recovery, he was attached as ordnance officer (orderly) on the staff of *General Kommando*, VIII Army Corps, on December 6, 1918, when the war was over and the army was in the process of dissolution.

On June 21, 1919, he was discharged from the service and returned to Hamburg, where he stayed with his family and secured a post as a pilot for one of the small commercial airlines then being established. He courted Ingeborg von Harlessen, the daughter of a family friend, a businessman, and married her on January 7, 1921. Later that year, his father died, leaving him responsible for the family—mother, wife, and unmarried sister.

Continuing in his flying career, he became the father of one son, Harald, born on May 14, 1922, and a daughter, Brigitte, born on November 28, 1927. On October 1, 1927, he was employed as a civilian aviator by *Wehrkreis VI* (VI Military District) at Muenster and served as an unofficial airman through the last years of the declining Weimar Republic.

No sooner had Adolf Hitler been named chancellor in 1933, and consolidated his power, than the new German Air Force, the *Luftwaffe*, came unofficially and clandestinely into being. On October 1, Jollasse was formally commissioned as a *Flieger Hauptmann* (flight captain), with the grade made retroactive to February 1, 1928. Although he had served as a pilot for so long, Erwin was basically an army man, and he eyed jealously the beginnings of military expansion. On April 30, 1934, he secured his release from the air service so that the following day, May 1, he could reenter the regular army, again with the rank of captain, retroactive to February 1, 1929. He was posted at once to the II Battalion, 18th Infantry Regiment, at Muenster.

Five months later, on October 1, 1934, he took command of the 2nd Company, I Battalion, Infantry Regiment Muenster, later to become the 64th Infantry Regiment of the 16th Infantry Division. On July 1, 1935, he was commissioned major. On November 1, 1936, with a second wave of expansion, Jollasse took over II Battalion, 39th Infantry Regiment, of the 26th (Muenster) Infantry Division. The next year, he attended a brief course for potential staff officers from November 13 to 29, 1937.

Posted with the division to the West Wall during the Austrian *Anschluss* and the Czech crisis of 1938, Jollasse also watched the Polish campaign of September 1939 from this far-off position. He was nevertheless promoted to lieutenant colonel on March 1, 1938.

Anxious to be employed in field duty, Jollasse twice secured official leave during this period, once in January and once in late August 1939, during which he was listed as *Offizier zur Verfugungs der Oberbefehlshaber des Heeres* (ordinance officer for the Army High Command). These periods at the High Command offices in Berlin finally resulted in a much better posting for the lieutenant colonel.

On February 6, 1940, he assumed command of the 52nd Infantry Regiment, erstwhile part of the 4th Infantry Division, which took part in the campaign in Holland under the IV Corps in May. Jollasse handled his regiment with considerable skill in the short but bitter campaign. After Holland fell, the corps was transferred south to take part in the June 1940 assault across the Meuse for the final subjugation of France. As a result of his services, Jollasse was awarded the 1940 clasps to his Iron Crosses Second Class (June 10) and First Class (June 21).

In the fall, the 4th Division returned to its home base of Dresden, where it was converted into the 14th Panzer Division; Jollasse remained in command of what was now the 52nd Rifle (*Schutzen*) Regiment, completely motorized. In November, along with his staff and troops, he was transferred to the 18th Panzer Division, which was being created from miscellaneous formations in the Dresden area. Maj. Gen. Walther Nehring had been given the task of forming and training this amalgam of units—all from different divisions—into a coherent whole. The 18th Panzer Regiment, commanded by Col.

Eduard Hauser, was brand new. Its battalions, I and II, came from the artillery and panzer training schools at Jueterbog and Krampnitz. Colonel Jollasse's 52nd Rifles had come from the old 4th Infantry, and Col. Hans Schreppfer's 101st Rifle Regiment had originally been attached to the 14th Infantry Division.[2] Col. Johannes Schraepler, in charge of the 88th Panzer Artillery Regiment, had previously commanded an antitank battalion in the 20th Motorized Division.[3] Maj. Max Sperling of the 88th Panzer Reconnaissance Battalion had served in France under the 10th Infantry.[4] The brigade commanders were Col. Max Fremerey of the rifles, who had commanded the 480th Motorized Regiment of the 164th Infantry Division, and Col. Rudolf Keltsch of the panzers, who had led the crack 1st Panzer Brigade.[5]

Nehring and his general staff officer, Maj. Fritz Estor, were not daunted by the task cut out for them, however. Experienced panzer officers, they introduced a rigorous program of maneuver and instruction, which, despite the onset of winter, ground through the next two months with a passionate intensity. Jollasse adapted rapidly to the use of motor vehicles, and by the time the entire division trekked through the snow-blanketed plains of Silesia to the new advance base at Breslau, it was part of the combined-arms strike force on which Nehring, like Guderian, put particular emphasis. "Infantry without tanks may hold, but hardly advance; tanks without infantry may advance, but hardly hold" became the motto of the division, to which was always added, "Speed, always speed!"

On March 1, 1941, Jollasse received his promotion to full colonel. Less than four months later, on June 22, the great invasion of the Soviet Union began on a huge front extending from the Baltic Sea south to the Black Sea in Romania. The 18th Panzer was under the command of the XXXXVII Panzer Corps (under Gen. of Panzer Troops Joachim Lemelsen) in Guderian's 2nd Panzer Group, posted between Legt and Pratulin, along the Bug River on the central sector. While Lt. Gen. Hermann Franke's 162nd Infantry Division made an initial bridgehead, the panzer regiment, using Snorkel tanks, forded the river and deployed preparatory to an advance eastward.

Jollasse's regiment was next across, in rubber dinghies, and while the engineers strung a pontoon bridge for the rolling stock, the men of the 52nd rode the backs of Maj. Count Hyazinth von Strachwitz's tank battalion and took the town of Maloryta by noon.[6] The rest of the division now pushed across the bridge and the whole force set out to secure the bridge across the Lesna, the next river barrier.

At Pruzana, the tank regiment ran into a congeries of Soviet tanks and came out the winner in the first major armor battle of the campaign. Jollasse's regiment occupied the town at sundown, while Hauser camped just beyond. Between June 23 and 26, the division swept rapidly eastward, seizing the Lesna bridge and the town of Slonim. It then pushed onward toward Baranovizce and Stolpce.

On June 28, Jollasse's infantry, with Strachwitz's tank battalion, bypassed Niewicz and headed for Minsk. Two days later, they captured the town of Borissov and secured the rail and road bridges over the Beresina, taking a sizable bridgehead. This position—unsupported by other troops, which were detained to keep the Bialystok Pocket closed—was assaulted viciously by heavy Soviet forces, including a battalion of T-34 tanks. This was the first appearance of this thirty-ton monster, whose existence was unknown to the Germans until the invasion began. Mechanically superior to any of the panzers, it was a very unpleasant surprise to the German soldiers. Jollasse's guns could not even dent the Russian behemoths. He undertook to use demolition packets from his engineer battalion and destroyed seven of the big tanks. The Soviets fell back at nightfall, leaving numerous dead troops and disabled vehicles. Jollasse's force had also sustained serious casualties. General Nehring hastily sent up his field training battalion to enable the group to exploit its costly success.

News of Jollasse's exploits filtered back to Supreme Headquarters, and on July 12, he received a letter of special commendation from Field Marshal Walther von Brauchitsch himself—one of only half a dozen such letters granted during the entire war. Jollasse had not remained idle, however; upon being reinforced, he pushed an advance party of Strachwitz's tanks out to the Natcha River and forced another bridgehead over that stream by July 5. On the sixth and seventh, he captured the burning township of Tolochino, west of the Dnieper, but was unable to secure a bridgehead across that big river. Nehring rushed the balance of the division up to the forefront. Meanwhile, Soviet forces from their strongpoints at Orsha and Kachanovo counterattacked, and Jollasse's forces were in serious peril before being reinforced by a mixed battle group under Maj. Gen. Johannes Streich.

By July 10, the Kachanovo enemy had been eliminated, and the entire division prepared for a crossing of the Dnieper the next day. Supported by the artillery, some of the Snorkel tanks were again able to ford the wide stream and so surprised the Soviet defenses that a bridgehead was secured with a minimum of casualties. On the twelfth, though General Streich now controlled the larger battle group of the division, Jollasse and Strachwitz still kept the lead in the advance along the river and took Dubrovno.

By July 16, Smolensk was seriously threatened by this spearhead, which fought a sharp little action with Soviet tanks and infantry in the Krasny-Gasino area, inflicting severe losses on the enemy. The next day, the battle group pushed through the soon-to-become infamous Katyn Forest and came to a halt for the next several days, covering the panzer group's flanks as it pushed eastward. By July 25, the infantry divisions had been able to move up into position, thus freeing the panzer forces for further advances, and the 292nd Infantry Division of Lt. Gen. Martin Dehmel relieved Nehring's forces.

The XXXXVII Panzer Corps was now under orders to move slightly north by east to provide assistance to the southernmost units of Hoth's 3rd Panzer Group, which was endeavoring to encircle a large Soviet force around Smolensk. But on July 28, the 18th Panzer Division was ordered to support the SS Division *Das Reich* on the flank of the Yelnia salient, which was under heavy attack by six or seven Soviet armies. By August 3, this task had been satisfactorily accomplished, and the 18th Panzer was pulled back to Prudki on the Smolensk-Bryansk highway for a brief rest and sorely needed reinforcements. These had been carried by train up to the Minsk railhead and pushed overland—a journey of some six days' duration. Jollasse received an increment of about 100 young trainees from the Chemnitz training center, but best of all, he was alloted twenty of the brand new *Leichter Gepanzerter Kraftwagen* SD 250s—seven-speed, sixty-mile-per-hour half-track vehicles. Although the tracks on these vehicles were not as wide as those on the Russian ones, they were excellent infantry carriers, particularly good for rapid reconnaissance work.

Returning to action with the direction of the assault south-southeast—to keep up with the fluctuating ideas of Hitler, who was now concerned with the Ukraine at the expense of the advance on Moscow—the 18th Panzer drove up on Pochep by way of Sergievskoye and took the town by August 20. Hereafter, however, the division was allocated to rear flank protection, while the rest of the XXXXVII Panzer Corps cooperated with the XXIV Panzer Corps in its drive south against Kiev. Thus for ten days, the 18th Panzer was engaged around Trubchevsk on the Desna River. Here on September 3, Jollasse's regiment had a fierce little combat with a Soviet tank brigade, which it destroyed almost totally, capturing four intact tanks, eighteen guns, and 1,100 prisoners. As a result of this—Erwin's third tank battle since the campaign began—he was awarded the Panzer Battle Badge in Bronze (*Panzerkampfabzeichen*) on September 5. This was the award given to motorized infantry and reconnaissance personnel; only tankers received this award in silver. Map 3.1 shows the German drive across the Desna and the subsequent battle of Kiev, where more than 667,000 men of the Red Army captured.

Early rains now fell periodically, fouling up the German movements and offering a preview of what they could expect later. Jollasse took this very much to heart: he proceeded to place his best troops in his surviving twenty-six SD-250s and "appropriated" ten captured Soviet half-tracks for his I Battalion, under Maj. Friedrich von Seydlitz und Ludwigsdorff. This move was to stand him in good stead later.

On September 10, the division began a southerly advance via Pogar to Yampol, where a renewed series of battles started on the nineteenth. By the twenty-fourth, however, the Soviets had been so severely battered that the front settled down to a static quiet, and the units of the German Army prepared to renew the drive toward Moscow.

Then, on September 30, with the motorized infantry division moving along behind them, the 17th and 18th Panzers lunged into the disorganized Soviet lines north and east of Yampol, capturing Sheravko in the first days' surge. At first, it was almost a cakewalk: Jollasse's spearheads crossed the Sev River on October 3 and seized the important road hub city of Karachev on the fifth. From here, the 17th Panzer was ordered across to Bryansk, while the 18th continued on a northerly course, threatening Chastovichi. Thus Jollasse was not in on the coup de main, which captured Bryansk on the sixth, and in fact was immobilized by concentrated Soviet attacks for two or three days. On the tenth, however, spearheaded by Strachwitz's tank battalion, Jollasse and his motorized infantry burst through the Soviet resistance, and on the eleventh, they achieved a linkup with advance

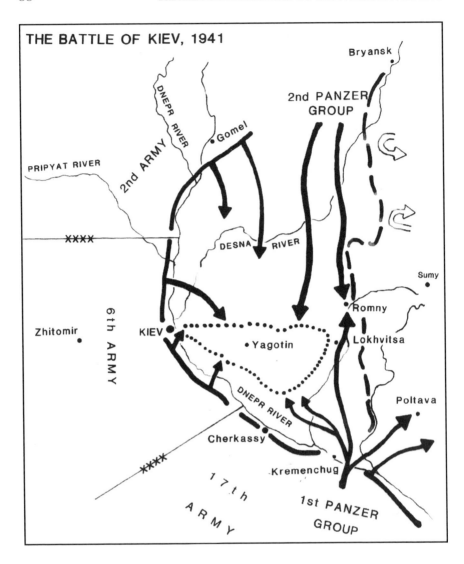

THE BATTLE OF KIEV, 1941

elements of the XXXXIII Corps to encircle a large Soviet army group to the north of Bryansk.

Russian efforts to break out caused Guderian to rush the Motorized Infantry Regiment *Grossdeutschland* to the assistance of Nehring's 18th Panzer, Lt. Gen. Friedrich Mieth's 112th Infantry Division and Lt. Gen. Dr. Lothar Rendulic's 52nd Infantry Division, and on October 17, the Soviets capitulated, giving up 50,000 prisoners and 400 guns of the 50th Army. Jollasse's initial endeavor to close this pocket resulted in his being awarded the Knight's Cross to the Iron Cross on November 2.

Meanwhile, the 18th had not rested on its laurels. It turned right on or about October 19, rushed down the one good road running via Kromy, and crossing the Swapa River, surprised and captured Fatezh on October 22, thus outflanking strong Soviet forces holding up the advance of the XXXXVIII Panzer Corps from Dmitriev. In close pursuit of the fleeing Russians, it swung north toward Speskovy and Yefremov.

But the advent of the rains virtually brought the motor units to a halt. Bogged down as the divisions now were, they were attacked from November 3 on by a powerful Russian force consisting of two cavalry divisions, five rifle divisions, and a tank brigade. The infantry divisions of the LIII Corps arrived at this time, however, and in the ten-day battle, the Soviets were severely handled and finally retreated through Yefremov.

Then subfreezing weather set in, creating different problems for the panzer units, but despite everything, Jollasse's group launched an attack on Yefremov on November 18 and captured the town after two days of bitter fighting. This was to be the last major success of this campaign. The Soviets were now bringing in dozens of their Siberian divisions, and their defensive positions became stronger and stronger. Jollasse's battle group was held stationary in a monthlong defensive, his men acting as plain infantry in the gradually deteriorating situation. By the first week of December, it was painfully evident that they needed to withdraw to a more readily defensible position, preferably the Don-Shat-Upa line. On December 12, the division regretfully abandoned Yefremov and made its way back to a better defensive position.

In the interim, the Panzer Troop Office (*Panzertruppenamt*) had recognized that in his two campaigns—France in 1940 and now Russia—Erwin Jollasse had sustained four wounds. All were relatively minor, and none of them kept him from duty for more than twenty-four hours. Nevertheless, he was awarded the Wounded Badge in Silver (*Verwundung Abzeichen im Silber*), more as a sign of respect for his abilities than anything else.

On December 25, with the entire panzer group under terrible pressure and being forced back toward Orel and Bryansk—which the troops were to hold despite everything the Russians could do—Heinz Guderian was summarily relieved of command by an angry Hitler, who would not face up to the truth. Rudolf Schmidt, another veteran panzer leader, took his place at the head of what was now the 2nd Panzer Army.

By January 6, 1942, the division was posted along the Zasha River with its headquarters at the Voin Collective Farm, its left flank at Mtsensk and its right at Novosil. Both towns, however, on the Soviet bank of the river, were in Russian hands. Although the front here was relatively stable, farther north, massive Soviet penetrations had isolated the German garrison at Sukhinitsi and were threatening Chvastovichi and Bryansk. The 18th Panzer Division was given the task of rescuing the garrison at Sukhinitsi.

The 18th was to be augmented by the single regiment of the 208th Infantry Division and the 12th Rifle Regiment of the 4th Panzer Division, as well as a few batteries of self-propelled guns from the army reserve, but considering the number of Soviet forces they were facing, it was a risky business altogether. Some thirty Russian units had been identified in and around Sukhinitsi (see Map 2.1).

Jollasse, the proven veteran battle group commander, was given one of the most powerful attack forces. It consisted of his own regiment of three battalions, commanded by Friedrich von Seydlitz, Hans Wolter, and Albrecht Aschen, in the mixed German-Russian half-tracks, backed by Panzer Company 3 under Capt. Georg von Stunzner, the 2nd Company of the panzer jaeger battalion, and a self-propelled battery of the 208th Artillery Regiment.

Because of the deep snow and frozen mud of the roads, it was a full ten-day journey for the attack forces to reach assembly points at Zhizdra, but the daring assault began at dawn on January 17. Jollasse's forces smashed two Soviet rifle brigades and captured the strongly held town of Lyudinovo. In an all-day fight, the now-dismounted infantry cleared the town and pursued the Soviets into the snow-covered forests beyond, capturing 150 prisoners and considerable numbers of weapons and vehicles. They counted 500 Russian bodies when night fell.

The rest of the attacking forces—Keltsch's tanks, Luettwitz's 12th Rifles, and the recon battalion and other rifle regiment of the 18th—made similar progress against furious but totally surprised Soviet formations. By January 25, they had reached Sukhinichi and opened a path of supply to it. Soviet losses were five to six times heavier than the Germans'. With tacit approval from the army group, the attack forces Sukhinitsi around February 1 and set up a more defensible position along the Desna River. Meanwhile, two Soviet armies, a cavalry corps, and a paratroop brigade were cut off in the German rear, and the battle of the Ugra began. It was not to be finished until the advent of spring. Enemy casualties were immense, but the German divisions lost heavily too.

Lt. Gen. Walther Nehring was recalled to Berlin on January 25, 1942, right in the midst of the Sukhinitsi rescue mission; his expertise was desperately needed now in North Africa.[7] Similarly, other senior officers in the division had left, either transferred or wounded. Streich had been put in Fuehrer reserve, Fremerey given a division, and Keltsch killed in action on the Ugra. Maj. Gen. Baron Karl von Thuengen-Rossbach now headed the division.[8] Colonel Schreppfer commanded the rifle brigade and Lieutenant Colonel Strachwitz was in command of the panzer regiment.

The division manned the positions around Orel for the rest of the winter, in relative quiet. Laboriously, reinforcements were moved up to the Desna and incorporated into the division's various units, not the least being Jollasse's crack 52nd Rifles.

On March 6, 1942, Colonel Schreppfer was injured in an auto accident behind the lines, and Jollasse was immediately appointed as commander of the rifle brigade. He in turn elevated Lieutenant Colonel Seydlitz to the command of the 52nd. Col. Hans Treptow was now commanding the 101st Regiment.

Jollasse's new command was short-lived. In April, despite the spring thaws, the Soviets made an assault to the south of Orel, with the aim of enabling their trapped comrades inside German lines to break out southeastward. The rifle brigade of the 18th Panzer was directly in the path of this attack and at once fought back. Colonel Jollasse, with his headquarters escort, hurried to reinforce the hard-pressed 101st Regiment and on April 26 was heavily engaged in the seesaw combat. Early the next day, the command half-track received a direct hit from a Soviet tank. It exploded and threw the colonel a considerable distance, inflicting numerous wounds and rendering him unconscious. Rescued by his escort, he was shipped to the Orel hospital and from there was flown back to Chemnitz for recuperation.

Kept in the main military hospital until April 1943, Jollasse recovered fairly rapidly. He was, however, incapable of using his left arm, which remained paralyzed for the rest of his life. Nothing daunted, he embarked on a rigorous physical fitness regimen and was able to report as fit for duty by early July.

On July 12, he was sent to the headquarters of Army Group Center for posting as a reserve divisional commander. At the climax of the ill-fated Operation Citadel, he was rushed up to the battle headquarters of the 9th Panzer Division near Orel. Here Lt. Gen. Walter Scheller had just been severely wounded in the desperate battles to stop the Soviet juggernaut, and Jollasse took over the hard-pressed unit on July 22.[9]

For the better part of six long weeks, the battered 9th strove to cover the withdrawal of the German forces to the Dnieper and suffered heavy casualties. Lt. Col. Walter Gorn, commander of the 10th Rifle Regiment, and Rittmeister Bunau of the recon battalion both fell on August 15; Gorn lived to tell about it.[10]

In early September, the 9th was relieved and pulled back to Smolensk for a brief rest and reinforcement before being rushed to the Pavlograd sector to counter a renewed Soviet attack.

On October 1, 1943, Jollasse was promoted to major general, and on the eighteenth, he was again severely wounded by machine-gun fire and flown to a Warsaw hospital. He was succeeded by the gallant Col. Johannes Schultz, who took the division south to support the Nikopol-Kiev defenses. Here on November 27, near Krivoi Rog, Schultz was killed in a fierce engagement with the Russians.

Although by no means fully recovered from his injuries, Jollasse left his hospital bed and commandeered a plane to take him south to resume his command. He relieved Col. Max Sperling within ten hours of Schultz's death, and then began a three-months series of battles of such ferocity that it is miraculous he and any of his men survived them.

Driven out of Bazaliuk on December 2, the division followed the river south under terrible attack from the air and ground, and reached Apostolovo, where it spent Christmas under unceasing assault. Pulled to Marinskoye in late January 1944, the remnants of the division staged a last-ditch stand until, on February 8, the Nikopol evacuation began. Jollasse had by now had an iron frame made for his useless left arm so that he could support a rifle if need be, and in the weeks that followed, he had many occasions to use it.

With his last four tanks and 600 weary men, he crossed the Dnieper to comparative safety on February 22 and was presented with the German Cross in Gold, awarded to him on January 7, for his brave leadership. Earlier, on November 26, 1942, he had also been awarded the *Ostmedaille*, given for long service in Russia. With his men, Jollasse was ordered to entrain to Lvov and then proceed to France, where the division was to be rebuilt.

On March 7, the major general was welcomed by his new operations officer, Lieutenant Colonel Friedel, at the divisional headquarters at Nimes, where the work of refitting and training was to take place. In most cases, Jollasse found that he would be serving with new officers, so devastating had been the losses of the last great battles. Reserve Lt. Col. Johannes Reich and Jollasse's old friend from the 18th, Col. Max Sperling, still commanded the two panzer grenadier regiments, the 10th and 11th. Lt. Col. Ewald Kraus, of the 102nd Panzer Artillery, had also survived. All of the other officers were newcomers.

Between April and the first of June, Jollasse received 74 *Panzerkampfwagen IV Ausf. H* (PzKw IV-Hs), 20 *Sturmgeschutz IV* (StuG assault guns), and 15 *Panzerkampfwagen V Ausf. A* (Panther Is)—all excellent fighting machines. Absorbing the training cadres of the 155th Reserve Panzer Division, Jollasse could count an effective force of 12,678 men, 130 tanks (the rest were rebuilt *Panzerkampfwagen IIIs*), and 200 other motor vehicles, including a good number of the efficient SD-250s.

When the Allies landed at Normandy, Jollasse's division was moved up to Avignon, but it was not called for service in the hard-fought battles for the beachheads. Air attacks began at about this time, which the general combated by widely scattering his units under heavy camouflage and massing antiaircraft guns near his headquarters, which took a toll of low-flying raiders for the following couple of weeks.

After the end of the war, General Jollasse wrote a manuscript on the operations of the 9th Panzer Division from July 24 to September 4, 1944, for the Historical Division of the Headquarters of the U.S. Army in Europe. As it is extremely relevant, I will now let Jollasse tell his own story of these critical days, with only minor modifications for the sake of clarity.

9th Panzer Division (24 July–4 Sep 1944)
by Erwin Jollasse, *Generalleutnant*

Preliminary Remarks. The rehabilitation of the division generally proceeded without difficulties or delays. By the end of July it had attained its full strength. The replacements were good, as was the morale of the troops. The rest had visibly refreshed them, after three years of arduous combat in Russia. The training of the troops was satisfactory. In particular, officer training in the type of warfare prevailing in the West, which differed from that in the East, had made good progress.

Employment on the Invasion Front. In the afternoon of July 27, the division was alerted, and its speedy transfer to the Normandy invasion front was ordered. The shipment at first proceeded smoothly. In spite of the numerous enemy air raids on the moving columns, there were no notable losses of personnel or materiel.

The last elements of the service troops of the division could not reach the division on account of the destruction of the Loire bridges and the rapid advance of the enemy troops who had landed on the southern French coast. They rejoined the main force only in the vicinity of Metz, much later. The 287th Flak Battalion, which was in part immobilized owing to lack of prime movers, only managed to reach the Loire River, where it was employed to protect the bridges and lost almost all of its materiel in the subsequent fighting.

On the evening of August 1, after a short briefing at 7th Army headquarters in Le Mans, the commander of the 9th Panzer Division [i.e., Jollasse] reported to the commander of the 7th Army at his advanced command post in the vicinity of Mortain, 30 kilometers (18.64 miles) southeast of Avranches. Here I was instructed that the 9th Panzer Division, after assembling in the area Alencon-Domfront, was to participate in a German counterattack to close the gap at Avranches. The rapid development of the situation in the area around Avranches and the eastward turn of the enemy in the general

direction of Laval-Le Mans prevented the planned employment of the 9th Panzer Division during the counterattack on
Avranches.

The threatening envelopment on the open southern flank
and the large-scale attack of the British forces induced the
commanders of the army group [Army Group B] and army to
commit the various elements of the 9th Panzer Division in
piecemeal fashion, very much to the detriment of the overall
situation during the further evolution of the situation.

On August 6 the elements of the 9th Panzer Division that
had already arrived (10th and 11th Panzer Grenadier Regiments; 33rd Panzer Regiment, minus its Panther battalion;
102nd Panzer Artillery Regiment, less some elements of the
heavy battalion; 9th Panzer Reconnaissance Battalion; 86th
Panzer Engineer Battalion; 85th Panzer Signal Battalion; and
elements of the service troops) stood along the general line
Domfront–Mayenne River–north of Montsurs, mingled with
elements of the position [static infantry] divisions and alert
units of the army and Luftwaffe.

The 9th Panzer Division elements were organized approxi-
mately as follows:

1. The reinforced 9th Panzer Reconnaissance Battalion was
   immobilized on both sides of Ambrieres (south of Domfront), which had particularly disagreeable effects during the further enemy advance northward, since as a
   result there was no longer any reconnaissance of enemy
   intentions by this unit, which was especially well equipped and trained for the purpose.
2. Battle groups of the reinforced 11th Panzer Grenadier
   Regiment in the area north of Mayenne.
3. Armored battle groups in the Mayenne-Montsurs area,
   including the armored personnel carrier battalion of the
   10th Panzer Grenadier Regiment, IV Battalion of the
   33rd Panzer Regiment, II Battalion of the 102nd Panzer
   Artillery Regiment, and the armored personnel company of the 86th Panzer Engineer Battalion.

The diversion of the Panther battalion of the 9th Panzer Division toward the vicinity of Falaise on August 8 was felt as a serious loss owing to the strained situation at the southern wing of the division.

A briefing of the divisional commander at the advanced command post of the Commander-in-Chief, West [Field Marshal von Kluge] at Alencon in the evening of August 9 yielded the information that Alencon, as a supply and withdrawal center for the units fighting north and west of it, had to be held under all circumstances. No further troops could be promised for the time being for the protection of the open southern flank. The Commander-in-Chief West summed up the assignment of the 9th Panzer Division as follows: "Le Mans may fall, but Alencon must not fall."

The renewed request on the part of the divisional commander to disengage the 9th Panzer Reconnaissance Battalion from the front south of Domfront and employ it for reconnaissance and security on the open moving wing under its commander was refused again, although the divisional commander pointed out that no additional troops would be needed for disengagement of the 9th Panzer Reconnaissance Battalion.

After interpolation of elements of the 708th Infantry Division and the Panzer Lehr Division on August 10, the 9th Panzer Division was operationally limited to the open southern wing, where enemy pressure continuously increased. The 9th Panzer Reconnaissance Battalion even at this point remained in the area around Ambrieres. The absence of reconnaissance made itself more and more unpleasantly felt. Therefore the division ordered two eight-bicycle patrols to the divisional command post so as to have at least some reconnaissance troops available. These patrols rendered excellent service during the following days and kept the division informed of the direction of enemy envelopments and attacks.

On August 10, as expected, the enemy veered northward from Le Mans. The 9th Panzer Division, its bulk now facing south and southwestward, engaged in bitter resistance in the area on both sides of Beaumont, 20 kilometers south of Alencon.

On August 11 fighting shifted to the area due south of Alencon, where as on the previous day, a large number of enemy tanks [belonging to the French 2nd Armored Division] were put out of action, though at considerable sacrifice to ourselves. Alencon was lost.

The pressure increased constantly as a result of the enemy's advance north and northwestward. From August 11 on, the 9th Panzer Division fought without control from the top, since the staff of the LXXXI Corps, as a result of shifting of the command posts, was now east of the menacing enemy envelopment.

On August 13, after hard battles north of Alencon the preceding day, the 9th Panzer Division stood near Cassonges, 25 kilometers northwest of Alencon. It was entirely alone, since the Panzer Lehr Division (on the right) and 1st SS Panzer Division (on the left) had suddenly withdrawn. Attacked in flank and rear by superior enemy forces, the bulk of the armored battle group and essential elements of the 11th Panzer Grenadier Regiment and the panzer artillery were lost.

On August 14 Group Eberbach was interpolated into the area north of Cassonges, with the remnants of the 9th Panzer Division being placed again under strict control. On August 16 the remaining elements of the 9th Panzer Division were released from the almost closed pocket by the commander of the 7th Army, with instructions to assemble in the area southeast of Paris.

The elements of the 9th Panzer Division referred to in the daily report of Army Group B of August 18 as having been committed against the advancing enemy between Vernon and Mantes on the lower Seine River can only have been the remnants of the Panther battalion, which had been dispatched to Panzer Group West [5th Panzer Army] on August 8.

Employment of the Remaining Elements of the 9th Panzer Division. Up to August 14, the remnants of the 9th Panzer Division assembled in the area south of Estanay and Sezanne. On August 21 it took over protection of the bridges south of the Seine River in a line from Nogent (excluded) to Mary (included), and engaged in reconnaissance in this area.

On August 24 the remnants of the 9th Panzer Division were committed at the eastern edge of Paris. Partisan action in the rear of the division was already flaring up everywhere at that time. After the enemy had broken through south of the division at Melem, the division formed a blocking line on the Marne River on both sides of Le Meaux and toward the south.

On August 26 a further withdrawal northeastward was ordered. The area around Metz was reached a few days later by way of Aisne (in the vicinity of Soissons)–Chemin de Dames (south of Laon)–the Oise and through Belgium.

From August 18 on, the division had ordered all unnecessary elements into this area. Rehabilitation of the division could thus be started immediately after the withdrawal ended.

Conclusion. Once more the 9th Panzer Division, as in February 1944, in the area Apostolovo–Krivoi Rog, had been dispersed almost over the entire front of the army and the army group. Since an armored division is at its best when employed as a combat unit, a great deal of its striking power had been lost in the process.

The refusal to disengage the 9th Panzer Reconnaissance Battalion from the area south of Domfront, with the result that it could not be employed on the open wing in the area around Le Mans, likewise had detrimental effects upon the course of the battle, although this could not have influenced the development of the situation as a whole.

The absence of tight control by the corps in the critical days from August 11 to August 13 resulted in serious losses.

From August 24 on the conduct of operations was made very difficult by the rapidity of the enemy advance and our own movements. Reports and orders, upon arrival at the division, in most cases were 24 to 48 hours behind actual events.

The daily reports of Army Group B from August 28 to September 4 also show that in the precipitate development of the situation, higher headquarters had temporarily lost their overall view of things.

During the retrograde battles east of Paris and on the way to Belgium, the 9th Panzer Division was not employed. The division staff, however, was still employed in the conduct of operations, while, as already mentioned, the remnants of the division proceeded to the area around Metz according to orders.

Jollasse appears to have been en route to report on the destruction of his force on August 8 or 9, but he was caught on the road by a fighter-bomber and his car was destroyed. The driver was killed, Lieutenant Colonel Friedel was slightly injured, the divisional adjutant lost a leg, and Jollasse was seriously wounded.

Jollasse remained with the divisional medical service while his senior colonel, Max Sperling, exercised acting command right up until the remnant finally reached safety near Metz on September 3. Jollasse was then finally medically evacuated to Germany. After he partially recovered, he was sent on recuperative leave.

In November, after being declared fit for limited service, he went to Berlin where, on November 28, he was given a desk job at the Inspectorate of Panzer Troops by his old friend Gen. Wolfgang Thomale. He was put in charge of the necrology branch—notifying the next of kin of deceased panzer officers and forwarding pension requests to the Army Payroll Office.

The critical developments of the new year of 1945, however, were too urgent to allow a general in moderately good health to remain in a desk job. General Burgdorff, now chief of the Army Personnel Office, therefore ordered him to Breslau—which was already menaced by the Soviet attacks across the Vistula toward the Oder—where he was to assume command of the 408th Replacement Division. He arrived in the city on January 25, after the Russians had already established bridgeheads both north and south of the city.

The division was one in name only. It administered training and miscellaneous replacement units, usually consisting of men en route to their parent formations.[11] During February, it became obvious that the headquarters was superfluous, so it was divested of its troops. They were attached to the 609th Infantry Division, assigned for the primary defense of the city—which meanwhile had been encircled by the Russians on February 15–16.

Jollasse took part in the breakout staged by Maj. Gen. Max Sachsenheimer's 17th and Lt. Gen. Hans Wagner's 269th Infantry Division, to link up with 4th Panzer Army on February 20–23.[12] Jollasse succeeded in crossing the Niesse and making his way to the headquarters of Col. Gen. Ferdinand Schoerner's Army Group Center.

On March 15, Jollasse was named to replace Maj. Gen. Rudolf Goltzsch as commander of what was left of the 344th *Volksgrenadier* Division, then fighting in Czechoslovakia.[13] On April 14, 1945, he became commander of Battle Group Jollasse, which included his own 344th *Volksgrenadier* and the decimated *Fuehrer Begleit* and 10th SS Panzer Divisions. These divisions were surrounded by the Red Army in Czechoslovakia, along with most of Army Group Center, when Adolf Hitler committed suicide on April 30, 1945. Jollasse, who had been promoted to lieutenant general on April 20, Hitler's last birthday, gave permission for anyone who wished to attempt to escape to do so. He and twenty-five men actually succeeded in eluding the Red Army and associated outlaw gangs and partisans. He was not captured until June 8, more than a month after the war had ended, and at which time he was in upper Bavaria. He was released from prison on June 30, 1947, and moved to Kochel am See, a lake in the Bavarian Alps. He died on March 14, 1987, in Kitzing, a former German town now located in the Lorraine province of France.

Baron von Elverfeldt, shortly after he was promoted to major general on September 1, 1944.

Erwin Jollasse, commander of the 9th Panzer Division on the Western Front in 1944.

Gen. of Panzer Troops Heinrich von Luettwitz, commander of the 2nd Panzer Division in the Normandy campaign and the XXXXVII Panzer Corps during the battle of the Bulge.

Baron Smilo von Luettwitz (1895–1975), cousin of Heinrich von Luettwitz and also a panzer commander.

An experimental German half-track, circa 1938.

The Panzer Troops School at Wunsdorf, near Zossen, south of Berlin.

Field Marshal Walter Model, commander in chief of Army Group B on the Western Front, 1944–45.

Baron Werner von Fritsch, commander in chief of the German Army from 1934 to 1938 and a close associate of Hans von Funck.

Gen. of Panzer Troops Ludwig Cruewell, the extremely capable commander of the Afrika Korps (1942–43) and deputy commander of Panzer Army Afrika (1943).

Hasso von Manteuffel, commander of the 5th Panzer Army on the Western Front, 1944–45. He had low opinions of both Luettwitz and Bayerlein.

An American infantryman captured a German *Landser* in Mortain, 1944. The town was the objective of Funck's unsuccessful counterattack in early August 1944.

Col. Gen. Heinz Guderian, "father of the blitzkrieg."

Field Marshal Erwin Rommel, the Desert Fox. He apparently lost faith in Bayerlein during the retreat from El Alamein.

Gen. of Panzer Troops Ritter Wilhelm von Thoma. Fritz Bayerlein was his chief of staff.

Gen. of Panzer Troops Hans Eberbach, commander of the 5th Panzer Army, Panzer Group Eberbach, and 7th Army during the battle of Normandy and the retreat from France.

Maj. Gen. Baron Kurt von Liebenstein, another of Guderian's highly capable staff officers.

Gen. of Panzer Troops Baron Hans Funck, commander of the 7th Panzer Division (1940–43) and XXXXVII Panzer Corps (1943–44).

Col. (later Gen. of Artillery) Bodewin Keitel, brother of Wilhelm and head of the Army Personnel Office and commander of *Wehrkreis XX.*

Fritz Bayerlein in the desert, circa 1942. He served as chief of staff to Rommel and Guderian and commanded the 3rd Panzer Division, Panzer Lehr Division, and LIII Corps and briefly served as acting commander of the Afrika Korps.

Baron Leo Geyr von Schweppenburg, commander of 3rd Panzer Division, XXIV Panzer Corps, XXXX Panzer Corps, LVIII Panzer Corps, and Panzer Group West.

A Panther tank from the 116th Panzer Division, damaged and abandoned in Argentan, August 1944.

A destroyed convoy near Falaise.

A German Sdkfz 234 reconnaissance vehicle, abandoned in Normandy.

A German Panther, considered by many panzer troops to be the best German tank of World War II.

Field Marshal Wilhelm Keitel, the "Nodding Ass," shaking hands with Adolf Hitler. He was commander in chief of the *Wehrmacht* High Command throughout the war.

A German infantry squad hidden in the snow near the French border, circa 1939–40.

A Tiger tank.

The "corridor of death" near Falaise, France. The 5th Panzer and 7th Armies were slaughtered here by U.S. and British forces in August 1944.

SS Col. Gen. Paul Hausser, commander
of the 7th Army in Normandy.

Gen. of Panzer Troops Hasso von
Manteuffel.

British fighter-
bombers provide
air cover for
ground troops in
Normandy,
June 7, 1944.

A German armed with a bazooka waits in ambush at the edge of a hedgerow, Normandy, 1944.

A German battle group forces a river crossing, France, 1940.

Caen, Normandy, 1944.

German infantrymen await an attack in Normandy, summer 1944.

An 88-millimeter antiaircraft gun after it has been hit by an Allied fighter-bomber.

Col. Gen. Hermann Hoth, commander of the 4th Panzer Army, shown here on the Eastern Front.

CHAPTER 4

Baron Heinrich von Luettwitz

Early natives of Silesia, the family von Luettwitz is first mentioned during the reign of Duke Heinrich I (1321–88). Another ancestor, Ernst von Luettwitz, was made a *Freiherr* (baron) by a patent issued by Frederick William IV, king of Prussia, in 1815 for his service in the war against Napoleon. His brother, Karl, born in 1779, was also raised to the same title at the same time and for the same reason. From these two brothers, the two separate branches of the family descended—both producing generals of panzer troops during World War II. Smilo von Luettwitz, grandson of Ernst and cousin of Heinrich, later commanded 9th Army on the Eastern Front.[1]

Baron Friedrich Karl von Luettwitz, who was born in 1849, served in the army until after the conclusion of peace at Versailles in 1871. He then retired as a captain and returned to the family's estate of Kruempen in Prussia to live the life of a gentleman farmer—a traditional *Junker*. He would not die until 1919.

The baron married Klara von Unruh, daughter of another prominent military dynasty, ten years his junior, and began to raise a modest family. Their second son, Baron Diepold Georg Heinrich von Luettwitz, the future panzer general, was born at Krumpach on December 6, 1896, and was soon entered in the standard German school system, in which he excelled. He became an avid horseman from the age of eight and was soon entering riding competitions, but his promising career ended when World War I broke out.

Apparently unable to get his father's support, despite the excitement of the war fever sweeping all of Germany, Heinrich volunteered for military duty on August 10 and joined the forces being rushed to the Western Front. After he served briefly as a simple private, his maternal uncle intervened in his behalf and had him brevetted as a *Leutnant* (second lieutenant) on December 4, 1914, two days before his eighteenth birthday.

Put through a quick officers' training course in early 1915, Heinrich was posted to the 48th Infantry Regiment, at first as a supernumerary with the rear area services. Though this allowed him ample time to enjoy his hobby of riding, it was scarcely the preferred placement for a patriotic young firebrand like Luettwitz.

It seems probable that the aging senior Luettwitz used considerable influence to keep his son out of danger; nevertheless, Heinrich began a letter-writing campaign to obtain an active posting, which finally, in the critical days of 1917, had the effect of earning him a transfer to a field platoon of the regiment, fighting in the bloody trench battles in northern France.

In several pitched battles during the summer, Second Lieutenant von Luettwitz received his Iron Cross, Second and First Classes, as well as a not-too-serious wound, which resulted in his being posted back to Germany and a hospital until the spring of 1918. By now his family had begun to use a little more influence with the War Department, and on May 2, 1918, Heinrich was posted as a squadron leader of the 3rd Troop of the 1st Ulan Regiment, a crack unit designed to exploit hoped-for breakthroughs in the front, initially made by the assault troops (*Stosstruppe*), a new German military development.

Regrettably, though the assault technique was fairly successful in the 1918 summer offensive conceived by Field Marshal Erich Ludendorff, no deep penetrations were achieved, and hence the cavalry, including the crack Ulan regiments, was never employed. As a result, Luettwitz spent most of 1918 in evolutions and maneuvers.

In October and November, heavy Allied pressure on the German lines—despite a last, costly German assault—drove the weary nation to eject its rulers and, in a state of turmoil and confusion, sue for an armistice. Though the German Army now virtually dissolved as dissatisfied draftees went home or joined the Communists, the Ulans, members of a largely volunteer and elite unit, returned quietly to their garrison post at Brieg/Oels in Silesia for disbandment under the Versailles mandate.

Fortunately for Luettwitz and several other highly placed subalterns, the new Reich Defense Ministry decided to retain the regiment—not as an elite Royal Prussian Ulan formation, but as the 8th *Reichswehr* Cavalry Regiment under its old commander, Colonel von Jagow, who was soon to be promoted to major general. Some

Allied military inspectors who were dedicated to the total eradication of the Imperial Army began to make protests, but the cunning German war minister, Gustav Noske, merely ordered the 8th Cavalry to the Polish frontier for peacekeeping duties until late in 1919, by which time the Allies had other things on their minds.[2]

On December 18, 1919, Second Lieutenant Luettwitz was commissioned into the *Reichswehr*, retroactive to September 1, 1915. He became the 245th former Royal officer thus commissioned into the new 100,000-man army and was also confirmed as squadron leader in the 8th Cavalry, now again quartered at Oels. At about this time, while socializing with the Silesian nobility, many of whom were still represented in the regiment, the twenty-four-year-old Heinrich began paying court to the sister of a fellow officer. Her name was Jutta von Engelmann, a lively and attractive young lady of twenty-one. On September 17, 1920, the two were married at the Engelmann estate of Pzybor, not far from Wohlau on the Frisches Hof in East Prussia. The couple spent a brief honeymoon at the Luettwitz estate at Krumpach before the cavalry officer returned to duty. Life at the garrison was pleasant enough; the regiment was a close-knit unit and its standards were high, thus ruling out undesirable recruits, both officers and men.

Jutta gave birth to the eldest son of the family, Hans von Luettwitz, on January 18, 1922, at Krumpach, and Heinrich returned home for the christening. Jutta seems to have been unhappy among the Luettwitzes, and in the spring, she and the baby returned to the Engelmann estate in East Prussia. It was the beginning of the end for the marriage.

On April 1, 1925, Luettwitz was at last commissioned *Oberleutnant* (first lieutenant). It was not unusual at all, particularly in the *Reichswehr* cavalry, for so many years to elapse before a raise in rank. It resulted in only a slight increase in pay. Heinrich continued in his same squadron command, which he had turned into a veritable showpiece of beautifully executed precision.

In 1926, Lt. Col. Baron Hans von Stein zu Kochberg, who had served in the 8th Cavalry as a captain in 1920–22 before being posted to Berlin, took over command of the crack regiment. He had always favored Luettwitz, and now they renewed their friendship. Dinners, fetes, and the theater in nearby Breslau became a part of the lieutenant's life.

Stein had a very beautiful young daughter, coincidentally also named Jutta. At the time, she was a fresh nineteen years of age, an accomplished pianist, well read in the classics, and an equestrienne of no mean ability. One can almost immediately predict the results.

Lieutenant Colonel Stein was a "retread," a previously retired officer who returned to active duty, and came up for permanent retirement as of November 1, 1927. His last official act was to have Heinrich posted to the senior regimental staff of the *Wehrkreis* Officers' Training School from October 1, and the lieutenant was enrolled in the school's training course two days later. During the Christmas season, Luettwitz filed suit for divorce in the Breslau Judiciary, which almost immediately issued a decree in his favor as of December 23, 1927—a marked contrast to what happened to Baron von Funck later, during the Nazi period. Luettwitz continued in his course until graduation on February 15, 1928, whereupon he remained at the school as an administrative officer. On December 11, at Ober Naundorf near Dresden, he and *Freifrau* (Baroness) Jutta von Stein zu Kochberg were married. Both returned to Breslau following a ski vacation in Bavaria.

Seven months later, on July 21, 1929, their first child, a daughter named Christa, was born in their comfortable quarters at the school. The father had taken another special course, between April 13 and May 4. It was a pilot program, probably initiated by Col. Oswald Lutz, for controlling fast-moving cavalry formations with radios mounted in trucks and cars.

Though Luettwitz continued his equestrianship and remained closely associated with horses and horsemanship throughout his career, he became a convert to the revolutionary innovation of motorized forces from this point on. In fact, on September 20, with the approval of his superiors at the school, he took an extensive part in a training exercise involving heavily armed infantry being speedily deployed for combat by motor vehicles. This maneuver came to a highly successful conclusion on October 18. Lieutenant Luettwitz was warmly commended by the exercise commander, Maj. Werner Kempf, commanding officer of the 8th Motorized Battalion.[3]

The school administration took due note of this young officer and for most of the next year, 1929–30, sent him on a series of lecture tours to the other *Wehrkreis* training centers, to introduce the new mechanized theory as much as possible. Regrettably, however, few of the commanders had the breath of vision possessed by Maj. Ritter Ludwig von Radlmeier of the Breslau center, and the tours were generally a failure.[4]

On February 1, 1931, Luettwitz was promoted to the rank of *Rittmeister* (cavalry captain). On the twenty-fourth, he took over a course in fire control for motorized units in action, combining artillery, truck-carried infantry with heavy machine guns, and a small group of dummy tanks—a course on which Lutz and some of his junior officers from the Motor Inspectorate commented favorably.

On completion on March 13 of the exercise, along with its accompanying lectures and written and oral examinations, Luettwitz was advised that he was to be posted back to his old cavalry regiment at Oels-Brieg. He took over the I Battalion on April 1. Now, however, this battalion was to be motorized—with trucks, cars, and motorcycles—though the rest of the 8th Regiment remained traditionally mounted. Regrettably, the commander and most of the other senior officers of the 8th Cavalry were ultraconservatives, who regarded the noisy vehicles, with their stench of petrol and grease, as gross insults to their fine horsemen and—despite Luettwitz's obvious predilection for horses—caused him considerable discomfort. The fact that Col. Baron Anton von Hirschberg, inspector of cavalry, was outranked by Major General Lutz, the inspector of motor troops, made no appreciable difference.[5]

The captain's problems were somewhat overshadowed on February 1, 1932, by the birth of his second son, Hans-Jurgen von Luettwitz, the first child by this happier marriage. The internal problems of Germany at this time—when the National Socialist German Workers' Party, led by a certain Adolf Hitler, was beginning to win power in the *Reichstag*—gave many forward-thinking officers a certain amount of hope. Hitler was openly promising to restore the army.

In January 1933, Hitler became chancellor of Germany, and the army began at once to experience a measurable improvement. Lutz and his chief of staff, Heinz Guderian, arranged for a large demonstration of their new motorized forces in October, and Luettwitz and his battalion were detached to participate. Beginning on October 24, the repeat of his 1929 maneuvers was viewed with great enthusiasm by the new chancellor, who was subsequently quoted as saying: "That's it! That's exactly what I want!"

Returning to the battalion garrison at Brieg on November 5, the captain was deluged with praises from the many motor enthusiasts, including the Austrian theoretician Ritter von Eimannsberger. The 8th Cavalry Regiment was forced to rethink its attitude, and the commander and cavalry battalion leader were posted to other stations.

As the *Reichswehr* began to evolve into a larger and better armed force, designations also began to change. The 8th Cavalry became Cavalry Regiment Brieg on October 1, 1934, much to the disgust of all of its officers. It was a full year later, on October 15, 1935, before the Defense Ministry thought better of its decision and restored their traditional numbers to the cavalry and infantry regiments. At the same time, Luettwitz was transferred to the command of *Motorisieren Kraftfahr Abteilung 3* (3rd Motorized Battalion), a squadron of the new Mark I infantry tanks.

On January 1, 1936, he became a major and officially changed his service color (*Waffenfahrbe*) from cavalry lemon yellow to the new panzer pink. This, however, did not prevent the honors-seeking *Reichswehr* from remembering his brilliance as a rider and posting him to the nebulous command of *Reiter Regiment 4* (4th Cavalry Regiment)— although there was already a 4th Cavalry at Insterburg in East Prussia.

This group was the German Olympic Equestrian Team, which, under Luettwitz's leadership, performed most creditably during the August games, earning several medals. Unfortunately, it did not do the Fuehrer's will and capture the elusive gold. As a result, on September 23, 1936, the unlucky major was abruptly posted to the real 4th Cavalry, as acting commander. Even this, however, was only temporary. On October 6, he was put on the supernumerary list— "attached" to the regimental staff. At this time, the 4th Cavalry was exactly that—cavalry—and one can thus understand the poetic punishment meted out to the officer who had failed the Nazi State.

Luckily, Hitler did not maintain this grudge for long, if it actually had been he who was behind Luettwitz's exile. The need for trained armored officers to implement the grandiose schemes being made led to a change just a year later. On October 12, 1937, Major Luettwitz was given official command of the *Kavallerie Regiment 4*, which was to be immediately converted into a motorized unit as part of the newly organized 1st Cavalry Brigade, stationed in East Prussia, and commanded by Luettwitz's old friend Col. Baron Wolfgang von Waldenfels, of the Breslau School.[6]

Luettwitz's efforts during 1938, while the Austrian and Sudeten crises were taking place, actually did him more harm than good. As the 4th grew in size, the Panzer Inspectorate determined that a more senior officer should command it, and Luettwitz ended up commanding only the I Battalion, on an equal footing with Maj. Hans Kaellner of the II Battalion.[7] However, on March 1, 1939, he was duly promoted to lieutenant colonel, and at the outbreak of the war with Poland on September 1, he took command of the 1st Reconnaissance Battalion (*Aufklarung Abteilung 1*) of the brigade. Alas, instead of taking part in the East Prussian drive into northern Poland, Luettwitz and his men were held as a reserve in the East Prussian capital of Koenigsberg. The lieutenant colonel protested, naturally, but to no avail. By the time his entreaties were processed in Berlin, he not only had missed the opening of the campaign, but also had to play catch-up to overtake the brigade outside Warsaw on September 14. To make matters even worse, he received a painful wound on September 16 and was sent back to Koenigsberg to recover.

Awarded the clasp to his Iron Cross, Second Class, on September 20, he also received the Silver Wounded Badge on March 2, 1940, by which time he had resumed command of the reconnaissance unit. In this capacity, he was left to kick his heels in the east, while the rest of the panzer forces were winning glory in the six-week French campaign. One may well understand the utter frustration of the patriotic soldier who saw himself being deliberately shunted into a backwater when he wanted nothing better than to lead a force in action. While maintaining his reconnaissance unit at peak efficiency, he buried his disappointment in long rides through the East Prussian countryside, also indulging his other passion: foxhunting.

With the war in an apparent stalemate in the fall of 1940, Lieutenant Colonel Luettwitz was ordered to Chemnitz in *Wehrkreis IV*, headquartered at Dresden, to take command of the new 101st Motorized Infantry Regiment, formerly of the 14th Infantry Division and now attached to the headquarters of the 18th Panzer Division. The divisional commander, Maj. Gen. Walther Nehring, had asked for him specifically to train the men who had never had any experience in trucks and half-tracks.

Luettwitz threw himself into the task and, in the two succeeding months, accomplished it with commendable results. His satisfaction in a job well done was short-lived, however. On January 3, 1941, he was abruptly ordered back to Koenigsberg as a reserve officer for armor under the *Wehrkreis* commander, Gen. of Artillery Wilhelm Ulex.[8]

Nehring wrote a letter of protest to the Army Personnel Office, as did several of Luettwitz's former associates. Urged also by Gen. Erich Hoepner and Gen. Heinz Guderian, the Personnel Office posted the unhappy officer to the headquarters of Maj. Gen. Friedrich Kirchner's 1st Panzer Division as a supernumerary motorized infantry regimental commander on February 1.[9] Unfortunately, both of the 1st Panzer's regiments were already headed by veteran officers, Lt. Col. Franz Westhoven and Col. Hans Christoph von Heydebrand und der Lasa, the latter of which had displaced Luettwitz in command of the 4th Cavalry Regiment in early 1939.[10]

When the onset of Operation *Barbarossa*, the invasion of Russia, took place on June 22, 1941, Luettwitz was attached to the headquarters of Field Marshal Ritter Wilhelm von Leeb's Army Group North in its drive into the Baltic countries and spent the first week of the great campaign as an observer. Then a death in action in Army Group Center on June 29 proved fortunate for the previously anguished lieutenant colonel. The next day, he reported to Lt. Gen. Horst Stumpff and his Ia (operations officer), Maj. Baron Rudolf von Gersdorff, at the headquarters, 20th Panzer Division, located near Grodno on the Niemen.[11] He was to assume command of the 59th Rifle Regiment of the division, which was slated to advance to the Dvina opposite Ulla over the next few days. Stumpff shook the lieutenant colonel's hand and bade him to take the point of the advance. Now Luettwitz was to justify his years of training.

On July 6, the regiment deployed along the southwest branch of the river while the commander reconnoitered the ground. He ordered an engineer unit to lay a couple pontoon bridges under the cover of darkness, over which he threw his two battalions, supported by artillery and a squadron of tanks. The following day, Ulla fell by storm, Soviet forces streamed away to the east and south, and Luettwitz continued in close pursuit of the enemy toward Vitebsk, which he succeeded in capturing in a coup de main on July 10.

Under heavy attack, the regiment hedgehogged to await the arrival of the rest of the division. Stumpff, with the recon detachment and elements of the 112th Rifle Regiment, reached the beleaguered battle group on the eleventh. The panzer regiment, the 21st, arrived in penny packets the next day. Together, the division first contained the Soviet attacks, then drove them back and destroyed several units. The 7th Panzer Division, operating farther south, had bypassed Vitebsk by some distance, and now Luettwitz, his command augmented by a panzer battalion, was sent on toward Velizh.

By July 21, the advance had reached the Smolensk-Moscow highway behind the Soviet forces now trapped in this area. As the German infantry moved up to solidify the huge pocket, Luettwitz and the rest of the 20th Panzer acted as a rear-guard defense, holding off Soviet attacks aimed at relief of the pocket. Following the eventual mop-up of the surrounded Soviet forces, Hitler shifted the emphasis of his attack toward the south, diverting most of Guderian's 2nd Panzer Group to help Kleist encircle and capture the Soviet defenders of Kiev. As a result, Hoth's 3rd Panzer Group spent a month in a holding pattern east of Smolensk, along the Dnieper River, facing the Soviets around Vyazma.

When at last the drive for Moscow was recommenced in September—much too late—the whole LVII Panzer Corps (commanded by Gen. of Panzer Troops Adolf Kuntzen), including the 20th Panzer, was placed under the headquarters of the 4th Panzer Group (led by Col. Gen. Erich Hoepner), which had been switched from Army Group North and inserted between Hoth and Guderian. On October 7, the advance began. Luettwitz's veteran battle group, much rested and reinforced, led the 20th Panzer's lunge to seize Spas-Demensk, which fell on the ninth. Heinrich von Luettwitz then drove toward Kaluga on the Oka, while the main forces forged a great pocket around Vyazma. Using exactly the same method he had employed earlier on the Dvina against Ulla, Luettwitz threw his tanks and infantry across the Oka during the night of October 12–13, and seized the city by noon on the thirteenth.

On October 15, the health of Lt. Gen. Horst Stumpff gave out at last, and he was invalided home, Lt. Gen. Ritter Wilhelm von Thoma taking his place. Luettwitz had meanwhile won his clasp to the Iron Cross, First Class, on August 1 and the bronze Panzer Battle Badge on the eighth. On October 1, he was promoted to full colonel (*Oberst*), retroactive to November 1, 1940. He thus became the third most senior officer in the division.

As the German forces smashed across first the Istya and then the Nara in inclement weather, the new colonel and his regiment were transferred to the command of the 19th Panzer Division, to consolidate the latter river crossing. With his usual élan, Luettwitz attacked and routed a Soviet brigade and opened the way toward Naro Fominsk.

The weather now grew progressively worse. The trucks of the 59th were immovable in the mud, and only a few half-tracks, including Luettwitz's command car, could still make any progress. Returned to Thoma, the regiment struggled through mud and slush toward Naro Fominsk, which ultimately fell in November. But as with all of the terribly taxed units in the German Army, this was the regiment's last success as the terrible winter brought everything to a halt, with Moscow less than sixty miles away.

Better acclimatized to the conditions, the Soviets launched their devastating counterattacks all along the front in early December. Despite Hitler's "stand fast" directives and wholesale dismissal of generals, the German forces reeled backward under the sledgehammer blows of the enemy. Outflanked and repeatedly in danger of being cut off and surrounded, the 20th Panzer—by now terribly understrength—fell back as far as Kirov, where it had been in mid-October.

On December 20, in the midst of the worst fighting, Luettwitz received the German Cross in Gold (*Deutsche Kreuz in Geld*), the intermediate award between the Iron Cross, First Class, and the Knight's Cross. By February 1, 1942, he and the rest of the division were pulled back to the line east of the Desna-Oka, and in March, when the spring thaws effectively halted all operations, Thoma was ordered to move his division to Bryansk for a brief rest and refit.

Colonel Luettwitz and his surviving officers worked diligently to integrate the raw recruits sent them among the 59th Rifle's surviving veterans, and they were overjoyed at being able to equip the I Battalion with some of the new half-track personnel carriers. As a result of their efforts, the 20th Panzer was able to return to the Orel sector by the end of April, where, under the 2nd Panzer Army, they were to lend some cooperation to the great summer offensive about to be launched to the south.

Although not directly involved, much to the commander's chagrin, the 20th was allowed to participate in a preemptive attack against the Soviet 13th Army above Voronezh, preventing it from assisting the other Russian formations under attack by 4th Panzer

Army. With infantry support, between May 2–10, Luettwitz's battle group attacked and recaptured the town of Livny. For this victory he was awarded the Knight's Cross on May 27.

During June and July, while the southern armies advanced to Voronezh and crossed the Don, Thoma's 20th Panzer and 18th Panzer Divisions battled against Soviet entrenchments in an effort to reach Yelets. With the attention of the High Command totally focused on the Volga and Caucasus, however, no real attention was given to this sideshow. When Voronezh was captured in mid-July, Col. Gen. Baron Maximilian von Weichs, the overall commander of the southern sector, ordered the two panzer divisions to stand firm and not press their advantage.[12]

Meanwhile, on June 8, Luettwitz had taken over the entire 20th Rifle (*Schutzen*) Brigade, comprising both the 59th and 101st Rifle Regiments. On June 30, Thoma was recalled to Berlin for a new assignment, and Maj. Gen. Walther Duvert took over his place in command of the 20th.[13] Durvert had just recovered from nervous exhaustion suffered in the November battles as commander of the 13th Panzer Division. Thomas later described Luettwitz to U.S. Army interviewers as "a passionate soldier, ambitious, sometimes more critical than necessary. With much combat experience, he joined the front line fight himself. A professional soldier capable of improvising. Socially courteous, he leads men by his personality and handles them well, both in theory and in practice." It is interesting to compare this glowing evaluation with the opinion of an American observer, given later.

In late July, Luettwitz, touring his forward positions along the Oka east of Livny, was caught in a sharp firefight and received a wound that required him to put in a fortnight at the forward hospital at Bryansk. On his return to duty on August 20, he received the *Ostmedaille* (dated August 15) and, later, the Wound Badge in Gold (August 29).

Fortunately for the 20th, the Soviets were too preoccupied by the great thrusts of the 6th Army and 4th Panzer Army on Stalingrad to put any further pressure on the Orel-Oka-Livny sector, where poor General Duvert was proving not to have fully recovered from his breakdown. Finally, on October 10, the army command ordered Luettwitz to assume temporary command of the division while Duvert returned to Germany for further medical attention.

In mid-November, the Soviets launched an overwhelming counteroffensive to the south, destroying most of the 3rd Romanian Army and encircling the 6th Army and much of the 4th Panzer Army in and around Stalingrad. Units of the 2nd Army, holding below Livny down to Voronezh, were alerted to a possible Soviet attack on them, and Luettwitz's 20th was pulled back to the environs of Livny for possible commitment either south or north, depending on circumstances.

On December 1, Luettwitz was promoted to major general and, since it was now obvious that Duvert would not be able to resume active duty, he was confirmed as commander of the division. The situation in the south worsened throughout December, as a new Soviet assault wrecked the Italian 8th and Romanian 4th Armies. As of yet, no enemy pressure had been felt on the Voronezh-Livny sector, although reconnaissance showed powerful forces being concentrated on the Don around Yelets.

On January 5, 1943, orders arrived from Col. Gen. Baron Maximilian von Weichs, commander of Army Group B, for the division to turn over its positions to an infantry division and move north to cover the important supply center of Orel. Thus once again the 20th came under the command of the 2nd Panzer Army. After three Soviet armies smashed westward from the Don on January 15, recapturing Voronezh on the twenty-second and then Kursk in February, the 20th Panzer became embroiled in heavy fighting south of Orel, bringing the Russians to a halt.

In mid-March, as usual, the spring thaw began, bringing general hostilities to a halt, and the 20th Panzer was withdrawn once again through Orel to Bryansk for another quick refit. As it was preparing to move back to the front lines in late April, orders arrived at Orel, instructing Luettwitz to turn over the command to Maj. Gen. Mortimer von Kessel and return to Berlin.[14]

Leaving Orel on May 4, the general landed at Tempelhof in the afternoon of May 5. He reported to the chief of staff, *Oberkommando des Heeres* (OKH), Gen. of Infantry Kurt Zeitzler, who assigned him to a special staff being formed to supervise the testing of the new panzers being readied to go to Russia.[15] Although by now Col. Gen. Heinz Guderian had been appointed inspector general of the armored forces—virtually independent of the other OKH commands—Zeitzler, who had high hopes for the success of the upcoming

Operation *Zitadelle*, wanted a group of experienced panzer officers to keep an eye on developments for him.

Luettwitz and the other specialists thus employed felt almost universally that they were duplicating efforts, and also that their loyalties should go to the Panzer Inspectorate. Nevertheless, they made a serious effort at warning Zeitzler—and through him Hitler—that the new Panther and Ferdinand tanks were full of defects and should not be relied upon too heavily. Meanwhile, on June 1, Luettwitz was promoted to lieutenant general.

In cooperation with several experts from Guderian's office, the OKH special staff submitted a report warning not only that the new tanks were uncertain, but also that the advanced season would render the proposed attack on the Kursk salient doubtful of success at the very best, and a possible disaster at worst. Guderian and Field Marshal Manstein both endorsed this report, but to no avail.

On July 5, 1943, the 9th Army from the north and the 4th Panzer Army from the south launched the attack, but within ten days, it thoroughly bore out the predictions of the special staff. Luettwitz and two or three junior staff officers were sent to the front on the fourteenth to report on the failures of the tanks by interviewing as many of the participants as possible. Map 4.1 shows the battle of Kursk and the subsequent Russian counteroffensive in the Orel sector.

Returning to Berlin by July 26, Luettwitz was able to confirm that the very things he had predicted had indeed happened in the battle of Kursk. This, of course, did not serve to endear him to the manufacturers, the designers, or the staffs at OKH and OKW. But Zeitzler, prompted by Munitions Minister Albert Speer and Guderian, refused to disband the special staff, instead ordering it to redouble its efforts to improve the designs of the new tanks and the Ferdinand self-propelled gun.

Upon completing this assignment, which was filed and forgotten by the Army Construction Bureau, Luettwitz was placed in Fuehrer reserve at the disposal of OKH, and from September 25 to January 1, 1944, he was allowed to spend some accumulated leave time with his family at the new home he had purchased at Neuburg, just east of Ingolstadt, in northern Bavaria. In January, he reported again to the OKH in Berlin and was sent on a two-week inspection of assembly points of refitting panzer divisions in France, to see whether the

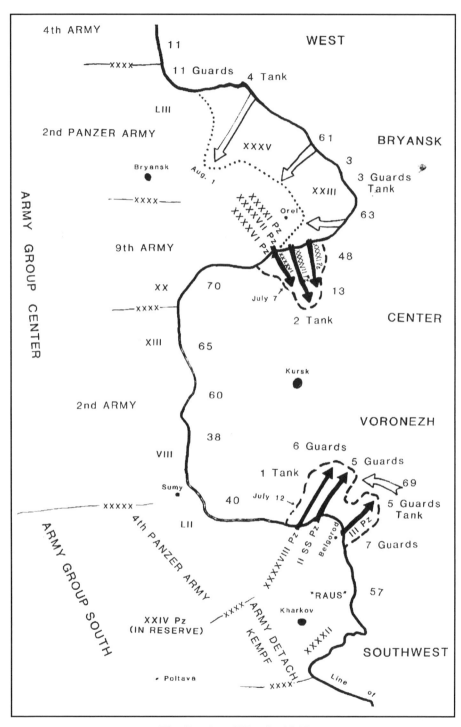

The Battle of Kursk, 1943

newly issued tanks were free of their early problems. Returning to Berlin on the twenty-fifth, he was almost at once summoned to the Personnel Office by Gen. Rudolf Schmundt.

At Guderian's suggestion, General Schmundt ordered Luettwitz to Russia to relieve the terribly depressed and overly exhausted Maj. Gen. Vollrath Luebbe in command of the decimated 2nd Panzer Division.[16] After a quick visit to his wife and children on January 27–28, Luettwitz boarded a plane for the southern sector of White Russia, reaching the railhead at Bobruisk on February 1.

As General Luebbe went off for an extended rest leave at Bad Toelz, Luettwitz supervised the entraining of the remnants of personnel from the division for speedy transfer to the west, leaving what equipment survived to be taken over by the panzer forces still in Russia. On February 17, he set up his new headquarters in a commodious chateau on the outskirts of Amiens and prepared for the monumental task of trying to rebuild the weary force. Map 4.2 shows the Western Front area of operations.

Of his officers, only one, Col. Gerhard Schmidhuber, was a veteran of any length of service in the division; deaths and serious woundings in the winter campaign in Russia had exacted a terrible toll.[17] Even his operations officer had been posted to the division at the same time as Luettwitz.

March, April, and May in France were peaceful and far more pleasant climatewise than the veteran NCOs and troopers had experienced in many months. They quickly adapted to the occasional air raids that were a fact of life in the west and were far more of a nuisance than a threat. The division adjusted well to camouflaging, and the practice of moving from place to place in the dark of night without headlights developed quickly into a habit.

General Luettwitz carefully kept in touch with his cadre of veterans through his personnel officer, Major Gudovius, and almost from the beginning instituted a rotation of leaves whereby the veterans were sent back to their homes in Germany in staggered shifts. He also kept a tally of the many Iron Cross, German Cross, and Wounded Badge bearers, frequently promoting them to higher ranks, where their ability would better serve the division.

Recruits, mostly boys of seventeen and eighteen, as well as some formerly exempted factory workers and a few "old Russian hands"

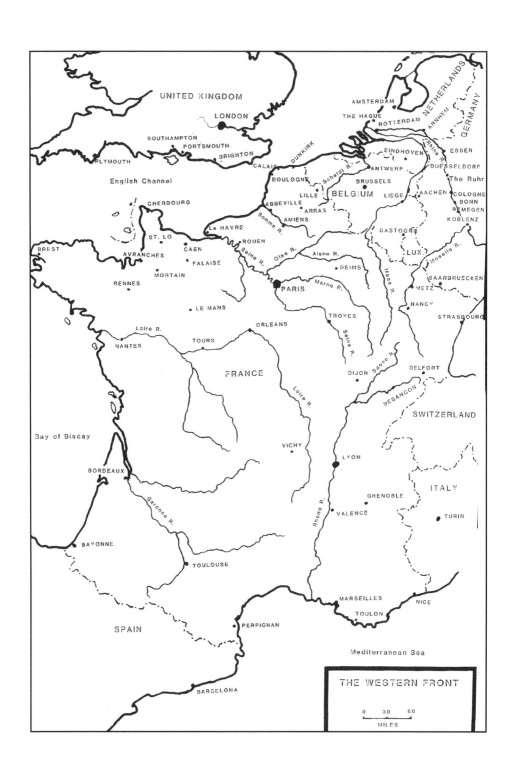

THE WESTERN FRONT

0   30   60
MILES

returning from the hospital, were carefully distributed to the several regiments and detachments, so that as far as possible, no unit would have too many greenhorns. Officers arriving to take up their posts were screened with even greater care. The general was not going to entrust even a platoon to anyone who did not measure up to his standards for a commander. In fact, so careful was he that no less than twenty prospective company and platoon commanders and one major were abruptly transferred or sent home because they did not possess the proper leadership qualifications. In short, the 2nd Panzer Division rapidly developed into a crack outfit, and Luettwitz was commended for his achievements by the commander of Panzer Group West, Gen. Baron Leo Geyr von Schweppenburg.

Because of the various different commands in France and the desires of Hitler back in East Prussia to keep control over the dispositions of the forces in the west, 2nd Panzer remained at Amiens as a Fuehrer reserve. The arrival of a new corps headquarters, the XXXXVII Panzer under Gen. of Panzer Troops Baron Hans von Funck, inserted still another command structure in the already overloaded west. The 2nd Panzer became one of the two divisions tentatively attached to it.

With the threat of imminent invasion by the Western Allies becoming increasingly close at hand, the several German commanders had occasion to meet and discuss events at home and in other theaters. Lt. Gen. Hans Speidel, the chief of staff to Field Marshal Rommel's Army Group B, in particular seems to have been flirting with a group of dissident officers bent on the overthrow of Hitler.[18] Actually, the bespectacled Speidel was almost as uncertain as was Field Marshal Kluge. He wavered to and fro, but it was not until after the war that he began to brag about his participation in the conspiracy, which was marginal at best. Rommel was also tangentially involved—possibly to a greater degree than his chief of staff. What does seem fairly certain is that several of the panzer commanders, including Luettwitz, agreed in principle on a course of action that would align them against the Nazis *if*—and that was a big *if*—some coherent force actually supplanted the Nazis in Germany and set up a new government. Otherwise, like most German generals, they were circumscribed by the principles once aptly stated by the American naval officer, Stephen Decatur, "My country; may she ever be right, but—right or wrong—my country!"

On May 1, Luettwitz bade good-bye, with considerable regret, to the capable Colonel Schmidhuber, who—largely as a result of his general's fulsome reports and recommendations—was named acting commander of the rebuilding 7th Panzer Division in Romania. Luettwitz was now surrounded by younger officers recently promoted to regimental command. These men were veterans and much decorated, but they had never before exercised their present rank. Luettwitz therefore undertook a radical approach in a series of evolutions conducted at night and during the long days of spring rain in May. Captains were given command of battalions, majors and lieutenant colonels acted as regimental commanders, and the four regimental commanders rotated as divisional commander. The general was everywhere, observing and evaluating performance and occasionally offering advice. As a result, in the end, he could only congratulate his young veterans for sterling performances.

The Allied avalanche hit the beaches of Normandy on June 6, but because of paralysis on high, it was June 10 before the 2nd Panzer was ordered to the battlefront, and even then with confusing and conflicting orders. After the war, General Luettwitz was prevailed upon by the U.S. Military History Commission to prepare a series of firsthand narratives of his activities in the west. They are succinct, professional accounts that should perhaps be published in their entirety.[19]

As it moved up to its most taxing battle, the 2nd Panzer's order of battle was as follows:

3rd Panzer Regiment, under Maj. Albrecht von Boxberg, who commanded II Battalion until late June, when the original, unnamed regimental commander was killed in action
2nd Panzer Reconnaissance Battalion, under Maj. Paul von Fallois
2nd Panzer Grenadier Regiment, under Lt. Col. Max Sieberg (killed in action on August 1944)
304th Panzer Grenadier Regiment, under Col. Siegfried Koehn (killed in action on July 20, 1944)
74th Panzer Artillery Regiment, commander unknown
38th Panzer Tank Destroyer (*Panzerjaeger*) Battalion, under Captain Habich

Now the extensive training and practice for movement under enemy air monopoly brought good results. Debouching from its camouflaged positions in and around Amiens and Abbeville, the division made a series of advances under cover of night, also taking advantage of cloudbursts and early-morning fogs. By June 15, it was in position along the Odon, ready for a counterattack toward Caumont and Caen. Allied statements pay tribute to this move. One in particular, Alexander McKee in *Caen, Anvil of Victory*, wrote of the "arrival of a new and totally unexpected formation . . . which had made a rapid march . . . without being detected."[20]

In *Six Armies in Normandy*, John Keegan stated that the division began its march on June 7, thus estimating that it covered 20 miles per 24 hours on its 120-mile journey.[21] Since Luettwitz averred that he did not receive orders until June 10, the daily average of the march is truly exceptional: 60 miles per 24 hours. No wonder the 2nd was so respected by its enemies.

In the battle of Villers-Bocage, General Luettwitz now put his forces into action against a veteran British armored division, the 7th, which had moved up to Cahagnes and occupied a strategic elevation, Hill 174, and was now threatening the anchor of the entire German line at Caen (Map 4.3). With his Russian-learned skill, he formed three combined-arms battle groups for the attack. To the right, he deployed the 2nd Panzer Grenadier Regiment, with a company of Tigers and the 1st Company, 38th *Panzerjaeger*. In the center was the bulk of the 3rd Panzer Regiment, with the heavier self-propelled guns of the artillery regiment. The recon battalion supplied infantry support. To the left lay the 304th Panzer Grenadier Regiment, supported by the 2nd and 3rd Companies of the *Panzerjaegers*, as well as a platoon of Tiger tanks.

On June 14, the Germans recaptured Hill 174, and the British fell back on their main force. At dawn the next morning, Allied artillery laid down a full-scale barrage in an effort to disrupt further advance, but the canny Luettwitz had pulled back his armor so the barrage was less than effective. By noon, the three battle groups pushed forward again. Lieutenant Colonel Sieberg's men captured Launay and St. Germaine d'Ector, in heavy fighting with severe losses. On the left, Colonel Koehn's forces pushed slowly forward against minor resistance.

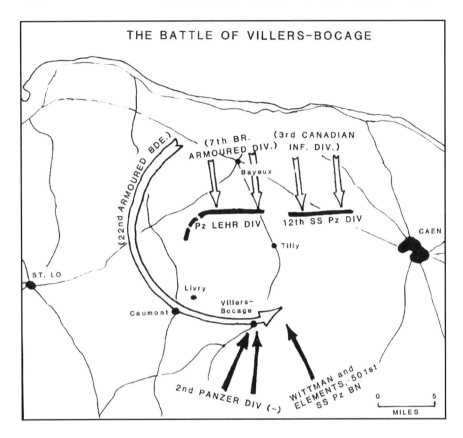

Both sides spent June 16 regrouping. The next day, Koehn, now temporarily supported by the artillery regiment, made an all-out effort to take Le Quesnay. Here was the fiercest fighting, stretched out over two days, in which the British were temporarily able to riposte, but then were driven back with unparalleled ferocity. The Germans seized Le Quesnay late on June 18, and a vanguard pushed toward Briquessard. Simultaneously, at nearby Villers-Bocage, a tank attack caused another British withdrawal.

Though the front now stabilized, and a sharp firefight around Briquessard on the nineteenth did not dislodge the British, Luettwitz could be well pleased with his results. The enemy had been forced to discontinue plans for an attack on Caen for an extended period. Losses in men and equipment, however, had been altogether too high, and the general at once importuned the corps for reinforcements. But these were not readily forthcoming because of Allied air strikes on the roads, bridges, and supply centers.

Toward the end of June, the 2nd was relieved of its station around Caumont and again successfully moved by night, this time southward toward Mortain and St. Lo, where an American offensive was now expected. Covering the short distance on interior lines, Luettwitz set up his new headquarters at Sourdeval, with his division dug in along the Vire River. He remained here for much of the month of July.

The U.S. attack broke into St. Lô in July. The 2nd Panzer fought desultorily until July 22, when it was again pulled out of the line and placed in reserve. Subsequently, five days later, Luettwitz was again moved up to the Vire, directly to the rear of the 352nd Infantry Division. At this point in the campaign, the general was uncertain of his overall superior. His division was briefly attached to the II Parachute Corps, then it was tentatively under the new headquarters, LVIII Panzer Corps, which proved to be too far away for efficient supervision. Finally, the 2nd Panzer was assigned to Funck's XXXXVII Panzer Corps which over the next few days also took control of the remnants of the 352nd Infantry Division at Beaucoudray and Panzer Lehr Division near Percy, as well as the 116th Panzer, which was moving hastily toward the Percy position. The XXXXVII Panzer also controlled what was left of the 2nd SS Panzer Division, deployed between the Sienne River and a hill east of Percy.

An attack was scheduled for July 29, to close the gap in the German lines between Notre Dame de Chenilly and the Vireo. Luettwitz crossed the Vire near Tessy-sur-Vire and assembled his units around Moyon, three miles to the northwest of his crossing. The Allies' air superiority enabled them to keep a close eye on German movements; they at once struck the division to forestall the anticipated attack.

Sharp battles around Tessay and Beaucouvray on July 29 and 30 failed to dislodge Luettwitz and his infantry screen, but the Allied air forces forced the cancellation of the counterattack. Even the tardy arrival of the badly battered 116th Panzer around Villebaudon only gave extra defensive power to the Germans; no offensive could be contemplated.

Gradually the situation stabilized, as Luettwitz assumed command over the remnants of the 352nd Infantry after Lt. Gen. Dietrich Kraiss, the commander, was mortally wounded on August 2 and most of his staff captured.[22] The Germans dug in behind the Vire, despite major air attacks and probes by Allied armor and infantry.

Nevertheless, Fuehrer Headquarters issued an order to attack despite its total lack of understanding of the real situation on the ground, and Funck reluctantly resolved to make the futile attempt at dawn on August 7.

Luettwitz, through his Ia, Maj. Rudiger Weiz, began to appeal for the tanks and self-propelled guns he had been promised. Losses since July 23 had eliminated half of his strength. Interdicted by attacks by the Allied air forces on railroads, highways and bridges in the rear, no reinforcements were forthcoming. On August 5, however, an isolated and understrength battalion of tanks from Panzer Lehr—in all, twelve Czech-built Skoda tanks—was attached to Maj. Albert von Boxberg's understrength 3rd Panzer Regiment.

The entire division had been badly hurt by its many engagements since the beginning of June. The original commanders of the 3rd Panzer, 2nd and 304th Panzer Grenadier, and 74th Panzer Artillery Regiments were dead, and four majors were now in acting command. Of these, Major Schneider-Kostalski of the 304th was killed within an hour of the beginning of the attack on August 7.

For this attack, Luettwitz divided the division into two columns. Both achieved relatively good penetrations, even if they were halted far short of their assigned destination: the sea coast. They reached St. Barthelemy and Le Mesnil-Tove, but here the stiffening U.S. resistance halted the plunge. Elsewhere in the attack, the 1st SS Panzer and 116th Panzer Divisions achieved little or no penetrations. Then, as fog blew away and clouds cleared, the massive power of the enemy air forces struck the strung-out German columns with devastating effect.

German commanders, in the course of August 8, admitted to themselves that the attack had failed. Funck, Eberbach, Hausser, and Field Marshal Kluge talked by telephone among themselves and resolved to hold fast at the forward positions they had captured and request permission to discontinue a now futile conflict. Hitler was not impressed by any of their explanations, however. A new attack must be prepared, he ordered, using still more of the precious armor.

Meanwhile, Allied attacks were threatening to outflank and then encircle the committed German forces at Avranches and Falaise. By August 10, Kluge had had to rethink his entire position and shuffle his hard-pressed armor to the threatened areas. The next day, the Germans abandoned the focal point of Mortain, and the XXXXVII

Panzer Corps, now under the newly created Panzer Group Eberbach, was moved to the Carrouge sector for a proposed new attack.

By now Luettwitz and the other divisional commanders had begun to realize that they had not the force to accomplish the chimerical dreams of the Fuehrer. The 2nd Panzer was a spent force with scarely enough tanks or guns to supply even a battalion. What the senior generals had known weeks earlier now became glaringly evident to the lesser commanders: "every man for himself" was the only possible hope. On August 13, down to twenty-five tanks, the 2nd division arrived in the Ecouche area, between the battered 116th at Argentan and the crippled 1st SS at Carrouges. Among them, the three divisions could place seventy tanks in the field, supported by an aggregate of three understrength battalions of grenadiers and perhaps fifty large-caliber guns. In 1940, the average German panzer division had had more than 200 tanks and 14,000 men.

On August 15, Luettwitz and his Ia, Major Weiz, reported the following strength roster to Panzer Group Eberbach: 1,874 officers and men, 5 self-propelled guns, and 7 Mark IV and Mark V tanks. This force, which still had a considerable number of half-track and wheeled vehicles for its infantry contingent, got under way to escape the great Falaise pocket after dark on August 16, driving steadily eastward in tight formation.

On August 19, under orders from Eberbach and Funck, Luettwitz deployed his battle group of survivors in the Foret de Gouffern, preparatory to an attack on the enemy cornerpost at St. Lambert-Chambois. Supported by the remnants of the 1st SS and 10th SS Panzer Divisions, this attack was designed to disorganize the U.S. advance sufficiently to allow the mass of infantry and supply services of the 7th Army and Army Group B to escape through the narrow gap over the Dives River to safety.

The breakout order, relayed from the confused army headquarters, failed to reach Luettwitz in time to coordinate with the two SS divisions. Aware of the congestion on all of the roads heading east, the general jumped off at 4 A.M. on August 20 instead. With fifteen tanks (several strays had been rounded up and one or two damaged panzers repaired), and using his armored cars as a spearhead, he set off for the last terrible battle to reach safety. As rear guard, the gallant Maj. Ernst von Cochenhausen's reduced 304th Panzer Grenadier

Regiment, augmented by the antitank battalion, moved in cautious pursuit toward the town of Chambois.

At first covered by a heavy fog, the 2nd Panzer came under heavy Allied artillery attack in the afternoon of the twentieth as it tried to cross the Dives River Bridge. Luettwitz generally lost control as the men and vehicles made a frantic drive to get across the river to safety, and he was fairly severely wounded trying to rally his men. Major Cochenhausen, reaching the western end of the bridge late in the afternoon, tried to cover part of the panicky flight. He subsequently cooperated with Gen. of Infantry Erich Straube of the LXXIV Corps and managed to restore temporary order by staging preemptive counterstrikes at the enemy artillery positions.[23]

Meanwhile, the wounded Luettwitz and his main body reached the safety of Orville early on the twenty-first, where Major Weiz tried to get his commander to go at once to the hospital—to no avail. Luettwitz sent his men on eastward toward the Seine, while he and his escort company awaited the arrival of the rear guard. At dusk, Cochenhausen and his grenadiers and antitank men reported to their pleased commander, who accompanied them in their march to the vicinity of Evreux.

Luettwitz refused to turn over the reins to his very junior officers, despite their entreaties, and insisted on remaining in command through a number of rear-guard actions en route to the Seine from August 22 to 25, and thence to the area of the West Wall in eastern Belgium and Luxembourg, where the division set up headquarters near Spa on August 28–29. On September 1, under direct orders from General of Panzer Troops Funck, the corps commander, who had travelled with the 2nd Panzer during the river crossing and the retreat to the Seine, Luettwitz finally turned over temporary command of his division to a staff colonel, Eberhard von Nostitz, and was flown to Wiesbaden for care. His wound, which medics had treated with sulfa during the previous week, was found to be healing well, and he was en route back to Spa on September 4 when a counterorder directed him to Metz, where he was to take over command of the XXXXVII Panzer Corps from General Funck, who had been summarily relieved of command on a whim of Hitler's.

On the third, while still at Wiesbaden, the lieutenant general received the Oak Leaves to his Knight's Cross for his bravery and skill in the recent battles of France. Luettwitz spent some hours with his predecessor at Metz on September 4 and 5, familiarizing himself with the problems of the senior staff, which in many ways were much more complicated than those at divisional level.

The lieutenant general inherited a fairly experienced staff, including Lt. Col. Hans-Gunther von Kluge as chief of staff, Maj. Arthur Eckesparre as Ia, Maj. Richwein Froelich as Ic (intelligence, or *Abwehr*). The twenty-two-year-old Lt. Hans von Luettwitz arrived from the Russian Front to serve as corps adjutant—a special gesture arranged by Colonel General Guderian. The general and his officers now bided their time awaiting a proper assignment, for by September 10, the corps had no attached divisions. All of them had been transferred to other units.

Luettwitz, anxious to continue active participation in the continuing campaign, visited the headquarters of Army Group G, under which he was territorially serving, and asked Col. Gen. Johannes Blaskowitz for activation with some units under command.[24] The imperturbable commander refused, on the grounds that he had no armor at the moment and that Luettwitz would doubtless be needed elsewhere very shortly. However, on September 21, Blaskowitz was summarily dismissed from his command by an order of Hitler's. The Fuehrer had been at odds with him since 1939 and seldom wasted a chance to deprive him of command. Gen. of Panzer Troops Hermann Balck was brought in from Russia to take over the army group.[25] Luettwitz immediately went to the new commander's headquarters to pay his respects and again appeal for an active field command.

Balck was pleased to receive an old friend and fellow panzer commander, but like Blaskowitz, he expected the corps headquarters to be speedily transferred to the northern sector, where most of the panzer divisions were employed. He did, however, authorize the staff to transfer from its Metz headquarters to a position behind Gen. of Panzer Troops Otto von Knobelsdorf's 1st Army, positioned along the Moselle from north of Thionville southward to Chateau Salins.

But the fact that a panzer corps headquarters with considerable experience in the type of battle fought on the Western Front was present and available quickly caused Balck to change his mind. A brilliant, highly adaptable tactician and strategist, the commander of the army group was still unfamiliar with the war of overwhelming air superiority and the Guderian-adapted armor tactics used by U.S. Gen. George S. Patton, so when a counterattack was projected on the Moselle along the Marne-Rhine Canal toward Nancy, he used not only Luettwitz, but also the headquarters of the 5th Panzer Army under Gen. Hasso von Manteuffel to conduct the battle.

At this time, in late September, Manteuffel was almost as unfamiliar with the Western methodology as Balck. (Both quickly learned, however; good panzer generals were nothing if not flexible in thought and were innovative enough to face any situation they met.) On September 21, therefore, Luettwitz was given control over the bulk of the understrength panzer forces already closely engaged with Patton's combat commands east of the Moselle.

General Manteuffel arrived at XXXXVII Panzer's Headquarters early on the twenty-second "to observe, to learn—pray do as you think best!" The 111th Panzer Brigade went in under fog and cloud cover and achieved a temporary victory at Juwelize, but the reappearance of the sun in the afternoon brought clouds of the dreaded Jabos (fighter-bombers), which virtually destroyed the 111th. The brigade lost its gallant commander, Col. Heinrich Karl Bronsart von Schellendorff, and all but seven tanks and eighty men, two of them officers: Major Klipphausen and Captain Eder.[26]

Luettwitz decided to regroup for a day, despite repeated orders from Fuehrer Headquarters for massive counterattacks to drive the U.S. forces back. Both Manteuffel and Balck, who had also arrived at Chateau Salins to observe the battle, agreed to the delay, and it was not until September 24 that Luettwitz again directed an attack, across the Seuille and into the Gramecy Forest. This time, however, he committed two regiments of the 559th *Volksgrenadier* Division, led by the capable Maj. Gen. Baron Kurt von Muehlen (1126th and 1127th Grenadier Regiments).[27] In support, the recently arrived 106th Panzer Brigade was thrown into the fray. Again the Germans achieved initial success, but at 10 A.M. the Allied aircraft disrupted the attack, inflicting serious casualties on the panzers.

Despite the obvious impossibilities of the entire situation, new orders from Fuehrer Headquarters arrived for the commitment of the 11th Panzer Division. The generals stared at each other in total disbelief; the 11th had suffered a terrible mauling as it covered the retreat of Army Group G from the Mediterranean coast in August and early September. So unhappy was Luettwitz that Manteuffel ordered him north to take over a quieter area, and headquarters, LVIII Panzer Corps, under the phlegmatic Walther Krueger, took over the new attacks.[28] Despite his anger at the foolishness of Hitler, Luettwitz was chagrined at being thus summarily relieved, and from his new headquarters at St. Avold, he sent a letter of apology to Manteuffel, who acknowledged its receipt in a most pleasant manner.

On October 1, orders arrived at St. Avold for the immediate departure of Lt. Col. Guenther von Kluge to Berlin. His replacement as corps chief of staff was Col. Albrecht Kleinschmidt. This was a disappointment to Luettwitz, who had formed quite an attachment to the capable young staff officer. Kleinschmidt proved able enough, but he never quite fit into the staff.

During mid-October, the entire 5th Panzer Army apparatus was pulled out of Alsace and sent north to the Rhine for regrouping. The XXXXVII Panzer Corps set up at Linnich, taking under its command the veteran 9th Panzer Division and the 15th Panzer Grenadier Division, both of which had been rebuilt and were almost at full strength. Luettwitz almost immediately received orders from the commander in chief of Army Group B, Field Marshal Model, to prepare for an attack against Allied forces in the Peel Marshes. The corps commander thereupon visited the headquarters of Maj. Gen. Baron Harald von Elverfeldt of the 9th Panzer. That gallant officer reported his formation as at slightly less than full strength but ready for action. Such was not the case with Col. Hans-Joachim Deckert of the panzer grenadiers, however.

Just recovered from a wound received in the summer, Deckert had replaced the veteran Eberhardt Rodt on October 9 and was still only acting commander (*mit der Fuhrung bei*) of a division that had driven and fought itself from central Italy via the Alps and the Alsace to the Roer River in a costly three-month uninterrupted move. The men were weary and in short supply. Their equipment was a real disaster. Nevertheless, Luettwitz felt confident that he could carry out the attacks as outlined and gave the principal role to Elverfeldt, with what success has been described in that general's biography.

As of October 30, Luettwitz directed the withdrawal of the burned-out 15th Panzer Grenadier into reserve, where it was to be extensively refitted. All in all, despite its lack of strength, it had acquitted itself very well. On November 1, while orders were being cut for the disengagement of the 9th Panzer as well, Luettwitz received a visit from his old commanding general, Hasso von Manteuffel, by which his acting status in XXXXVII Panzer Corps command was formalized. On November 9, while he and Elverfeldt were taking the last units of the 9th back to the reserve position, Luettwitz was formally promoted to general of panzer troops (*General der Panzertruppen*), retroactive to November 1. Thus he was made aware that his protests of September were not being held against him.

By mid-November, the corps was posted a short distance behind the main German lines, covering the adjoining flanks of the XII SS and LXXXI Corps west of the Roer River around Geilenkirchen. Luettwitz was able to report that his two divisions aggregated sixty-six tanks, forty-one assault guns (SP), and sixty-five towed howitzers (105-millimeter and 150-millimeter), plus almost a full complement of other armored vehicles, with a manpower totaling nearly 24,000 officers and men.

Once again, on November 16 and 17, it fell the lot of Elverfeldt's division to relieve the hard-pressed infantry by launching a series of successful, if fairly costly, spoiling attacks on the U.S. 2nd Armored Division. On the seventeenth, Deckert's units were committed to his support, and Luettwitz employed his own escort company the following day. In fact, though both divisions suffered heavy casualties, Luettwitz could be justifiably proud of the confusion and losses they inflicted on the cocky Americans in the six-day attack from November 16 to 21.

On November 24, the two divisions were attached to the XII SS Corps of Lt. Gen. Gunther Blumentritt, and the XXXXVII Panzer Corps headquarters was directed to relocate for new duties, controlling new formations.[29] Counterorders halted Luettwitz on November 29, however, and sent him back near the town of Lindern, where an Allied force had seized control of the village and its advantageous hill.

Two days later, on December 1, the general personally led a battle group of tanks taken from the 9th Panzer Division and 508th Tiger Battalion in a fruitless effort to retake the by-now well-defended American positions. Despite being able to cut off two company-size U.S. units in Lindern, which were resupplied by airlift, the lack of infantry support doomed Luettwitz's efforts, and the next day, he was recalled to his new headquarters at Gerolstein, where—unknown to him—

preparations for Hitler's great winter offensive were under way. It was not until December 8, at a conference of commanders at Manteuffel's 5th Panzer Army headquarters, that Luettwitz and Krueger of the LVII Panzer Corps were made aware that an offensive was even planned, and it was noon on Monday, December 10, before any of the divisional commanders were let in on the secret. Then, on December 12, much of the command echelon, including Luettwitz, his chief of staff, and his two divisional commanders, were taken by roundabout routes from Ziegenburg Castle, Rundstedt's headquarters, to the elaborately camouflaged Fuehrer Bunker at Adlershorst. Here they listened in grim silence to Hitler's rambling peroration on his hopes for the campaign. No one was particularly sanguine about his exaggerated expectations, but naturally no one dared make any comments.

On his return to Gerolstein, the general ordered the divisional commanders and their operations officers to attend a special planning conference. Besides Luettwitz, Colonel Kleinschmidt, and Lieutenant Colonel Eckesparre, present were Maj. Gen. Henning Schoenfeld (just promoted on December 1 and confirmed in command of Luettwitz's old 2nd Panzer Division), Lt. Col. Rudiger Weiz, Col. (later Maj. Gen.) Heinz Kokott of the 26th *Volksgrenadier* Division with his Ia, Major Gradl, and Lt. Gen. Fritz Bayerlein of the Panzer Lehr Division and his operations officer, Major Kauffmann.[30] Though the Lehr was technically a reserve unit, it would eventually be committed in the XXXXVII Corps' sector.

With his maps spread across the camp table, the corps commander went over the proposed plan of attack with methodical care: the 2nd Panzer would cross the Our on bridges laid by its engineers early on December 16 and drive toward Houffalize, which should be captured by the evening. On its left, Kokott's grenadiers should also cross the river and then seize crossings over the Cleve, whereupon the Lehr's armor would dash through the gap and push for Bastogne.

General Schoenfeld ventured the observation that he did not know the capacity of his engineers, nor was he sure that the grenadiers were sufficiently numerous to secure a probably well-defended town without some assistance. Was it possible to get the *Fuehrer Begliet* Brigade released from reserve to back up his attack?

Luettwitz demurred. He would check into the situation of the 2nd Panzer and talk to its officers, most of whom he knew from his own time as commander. But it was not feasible to commit the brigade so early, even if army group should agree, which he doubted.

True to his word, Luettwitz arrived at the assembly area of the 2nd Panzer well ahead of its returning commander. His old subordinates—Lt. Col. Rudolph Monschau of the 2nd Panzer Grenadier Regiment, who had been a major during the Falaise battles; Maj. Ernst von Cochenhausen of the 304th Panzer Grenadier; and Boxberg of the 3rd Panzer—gripped his hand in pleasure and were quick to disagree with Schoenfeld's estimates of the division's capabilities. The general awaited the division commander's return by looking over his former pride and joy, and the numerous veterans of the unit heartily cheered him.

Schoenfeld was somewhat taken aback at finding his commander there ahead of him, but he proffered estimates of the relative strength of his component units and renewed his request for assistance, stating that perhaps only a regiment of regular infantry or the corps' engineers company might be sufficient. Luettwitz merely observed that he would evaluate the situation and render a final answer within twenty-four to thirty-six hours.

His next stop was the 5th Panzer Army headquarters at Manderscheid to apprise General Manteuffel of his observation of the 2nd Panzer Division. Manteuffel listened in silence, then nodded. He had, he said, already had his doubts about Schoenfeld, whose background was largely as a panzer grenadier commander with little knowledge of the tanks. He had a solution, however: an officer who had served brilliantly in Russia in the *Grossdeutschland* Panzer Division during late 1943 and had subsequently commanded the Tiger brigade of the 11th Panzer Division. Col. Meinrad von Lauchert, a forty-four-year-old holder of the Knight's Cross with Oak Leaves, recently returned from a rest leave, was present at the headquarters and was quickly introduced to Luettwitz, who liked what he saw. Together they returned to the staging area of the 2nd Panzer Division and Major General Schoenfeld was relieved of his post as of 9 A.M. on Saturday, December 15. Lauchert at once began a series of inspections in his division and was able to assure his commander that he was in agreement with the junior officers: the 2nd Panzer should have no difficulties, as far as he could see.

Famous last words!

In fact, the several U.S. military historians who wrote on the Bulge battles generally described the performance of all the XXXXVII Panzer Corps commanders as uncertain at best, poor at worst. Considering, however, that the overall plans that Hitler and his desk-bound general staff insisted on were impossible to carry out, it hardly mattered who was in command. From the very start, snafus multiplied to render the German advance a complete confusion.

Here it may be a good idea to note what the Germanophobe U.S. historian S. L. A. Marshall had to say about Luettwitz after the war, and how closely he agreed with Thoma, quoted earlier. "Luettwitz," Marshall wrote, "is an old time cavalryman. Now past 58, he is large, gross and paunchy. His monocle and his semi-belligerent manner of speech would suggest that he is the typical arrogant Prussian, but among other German commanders he had the reputation of being especially kind to troops. He would talk only when he had a map before him. . . . What was most remarkable about him was that in battle he seemed to have concerned himself more with the movements of squads and companies than with the employment of divisions. He was frequently hazy about how his regiments had been disposed but he could invariably say what had been done by a particular patrol or outpost . . ."[31]

Colonel Lauchert succeeded in getting his 2nd Panzer across the Ourthe and was well on the way to capturing Clairvaux during the first twenty-four hours on December 16–17, 1944, but Kokott's grenadiers had less luck and delayed Bayerlein's forces, which were supposed to follow them across the river. By late on the seventeenth, however, Bayerlein's tanks and grenadiers were finally on the move, heading for the central town of Bastogne, which had been made the top priority for von Luettwitz in his briefings.

The 2nd Panzer, swinging north instead of capturing Longvilly, ran into what Lauchert mistakenly believed was a powerful defensive force at Noville, until Luettwitz appeared to direct the attack, the colonel awaited the arrival of his badly strung-out full force. The corps commander, however, on considering the enemy positions, realized that they were only lightly held and ordered a prompt attack with tank support.

For once Luettwitz was wrong—not because Noville was strongly held, but because it was held by brave and determined American troops who delayed the entire 2nd Panzer for a full forty-eight hours, inflicting disproportionate losses on Lauchert's forces. It was not until the evening of Wednesday, December 20, that the young colonel and Luettwitz met on the gutted main street of Noville.

"I propose to drive south in pursuit of the enemy and capture Bastogne," Lauchert suggested.

"Forget Bastogne and head for the Meuse," Luettwitz snapped.

By this time, he was a full three days behind schedule. None of his divisions had done what they should have, and from higher head-quarters, Manteuffel and Model were becoming more and more annoyed. Nor had things gone any better with his other two divisions.

Left to his own devices by Luettwitz, whose affinity to his former command caused him to bulldog the 2nd Panzer, Fritz Bayerlein with the Panzer Lehr endeavored to pursue his own idea of the attack, and Kokott, his junior in rank, was along willy-nilly. Having gotten across the Clerf River during the night of December 17–18, the "feisty, terrier like" Bayerlein split his forces and determined to drive directly into Bastogne. Half of his force made for Longvilly, while the panzer division commander, with a sizable task force, took a back road via Niederwampach to Mageret. By 2 A.M. on the nineteenth, he had secured the latter town, capturing an American hospital, but badly informed on U.S. strength, he first dawdled until 5:30 A.M., moved toward Waffe, and again halted for the better part of the day.

Kokott's slower-moving infantry got involved with the U.S. defenders of Longvilly through the two days, thus frustrating any hope of capturing Bastogne, which was reinforced during these delays. (This was not known by the German commanders at the time.)

By nightfall of the twentieth, when Luettwitz gave his order to Lauchert and returned his attention to his other two divisions, he discovered that the U.S. perimeter around the junction town was fiercely held, and neither Bayerlein nor Kokott seemed to be making much headway. He read their reports with considerable annoyance—particularly the fact that Panzer Lehr had taken to almost impossible backroads.

"If Bayerlein can't read a map," he growled to Colonel Klein-schmidt, "then he should have let one of his staff officers do it!" All in all, it was a rather unfair judgment, but not completely ill-founded.

During the next few days, however, Bastogne was completely sealed off from the main American lines by fast-moving armor, carrying with it the *Volksgrenadier* infantry. The Neufchateau road, the last supply line out, was cut within minutes of the return of Brig. Gen. Anthony C. McAuliffe, the acting commander of the 101st Airborne Division, from his corps headquarters (under Lt. Gen. Troy Middleton) in Neufchateau.

During the twenty-first and twenty-second, the Germans pressed their attacks only desultorily, which incensed Manteuffel when he visited Luettwitz's headquarters at noon on the twenty-second. Somewhat earlier, Luettwitz had ventured a maneuver that was to annoy his fellow commanders, amuse his enemy, and win for him a dubious place in the history of war for all time. Selecting a major and a lieutenant from his headquarters staff, he had directed them to bear a summons to surrender to the American commander in Bastogne. They reached the forward U.S. positions by 11:30 A.M., and an American captain took their ultimatum to General McAuliffe's headquarters in Bastogne.

General Luettwitz had been careful in the composition of this summons, writing tongue in cheek:

To the U.S.A. Commander of the encircled town of
Bastogne:

The fortunes of war are changing. This time the U.S.A.
forces in and near Bastogne have been encircled by strong
German armored units. More German armored units have
crossed the river Ourthe near Ourtheville, have taken
Marche and reached St. Hubert by passing through Hompre-
Sibret-Tillet. Libramont is in German hands.

There is only one possibility to save the encircled U.S.A.
troops from total annihilation: that is the honorable surrender of the encircled town. In order to think it over a term of
two hours will be granted beginning with the presentation of
this note.

If this proposal should be rejected, one German artillery
corps and six heavy A.A. battalions are ready to annihilate
the U.S.A. troops in and near Bastogne. The order for firing
will be given immediately after this two hour term.

All the serious civilian losses caused by this artillery fire would not correspond with the well-known American humanity.

—The German Commander

Typed on a confiscated U.S. machine, the ultimatum was in both German, with penned-in umlauts and other of that language's printing peculiarities, and English. McAuliffe, informed by his staff officer of the contents, made his classic monosyllabic retort: "Nuts!"

This was soon placed in large scrawling handwritten letters by the general himself: "To the German Commander: Nuts! From the American Commander."

The general staff major, who spoke no English, did not understand this. First Lt. Willi Henke of the Panzer Lehr asked the U.S. plenipotentiary, Colonel Harper, if this was an affirmative or a negative. Told it was "definitely not an affirmative," the two German officers were led back to their escort at the outpost.

"If you don't understand what 'Nuts' means," Colonel Harper then told them, "in plain English it's the same as 'Go to Hell,' and I'll tell you something else: if you continue your attack, we'll kill every Goddamn German who tries to break into this city."

"We will kill many Americans!" Henke retorted, saluting sharply. "This is war!"

"On your way, Bud," Harper snorted, turning on his heel, and then thoughtlessly added: "And good luck to you."

Meanwhile, Hasso von Manteuffel, apprised of this unauthorized sally, was furious. According to postwar interviews, this was the almost unanimous reaction of all the German commanders on hearing it. When the parliamentaries returned with the short, sharp refusal, the commander of the 5th Panzer Army was more outraged: the bluff had been called.

Desperately, he informed Army Group B headquarters and called for as much artillery as Model could spare, failing which he directed in *Luftwaffe* bombing attacks.

Model was unable to comply with the first request; in fact, because of a lack of fuel and the horrible Ardennes road network, much of the artillery attached to the three divisions had failed to get up to the front after six days. The *Luftwaffe*, however, did manage a series of none-too-effective strikes against the town over the next four days, but these were far from the overwhelming punishment Luettwitz had unwisely threatened.

The unfortunate corps commander was not allowed to forget his rash deed for some time, either. Manteuffel spent as much time as he could breathing down Luettwitz's neck, and when forced to headquarters, he delegated Maj. Gen. Carl Gustav Wagener, his chief of staff, to oversee his disgraced subordinate.[32] In fact, it seems certain that Manteuffel would have relieved Luettwitz of his command, except that he apparently thought even less highly of the next senior officer in the corps: General Bayerlein.[33]

Despite the urgency earlier expressed by the entire plan of the campaign for a rapid drive to the Meuse, the thorn represented by the encircled garrison at Bastogne took on an almost exaggerated importance in the minds of the commanders in Army Group B. Though Lauchert's division was making fairly steady progress in the right direction, Manteuffel ordered one grenadier regiment, with artillery support, to be employed against the pocket.

By Christmas Eve, the crack *Fuehrer Begleit* Brigade—a legion of heroes specially chosen for their deeds of bravery to make up the bodyguard for the Fuehrer—was committed to the attack. This was followed in succession, as December turned into January, by the 9th Panzer Division, 15th Panzer Grenadier Division, and even some units of the 116th Panzer Division. All of this was to no avail; not only was the inimitable Gen. George S. Patton able to break the siege and open a supply route to McAuliffe's gallant defenders, but the drive of the 2nd Panzer Division bogged down before Celles, and across the Lesse River, and by late December, a combined battle group under the able Major Cochenhausen was surrounded and forced to break out to the rear, leaving all of its vehicles, heavy weapons, and heavy equipment.

By January 16, 1945, the German forces had their backs to the West Wall and the Roer River—almost where they had started (Map 4.4). The last great offensive had blundered to an ignominious halt at great loss and expense—and with little to show for it all. Few decorations were passed out, despite some valiant endeavors; Hitler was even more disenchanted with most of his army commanders than before.

By now, Luettwitz's corps headquarters, with the decimated remnants of the 2nd Panzer and Panzer Lehr Divisions, had been switched south to the area of Gen. of Panzer Troops Erich Brandenburger's 7th Army, at Vianden on the Our, where the hard-pressed infantry divisions were being chopped to bits by Patton's powerful forces.

Luettwitz was by now thoroughly despondent. After a frightening series of air attacks throughout January 22, his available troops were down to pitiful levels. On February 1, therefore, Model pulled him out of the area and sent him northward to the Issel River, headquartering at Terburg. At first the staff had no attached units, but toward the end of February, first the 15th Panzer Grenadier Division and then the 116th Panzer Division were assigned to it.

The commanding general visited both headquarters during February 26, conferring with Col. Wolfgang Mauck, the senior officer of the grenadiers, and Maj. Gen. Siegfried von Waldenburg, of the 116th.[34] Luettwitz knew the latter fairly well, but was soon impressed with the abilities of the former. Between them, however, the divisions could muster a total of only thirty-five tanks and seriously understrength troop formations, most of which had no veterans.

Among them, the three commanders instituted a hasty training program to get as much efficiency out of these dregs as possible, all the while expecting to be thrown into action again soon. As it was, the XXXXVII now served as the whole reserve for the recently formed Army Group H, commanded by the overworked, underpromoted Col. Gen. Johannes Blaskowitz.

Opposed to this makeshift army grouping was the massive concentrations of guns, tanks, and infantry of British Field Marshal Bernard Montgomery's 21st Army Group, which, in true "Monty style," was being readied for a set-piece crossing of the Rhine. The British commander was nothing if not methodical; he crossed every *t* and dotted every *i* before moving a single Tommy.

On March 29, this huge force was at last ready, and it began to cross the river at Rees and near Wesel with a ponderous, absolutely impermeable strength that was impossible to resist. Blaskowitz at first tried to interpose Mauck's grenadiers at Rees, but with negligible results. The British were well across by the morning of the twenty-fifth.

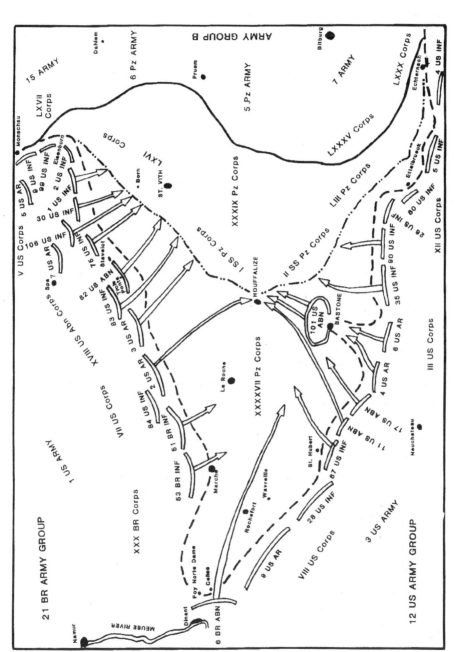

The Battle of the Ardennes: December 26, 1944–January 16, 1945

Luettwitz's headquarters with the 116th Panzer was sent into battle south of Lippe against the American wing of the great army group, and by nightfall much of the 60th Panzer Grenadier Regiment had been killed or captured. Nevertheless, this area east of the Rhine became Luettwitz's responsibility. He was given the newly arrived 190th Infantry Division, rushed south from Holland. Its commander, Lt. Gen. Ernst Hammer, was a recuperee from the east and an ardent National Socialist.[35]

During the next three days, the irresistible mass of Montgomery's armies rumbled forward, pushing before it everything in its path. On March 29, Blaskowitz abruptly informed the new commander in chief, west, Luftwaffe Field Marshal Albert Kesselring—and through him Hitler—that he was swinging his forces north of the Weser River to hold it against continued British advances.[36] He would therefore give over command of the XXXXVII Panzer and LXIII Corps to Army Group B, which was being driven inexorably back into the Ruhr industrial area.

When Kesselring rejected the idea, despite Blaskowitz's efforts, the British merely made the whole thing academic by smashing eastward along the Weser and completely cutting off the two corps to the south on March 30-31, whereupon Model, still commanding Army Group B, gave Luettwitz overall command of both corps as *Gruppe von Luettwitz* (Group von Luettwitz). The group was holding from north and east of Lippstadt and in an arc down the Lippe to Moehne reservoir. Under him, for the first few days of April, were—in north to south order—Special Division Hamburg and the 2nd Parachute Division (both now commanded by colonels), 116th Panzer, and 190th Infantry. Luettwitz shared the general opinion within the pocket that the war was lost—further resistance would be useless.

It was, however, April 15 before Model actually conceded defeat by dissolving the army group: every man for himself and good luck! The following day, Luettwitz with his staff joined Lt. Gen. Fritz Bayerlein of the LIII Corps in surrendering to the U.S. forces. Gen. of Infantry Erich Abraham, lately the commander of the LXIII Corps, acting as Luettwitz's deputy, also gave himself up.[37]

Now began an extended period of imprisonment for Luettwitz and his associates, during which Luettwitz cooperated with the U.S. Historical Commission. As is evident from S. L. A. Marshall's remarks, many of the German generals did not care for each other—and several had it in for the unfortunate von Luettwitz because of the Bastogne affair. This appears to have been particularly true of Bayerlein.

Released in 1946, the now-retired general finally reached his home of Neuberg in Bavaria, a bone-tired man, considerably overweight from months of inactivity, and with no real place in the world as it now was. He began again to cultivate his horsemanship, so long forcibly neglected, and with funds saved from the Luettwitz lands in the now occupied east, again acquired a stable. Thus he passed the rest of his life, finally dying at Neuburg on October 9, 1969, at the age of seventy-three. His two sons and one daughter, as well as his widow, survived him.

CHAPTER 5

Fritz Bayerlein

Gen. Fritz Bayerlein is the second of that group of some twenty panzer commanders about whose career a great deal has been written. Not only was he considered an excellent commander, but as a general staff officer, he was associated with the best known of the panzer generals—first Heinz Guderian, and then the legendary "Desert Fox," Erwin Rommel. Later on, he served with Field Marshal Walther Model. "He has been an enigma to me," Friedrich von Stauffenberg wrote later. "I started out believing him to be a splendid officer, only to discover from numerous firsthand accounts that much of what he has said of himself is either pure braggadocio, or downright prevarication."[1]

Fritz Bayerlein was born in Wuerzburg, Bavaria, on January 14, 1899, the son of Donat Bayerlein, a senior inspector, and his wife, Luise, nee Denkmann. Fritz entered the army as a *Fahnenjunker* in 1917 and took the field in May 1918 with the 9th Infantry Regiment. He remained in the *Reichswehr* following the Treaty of Versailles and was commissioned a second lieutenant (*Leutnant*) in 1922.

He commanded the machine-gun company of the 21st Infantry Regiment in 1926, was promoted to first lieutenant on January 1, 1927, and was assigned to command the motorcycle detachments of the regiment at the same time. In 1930, he became battalion adjutant.

He took the *Wehrkreis* examination for staff officers in May 1932, and having scored in the upper 15 percent, he was assigned to the staff of the 2nd Infantry Division at Stettin as assistant English translator, a language in which he was fluent. The following May, he was assigned to the Berlin *Heeresleitung* (Army Command), where he began his general staff training. During this tour of duty, he was promoted to captain on March 1, 1934.

Early the next year, he was reassigned to the artillery staff of *Wehrkreis V* at Stuttgart, and on June 1, he joined the staff of the 15th

Infantry Division, stationed at Kassel. He rose to the post of operations officer by 1936. At about this point in his career, he transferred to the motorized service, still with a reputation as a brilliant staff officer.

In October 1937, he was given a field assignment in the routine manner of the prewar staff, where a good officer was rotated to give him a broader knowledge of both staff and field responsibilities. He took over a company of armored cars attached to the division.

Bayerlein was promoted to major on June 1, 1938, and finished his advanced course in senior staff work prior to being assigned on November 1, 1938, as intelligence officer (Ic) of the XV Motorized Corps of Gen. Hermann Hoth. At the outbreak of the war, however, he was transferred to the 10th Panzer Division as chief of operations (Ia), serving under Generals Schaal and Stumpff and receiving the Iron Cross, Second and First Classes.

Major Bayerlein was assigned as the Ia of the XIX Panzer Corps on February 25, 1940. On May 10, he accompanied the rapidly moving staff headquarters into Belgium, through the Ardennes. He had established a considerable rapport with Guderian's veteran chief of staff, Walther Nehring; in fact, the entire staff operated in a close-knit manner. All were thoroughly aware of the desires of General Guderian, who had worked diligently to have his entire force ready for any eventuality in the campaign.

From the very beginning of the campaign, Nehring, Bayerlein, and the intelligence and logistics officers, Major Korff and Captain Seidel, as well as the adjutant, Lieutenant Colonel Riebel—being completely aware of the daily situation—were posted hither and thither to the component divisions and brigades, or to group or army headquarters, to thrash out future operations, to take and give reports, and often to argue for a specific objective or permission.

Bayerlein was promoted to lieutenant colonel on June 1. The campaign in France ended three weeks later on June 22, and the panzer group was dissolved effective June 30–July 1, but the staff accompanied Guderian to Paris, where it was supposed to cooperate in arranging a great victory parade for Hitler—a celebration that was never held. On July 19, the staff followed the general to Berlin for the triumphant *Reichstag* session, at which Guderian was promoted to colonel general. Bayerlein and Korff returned to Paris for the rest of the month to supervise the packing of all the papers for headquarters, now set up in Berlin.

Although technically at liberty, Guderian decided to take over the job of supervising the training and equipment of several of the newly authorized panzer divisions in and around the capital. Thus the staff was kept employed and able to see firsthand the problems now facing the new German panzer forces, which had been cut in half as far as their tank forces were concerned, although on paper the number of panzer divisions appeared to have doubled. In addition, the equipment necessary for such a large force was greatly lacking and captured French, British, Polish, and Czech vehicles had to be incorporated into the new units—rolling stock totally unfit for the type of combat the panzer forces would soon be embarked on.

In late October, Colonel Nehring was promoted and transferred to the command of one of the new panzer divisions. Lt. Col. Baron Kurt von Liebenstein[2] was brought in to take his place—which seems to say something about Guderian's opinion of Bayerlein, who easily could have been moved up a notch—and in early November, both he and Bayerlein were summoned to a special meeting for staff officers of the High Command. Here Hitler, Field Marshal Brauchitsch, and Franz Halder, the chief of the general staff of the army, for the first time revealed the plan for Operation *Barbarossa*. Their explanation was so plausible that both officers returned to Guderian thoroughly sold on the idea.

They were shocked, according to the general's own account, that he was not only unenthusiastic, but completely critical of the idea. Opposed or not, the campaign was definitely on, and Guderian worked all the harder to prepare his new units. The staff left Berlin for Warsaw on June 7, and moved up on the eighteenth to its advance position near Bohukaly in Poland, slightly to the north and west of Brest Litovsk—the earliest objective and a potential problem spot. In the course of the training, Guderian had rigged up an entirely new system of command. The headquarters was now fully motorized, with command armored cars, half-tracks, regular vehicles, and at least one prime mover in the event of breakdowns. Though it would set up nightly or binightly at given towns in the wake of the advancing panzers, it could also keep up with the fast-moving forces as long as necessary. Bayerlein in particular was devoted to this idea; later he would try—and fail—to arrange a similar mobile headquarters in North Africa.

The Russian campaign began on June 22, 1941, and Bayerlein worked closely with Guderian during the first three months of victorious advance. On August 30, however, he was ordered back to Berlin for reassignment and replaced by a Major Wolfe. Guderian comments on this deprivation in his book. Actually, by now, some faults of the staff lieutenant colonel appear to have been surfacing. Guderian does not say that he was aware of any, but from later comments, Bayerlein seems to have had his problems, and even as early as the 1940 campaign, Walter Nehring may have sensed something amiss. Now, however, Bayerlein reported into the OKH offices at Berlin and was placed on Fuehrer Reserve; thus it seems evident that Guderian was unaware of circumstances, for he believed—even after the war—that Bayerlein was recalled for immediate service in Africa. In fact, the Afrika Korps commander, General Rommel, was upgraded to Panzer Group Afrika commander as early as August 15. He took over the entire special operations staff, headed by Maj. Gen. Alfred Gause, while command of the Korps, which consisted of the 15th and 21st Panzer Divisions, eventually devolved on Lt. Gen. Ludwig Cruewell, a capable armored commander from Russia. Cruewell inherited Rommel's much put-upon chief of staff, Lieutenant Colonel von dem Borne. This man had already sent home several plaintive complaints about Rommel's high-handed and erratic conduct. His continuing presence—even at a distance, with Cruewell's staff—would prove embarrassing.

Thus, on October 1, 1941—more than a month after his departure from Russia—Fritz Bayerlein was alerted to fly to North Africa, to relieve Lieutenant Colonel von dem Borne, who was thankfully being recalled to Europe. After stops at Rome and Tripoli, the new staff officer reported to Cruewell near Tobruk, just in time for the great battles of the following month.

Officially taking over as chief of staff of the Afrika Korps on October 5, Bayerlein seems at once to have run afoul of Rommel. Several authors mention his complaints being forwarded to Berlin, where OKW had begun to handle affairs. Nothing mattered; Rommel was too much the Fuehrer's favorite to worry about complaints. At this time, observers had different opinions of the new chief of staff. One authority describes him as obsequious to senior officers, notably Rommel, Cruewell, and later Kesselring and Armin; other sources are unanimous in styling him as "loud, coarse and arrogant" to his inferiors. This does not detract from his organizational ability or his leadership, however.

He served in the fierce battles of November 1941, when the British were initially defeated, but Rommel's losses eventually compelled him to retreat from before Tobruk all the way back to Agedabia. Meanwhile, on December 18, Bayerlein was awarded the Panzer Battle Badge, and on December 26, he received the Knight's Cross of the Iron Cross. Finally, on January 23, 1942, he got the German Cross in Gold.

It was in the course of "winning" these awards that we have an eyewitness testimony of his activities during the retreat through El Duda on the night of December 8–9. Riding in a regular tank, carrying the corps' orders and papers, the crusty chief of staff was asked by his driver to identify the proper color flare they were suppose to follow.

"Are you out of your mind?" raged the Bavarian. "The fellow thinks I've nothing else to do! What the hell do I know about your blasted flares?"

As a result, the panzer commander was forced to try to follow the main stream of withdrawal, but without lights, he soon wandered unaware onto an Italian bivouac, careening right in among the sleeping troops and getting some unknown object caught up in the treads. Hearing the thing banging against the armor, the tank commander shouted, "Halt!" At once, from deep inside the tank, Bayerlein roared: "Keep going! Get me out of here! Have you all taken leave of your senses?"

The tank commander climbed back up to call in and explain that they were right in the middle of an Italian bivouac, and the tank treads could do untold harm.

"Drive away!" shrilled the chief of staff. "Run them all down, for all I care, but I've got to get out of here. I have the secret bag here, can't you understand?"

The tank continued on its way, its crew hoping all the yelling had scared off any other Italians in their path.

Yet in contrast, approaching Benghazi on December 19, when an English cavalry regiment in Cruiser and Honey tanks made a surprise attack on the endless German retreating column, Bayerlein commandeered the same tank and rushed up and down the German-Italian column, picking out self-propelled guns (SPs) , field artillery, and the big 88-millimeter antiaircraft guns and inflicting severe losses on the impulsive Englishmen, who hurriedly beat a retreat.

Though driven back some distance, the German-Italian Army was still able, in late January 1942, to inflict a sharp defeat on an incautious British armored division, thus bringing the Allied pursuit to a screeching halt. Nor was Rommel prepared to accept this setback for long. He began a steady buildup of resources preparatory to a renewed attack toward Egypt.

On March 1, Bayerlein was belatedly inserted in the day's promotion list, at 25-A (between numbers 25 and 26) in the colonels (*Obersten*) of the day. He continued in the post of chief of staff to the Afrika Korps, even when General Cruewell came down with an infection and on April 1 was flown back to Germany for medical treatment, there to find his wife at the point of death. In his place, a former associate of Bayerlein's, Walther K. Nehring, now a lieutenant general, arrived from Russia as acting commander of the Afrika Korps.

The renewed offensive to drive to Egypt began on the night of May 25–26. Bayerlein, asked by Rommel what he would do if he were the British commander, claims he annoyed the colonel general by employing some of Rommel's own tactics. As it was, the British commanders did not possess the colonel's imagination.

Though in critical positions much of the time and suffering appalling losses, the panzer army thoroughly disorganized the British in a fierce succession of battles. On May 28, however, Cruewell—back from leave and in command of the Italian forces in the north—was shot down and captured. A few days later, on June 1, Maj. Gen. Alfred Gause and Col. Siegfried Westphal were seriously wounded in separate attacks.[3]

On June 2, Bayerlein reported to Rommel as his acting chief of staff, leaving Nehring to make do with his deputy, Lt. Col. Wolf Stefeldt. The following confusing days saw the British badly battered, and finally, on June 21, the capture of Tobruk resulted in the immediate promotions of Rommel to field marshal and Nehring to general of panzer troops.

The euphoria—which even brought Mussolini to Derna, complete with white horse for a triumphal entry into Cairo—was rudely dissipated at the first battle of El Alamein in early July, when the British effectively halted a disorganized and understrength panzer army. By July 15, even the usually sanguine Rommel accepted the necessity of a halt and regrouping just west of the Alamein line.

On or about this date, General Gause was able to resume his post, and Fritz Bayerlein resumed his duties with Nehring, who had found Stefeldt a much more congenial staffer. Thus Bayerlein found himself somewhat persona non grata and spent much of his time sending off critical reports to Gause at army headquarters. Thus passed the hot desert summer.

The battle of Alam Halfa, fought between August 29 and September 2, 1942, was in reality the last flicker of hope for the Germans in Africa. Had they won it, if they could have, history might well have been different. The battle has been treated at length in many excellent works and will only be touched on here for its effect on Bayerlein.

Rommel lost three of his generals on the first day of battle. Georg von Bismarck, commander of the 15th Panzer Division, was killed, and Maj. Gen. Ulrich Kleemann, commander of the 90th Light Division, and Nehring were severely wounded. It became the only option that Bayerlein should take over acting command of the Afrika Korps for the thirty-first, and with an impetuosity at least as fierce as Rommel's own, he persuaded the marshal to allow him to continue an attack on the Alam el Halfa Ridge. But as he subsequently said, "I was sure I could take it and went on attacking it much too long."[4]

Gustav von Vaerst hastily took over acting command of the Afrika Korps on September 1 for the rest of the battle, and Bayerlein was again chief of staff. The unfortunate Stefeldt had been killed in the same air attack that had temporarily crippled Nehring. With the battle over and no victory won, it is almost as if Rommel suddenly lost his energy. His health, uncertain for several months, took a decided turn for the worst, and he was ordered back to Germany for medical attention.

Meanwhile, a whole galaxy of new appointees arrived in Libya to take over the vacant commands, and the dour armor pioneer, Gen. of Panzer Troops Ritter Wilhelm von Thoma, took command of the Afrika Korps, allowing Vaerst to resume command of his 15th Panzer Division. Maj. Gen. Heinz von Randow took over the 21st Panzer, and on September 19, Gen. of Panzer Troops Georg Stumme, accompanied by Col. Gerhard Franz, arrived to substitute for Rommel and the still ailing Gause, both of whom departed for Europe by September 23.

It would have been understandable under the circumstances that the senior general staff officer in the area—namely, Fritz Bayerlein—

automatically would have taken over the post of chief of staff, Panzer Army Afrika, but this was not the case, at least not at this point, although one or two authors seem to have assumed it happened.

Obviously Stumme worked congenially with Franz. They had been through a lot together in Russia and later, at a court-martial hearing in Germany, where both narrowly escaped death or life imprisonment for a security violation in June 1942. Pardoned thanks to the good offices of none other than Hermann Goering, they had been sent to North Africa to substitute for Rommel, possibly at the field marshal's own suggestion. Rommel and Stumme had exchanged commands of the 7th Panzer Division in February 1940 and probably had kept up a friendship since, though no proof of this exists.

Franz and Westphal cooperated very well together, but both came in for resentment by Bayerlein, who was furious at being overlooked. Subsequent indication makes it appear that both chiefs developed a lively antagonism toward one another. In any case, on October 12, Bayerlein took an extended leave and went to Tripoli, where he probably applied for help from Kesselring's staff, returning in a disgruntled state on October 23—just in time for the British surprise attack.

Gen. Sir Bernard Law Montgomery had taken over the command of the British 8th Army somewhat earlier and had meticulously prepared an overwhelming and technically infallible attack. Made aware by Ultra intercepts of the German code that Rommel was absent, the British commenced an all-out attack on October 23, with concentrated artillery barrage beginning, of all times, at 9 P.M. Map 5.1 shows the battlefield and the initial British attacks.

Such havoc was wreaked in the Italo-German lines that the infantry began its attack at 1 A.M. on the twenty-fourth; despite severe casualties, however, the surviving defenders fought back desperately. To the south, a further English assault ran upon fanatical resistance, including two of the Italian divisions, the Folgore Parachute and the Ariete Armored, and was temporarily halted.

General Stumme rushed up to the front, à la Rommel (most German armored commanders practiced this form of leading from the front, though this is usually overlooked by historians, who attribute the method entirely to Rommel). Under heavy machine-gun fire, the general fell from the running board of his car, the victim of a heart attack brought on by high blood pressure. No one was quite aware of

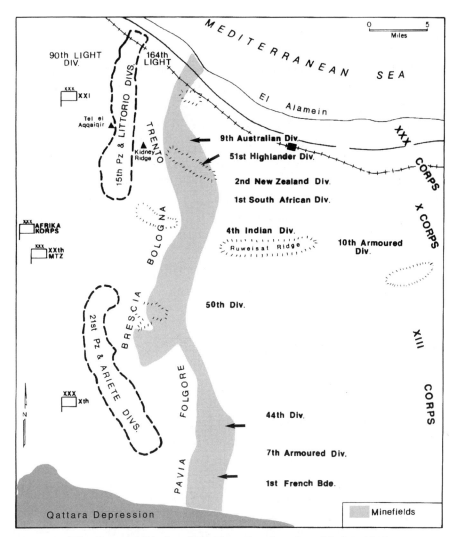

The Second Battle of El Alamein, October 23–24, 1942

his fate for several hours, but Franz phoned Thoma and told him to assume command of the operations.

Though both Franz and Bayerlein seem to have decided to leave the battle to Thoma, it was not so with Siegfried Westphal. Late in the evening, the colonel radioed Berlin to notify Rommel, who was still in Austria undergoing treatment. Keitel phoned the field marshal at once: Could he go back to take command? He certainly could! Keitel then got hold of the Fuehrer, who gave his consent.

Rommel reached the battlefield late in the afternoon of October 25. General Thoma, who had committed every available man and machine in order to stabilize the front, briefed the field marshal and then gave over command shortly before midnight. Thus the one-sided battle entered eleven days of bloody fighting, which is so well documented in first-class sources that it need only be sketched in here.

Fritz Bayerlein reasserted his predominance after the receipt of an order from the Fuehrer, which most believe was sent by mistake during the night of November 3–4, ordering the panzer army to fight to the last bullet without a step backward. Though this was quickly rescinded when the Fuehrer Headquarters ascertained the true state of affairs, it gave the German and Italian troops just enough time to be hammered into an almost impossible state of loss and demoralization, from which they could not recover.

Thoma in particular could not accept such a patently stupid order. He summoned Bayerlein to his emergency headquarters and directed him to move the staff all the way back to El Daba, while he obeyed the suicide order with his surviving troops. Bayerlein claims that he was impressed by the fact that Thoma had changed into his dress uniform, proudly bearing his recently awarded rank as general of panzer troops and his many wounded badges, his *Pour le Merite*, Max Josef Order, Knight's Cross, and Iron Crosses of both wars.

Obedient to his orders, the colonel skillfully moved his mobile headquarters apparatus to the rear area and got a telephone link to Rommel's headquarters to report what had occurred. He probably talked to Gerhard Franz (Rommel was as usual rushing about his positions), and this may well have been the occasion, reported by Franz after the war, when the infuriated Afrika Korps chief of staff shouted, "Hitler is a fool, a madman!"

Shortly thereafter, Thoma's adjutant, slightly wounded, turned up at the headquarters, ostensibly sent to comparative safety by his gallant superior. Bayerlein now feared the worst. Commandeering a reconnaissance vehicle and driver, he rushed back to the battlefield, only to have the car disabled almost at once. The colonel nevertheless made his way as close to the hell of the front lines as he could, arriving just in time to see Thoma, miraculously unscathed in a hail of fire, captured by British vehicles.

Bayerlein, weary and footsore, reached El Daba just moments before Rommel put in his appearance there. The marshal listened dumbly to the colonel's report on Thoma's capture and the destruction of his headquarters unit at Tel al Mampra. Then, according to Bayerlein much later, Rommel gave the colonel acting command of what was left of the Afrika Korps, with the added note: "The Fuehrer's order has become meaningless. . . . If we are court-martialed for disobeying it, now, we must abide by our decision. Do your duty well. All your orders must be given in my name."[5]

The only trouble with this lies in the interview Bayerlein gave to Desmond Young in 1950. At this time, the colonel claims he asked Rommel, "What can I do in the face of this order of Hitler's?" to which the marshal replied unequivocally, "I cannot authorize you to disobey it."[6]

Whatever the case, Hitler, advised of what the situation actually was, sent his authorization to retreat, which reached the shambles of the army during the morning of November 5. By now, willy-nilly, the panzer army was already in the process of trying to save what was left of itself, and a retreat was the only recourse.

Bayerlein says that he rose to the occasion: From November 5 to 21, he alone was responsible for the orderly withdrawal of the ruined Afrika Korps. When finally Gen. of Panzer Troops Gustav Fehn arrived from Russia via Berlin, Rome, Naples, and Tripoli at the newly established Mersa el Brega positions late on November 21, Bayerlein had managed an exceptional recovery for the two panzer divisions of his corps. The only trouble with this account is that when Fehn arrived, he was assured that Colonel Bayerlein had been ensconced at Mersa el Brega—far to the rear—ever since November 9.[7]

Although he resumed his post as chief of staff to Fehn, Bayerlein was also formally designated as deputy corps commander by Rommel, who does not seem to have had a particularly high opinion of the new Korps commander, even though Fehn had won his Knight's Cross in France as commander of the 4th Rifle Brigade of the 4th Panzer Division and later was awarded the German Cross in Gold and the East Medal for his service in Russia. In fact, Fehn was quite capable of his duties, and he and Bayerlein worked very well with each other.

After fruitless consultations with the Italian commanders and Kesselring, and a stand-fast order from Mussolini, Rommel impulsively tossed the temporary command of the army into Fehn's astonished hands and took an airplane for Hitler's headquarters in East Prussia.

He left on November 26 and returned—much chastened and angered by the cavalier treatment he had received—at 6:30 A.M. on December 2.

It seems to have been during this absence by the field marshal that Bayerlein managed to secure the recall of Gerhard Franz to Europe. Although he had remained as chief of staff after Stumme's death, the job of chief had really devolved upon Siegfried Westphal, who enjoyed the confidence of Rommel. Now, as of December 1, Bayerlein was assigned the post of chief of staff of the German-Italian Panzer Army. His machinations did not stop here. Although Rommel resumed command of the army on his return on the next day, Bayerlein seems to have been successful in shunting the loyal Westphal to the acting command of the 164th Light Afrika Division, thus leaving himself the undisputed staff senior in North Africa. And such he remained, despite the changes made in command subsequently.

Although intimately associated with the doomed effort to hold out in Tunisia, Bayerlein does not particularly seem to have exerted any real influence on events. When Italian Marshal Giovanni Messe took over command of the former Panzer Army Afrika on March 1, 1943, Bayerlein remained as his German staff officer—virtually deputy commander. And as the end came near under heavy Allied pressure, on May 2, the colonel secured permission to return to Europe, rather than being left to surrender to the Anglo-American forces. The colonel reported to the headquarters of *Wehrkreis XIII* at Nuremberg, where he was placed in Fuehrer Reserve temporarily, pending a new assignment. His conduct in North Africa had decidedly won him very few friends, just as Rommel had had a number of complaints lodged against him. Still, his supposed conduct of the retreat of the Afrika Korps from El Alamein could not be overlooked, and as Rommel was now attached temporarily to Fuehrer Headquarters, and as General Schmundt was still one of his good friends, Bayerlein was due for some belated recognition.

On July 1, 1943, he was apprised of his promotion to major general, retroactive to May 1, with a seniority of twenty-eight (the last in place; originally only twenty-seven colonels had been promoted that day). The next day, he was summoned to Rastenburg for the belated presentation of his Oak Leaves to the Knight's Cross (awarded on July 8), and he and Rommel were able to renew their acquaintance.

The field marshal was still bitter over the needless loss of men and equipment in North Africa, but in the next two weeks (prior to a personal interview of Bayerlein by the Fuehrer on the eighteenth), Rommel endeavored to secure for his loyal staff officer the post of chief of staff to Gen. of Panzer Troops Hans Valentin Hube, whose XIV Panzer Corps was charged with the defense of Sicily. Hube had his own choice in the matter, however. Although he had Rommel's influence to thank for his position, he felt much more secure with a staff he knew and trusted; hence Bayerlein returned briefly to Nuremberg on July 20 and cooled his heels there as summer turned into autumn and disasters befell the German armies in Russia and Italy.

On October 10, 1943, he was again summoned to Rastenburg for an interview with Rudolf Schmundt, who by now was acting not only as Hitler's military adjutant, but also as chief of the Army Personnel Branch. Schmundt explained that there were few staff duties for a major general—especially, he hinted, for one who had trodden on not a few toes—but that Bayerlein's exploits as a field commander in North Africa definitely recommended him for an active-duty command. The general was enthusiastic; as a result he was flown to the headquarters of Army Group South during October 16–18, and on the twentieth, Field Marshal Erich von Manstein ordered him to take over command (initially as acting commander) of the 3rd Panzer Division of the XXXXVIII Panzer Corps, which was committed to the containment of the Russian bridgehead at Pereyaslav on the Dnieper. The regular commander, Lt. Gen. Franz Westhoven, had been wounded on the first day of the division's commitment, and the senior regimental commander, Col. Ernst Wellmann, had assumed temporary command.

Bayerlein reached the front late on October 20, only about six hours after Westhoven's incapacitation, and was briefed on the situation, which was critical. Masses of Soviet troops were assaulting the German front, assisted by powerful, if generally inaccurate, artillery curtain fire and the equally ineffective Soviet Air Force.

Acting corps commander Lt. Gen. Dietrich von Choltitz visited the front on the twenty-first and expressed serious concern over the badly mauled division's ability to withstand much more of such violent attack.[8] Bayerlein, though new to the scene, was less concerned. Sure enough, on October 24, the Soviet offensive broke down, and the Germans were able to breathe easier.

On October 27, when it was obvious that the Pereyaslav front was going to remain quiescent for the time being, the 3rd Panzer Division was ordered away from the front and sent northward, to the sector of Gen. of Panzer Troops Joachim Lemelsen's XXXXVII Panzer Corps, screening the crossings of the Ingul River from the Soviet forces in the Bukhain bridgehead. Here, despite powerful enemy assaults to the north and south, at Lyutezh and Kiev and at Dnepronovinsk, the German forces remained untroubled throughout November and into December.

Bayerlein was confirmed as full commander of the division on December 15 and took up positions through Christmas at Lelekovka on the Ingul, a suburb of the major rail and road junction of Kirovograd. The Soviets remained unusually quiet through the frigid holiday season, building up their strength, but shortly after the New Year, they launched tandem assaults to the north and south of the city with powerful armored forces.

Bayerlein received orders from OKH to turn over his command to the veteran Col. Rudolph Lang on January 4, 1944, but by the next day, radio and telephone communications were out and the supply route had been cut. Four German divisions were encircled in the narrow pocket of Kirovograd, while outside it, the XXXXVII Panzer Corps headquarters was almost captured by a Soviet armored column and was driven all the way back to Malaya Viska, where the Russians surprised it once again two days later. Bayerlein was unable to leave Kirovograd, and Lang was unable to enter it.

In his exceptional book *Scorched Earth*, Paul Carell gives a compelling account of the battles of Kirovograd, but he seems to attribute a bit too much credit to Bayerlein. The Stauffenberg Papers give a slightly different version of the events of January 4–10.

Bayerlein had toured his perimeter during the first days of the attack, and on the evening of January 6, he called a conference of his officers to decide on a course of action. Carell is correct here in stating that the general was not as bound by orders as many other Eastern Front generals; hence he was perfectly willing to listen to the advice of his juniors. In this battle, Bayerlein had some outstanding subordinates. Two especially deserve mention: Wilhelm Voss and Ernst Wellmann.

Lt. Col. Wilhelm Voss had been operations officer of the division since November 1942, serving under Gen. Hermann Breith and Gen. Franz Westhoven. His reputation as a tactician was respected throughout the southern front. Col. Ernst Wellmann had commanded the 3rd Panzer Grenadier Regiment since September 1942 and received both the Knight's Cross and the Oak Leaves for his daring, plus the German Cross in Gold and two Panzer Battle Badges. He was unique in that he had declined reappointment to other panzer divisions as acting commander and refused a training course in senior leadership.

A plan was carefully sketched out, and now it was up to Bayerlein to sound out the other divisional commanders in the pocket: Lt. Gen. August Schmidt of the 10th Panzer Grenadier Division, Maj. Gen. Martin Unrein of the 14th Panzer, and Col. Otto Schwarz of the 346th Infantry Division.[9] Though Carell did not say so, the conference was arranged to secure the approval of Schmidt, the senior officer in the pocket.

Schmidt evaded the issue. He felt constrained to hold fast, since this had been his order earlier, but he agreed that Bayerlein might make the attempt to break out—whereupon, in a counterattack to relieve the pocket, the other three divisions would be free to assist their "rescuer" in escaping the trap. It was a clever piece of subterfuge, designed to frustrate the Fuehrer order—and it worked.

With units of the 10th Panzer Grenadier taking over its perimeter, the 3rd was formed into five battle groups (*Kampfgruppen*): A, under Bayerlein and Voss, with the tanks, the headquarters grenadier company, its engineer section, and a battery of self-propelled guns; B, made up of divisional engineer battalion, more artillery, and the 3rd Grenadier Regiment, all under Colonel Wellmann; C, with supply units, the damaged vehicles under tow, the medical staff, and the wounded; D, the reinforced 394th Grenadier Regiment under Lieutenant Colonel Beuermann); and E, the rear guard, consisting of Maj. Charly Deichen's antitank (*Jaeger*) battalion, with the antitank and self-propelled Flak squadrons, ready to rush to any threatened part of the columns.

When the signal to advance was given at 5:30 P.M., the canny Voss authorized the following radio signal: "3rd Panzer is bursting through the encirclement in a northwesterly course in order to seal the break in the front and to maneuver at the enemy's rear to relieve the encircled town." Though unable to receive messages, the Ia was reasonably sure that he could send and be heard; hereafter, no radio was operated.

The column moved off quietly and efficiently, blacked out on a moonless night of seven degrees Fahrenheit. At first all went well, but shortly before midnight surprised Soviets opened a wild fire on the forward units, inflicting the only casualty of the battle—on the lead tank. With irresistible force, the 3rd's panzers crashed in among the startled Russians, scattering them in confusion and destroying their guns and supply vehicles.

By daybreak, the Germans had recaptured the township of Vladimirovka in a coup de main, and once again sealed the breach to the north, and encircled the Russians, or at least cut them off. Taking full advantage of his momentum, Bayerlein about-turned his enthusiastic units and smashed into Russian positions around Osikovata, which were blockading Kirovograd.

While the XXXXVII Panzer Corps headquarters (now under Gen. Nicholas von Vormann) was being rousted out of Malaya Viska by a Soviet tank corps, the 3rd Panzer—well behind it—smashed the major portion of the VII Mechanized Corps at Osikovata, before wheeling south to destroy the commander and most of the armor of the Russian VIII Corps at Gruzkoye, thus opening the way to evacuate Kirovograd. While the audacious Colonel Wellmann ate a late supper with General Schmidt on the outskirts of Kirovograd on January 9, orders finally arrived from Rastenburg granting freedom of movement to the blockaded units. The next day, all three divisions, supported on the left by the 3rd Panzer and on the right by the elite *Grossdeutschland* Panzer Division, drove the remnants of the Soviet corps eastward, and then successfully evacuated Kirovograd down to the least essential stores before forming a contiguous line on the west bank of the Inguls. The immediate danger was over.

In the OKH communiqués, the 3rd Panzer and its component regiments were officially commended for their exploits. Significantly, not an officer was mentioned by name—in theory, the 3rd Panzer had disobeyed a direct order. On the other hand, on January 23, Lt. Gen. August Schmidt was ostentatiously awarded the Oak Leaves to his Knight's Cross, a backhanded compliment to the officers and men who had snatched victory from defeat.

In the course of events, Fritz Bayerlein was rapidly spirited out of the area late on January 10 and sent briefly to Berlin, while Rudolph Lang arrived to take over the division. So carefully was this transfer done that many people in the division were not even aware of the change of command, and long after the war Paul Carell was under the misapprehension that Bayerlein remained in command of the 3rd until late April or early May. Such was not the case.

Conditions in the east and in Germany were so poor in January 1944 that Bayerlein's progress back to Berlin for reassignment was considerably delayed. On January 10, Heinz Guderian had already asked for him as commander of the newly forming Panzer Lehr Division in France, and General Schmundt, chief of the Army Personnel Office, had accordingly cut his orders to that effect. Yet the major general only reached Berlin toward the end of the month, and then set out by rail and car for Nancy in Lorraine—the divisional headquarters—the next day. He did not arrive at his goal until February 4, according to the divisional history, by which time the former divisional commander, Maj. Gen. Oswin Grolig, had left to take temporary command of the 21st Panzer Division, and the brand new operations officer, Major Kauffmann, had had the difficult task of running the organization.[10]

The first thing Bayerlein did was to issue his first daily bulletin to the officers and men of his scattered unit. Dated February 4, 1944, this notification was something as follows:

> As of this very day I have been appointed to the command of the Panzer Lehr Division. The Panzer Lehr Division comes into existence due to the demand of the Fuehrer for an armored formation to be created which will be absolutely first class in its equipment.
>
> This fact alone compels the division to exhibit willing obedience and outstanding performance for its goal.
>
> Furthermore, you must first earn your title as the Panzer Lehr Division. Hence I expect of you that you shall go into this building period with all your strength and your total enthusiasm, that the foundation which you are laying will entitle you in your daily duties, the full right and privilege of claiming to be—THE BEST!
>
> Signed, Bayerlein.

The results of this exhortation seem to have been more than gratifying: twice, in February and May, Guderian commented on the spit and polish of the unit. In early March, the entire division was ordered out of the Nancy area and rushed eastward into Hungary, to support the German military takeover there. It did not have to be committed to action, as the Hungarians peacefully acquiesced to the demands of Hitler. So once again, on April 29, the division packed up and moved off west to France. En route, on May 1, Bayerlein was notified of his promotion to lieutenant general.

Save for the Tiger battalion, which had not yet arrived, the entire division was deployed around Nogent-le-Rotrou as a reserve for *Oberbefehlshaber* West (OB West) from May 21. The tanks were stationed at Brou, the 901st Panzer Grenadier Regiment went to Illers, and the 902nd Panzer Grenadier Regiment bivouacked in the vicinity of Vibraye. Everyone knew that an Allied invasion was imminent and Bayerlein was in close touch with his immediate superior, General Funck, on a daily basis.

On June 6, news of the attack was relayed to Nogent, and the division was ordered up to the coast to support the I SS Panzer Corps at Caen. Losses began to occur. Bayerlein's scout car was hit by a fighter-bomber on the eighth. Although he emerged unwounded, his driver and aide were both killed. Later on, a sharp attack by Canadian troops captured the Lehr's artillery commander, Colonel Luxenberger, along with his staff and one of his battery officers. Though liberated by SS troops on the ninth, Luxenberger was so severely wounded that he subsequently died, and the battery commander took charge of the regiment.

Meanwhile, the 902nd Panzer Grenadiers were severely handled at Brouay, where the unit's commander, his adjutant, and two company commanders were severely wounded. The 901st made little more headway at Norren en Bessin. The II Panzer Battalion did secure Ellion on the Bayeux Road but was forced to give it up after dark.

The battles in this area raged throughout most of June, taking heavier and heavier casualties on the division's equipment and men. As the disaster unfolded, Bayerlein became ever more aware of the meddling by Hitler's headquarters in affairs of the front. All rights to maneuver and effect timely pullbacks were curtailed, and the division—along with the rest of the army—was forced to stand and bleed uselessly.

After the war, while in U.S. captivity, Bayerlein, with his excellent command of the English language, wrote several lengthy reports on the operations in Normandy and France—not only those of his division, but covering much of the rest of the German Army as well.[11] Based on these writings, several later historians composed very good histories of the several phases of the western war.

I will not rehash the much more exhaustive works, not the least of which are the official U.S. Army history volumes; instead, I will use two German sources, one the history of the Panzer Lehr by an officer who served throughout the war, and the other another book by Paul Carell, titled *Invasion: They're Coming.*[12] As early as June, Bayerlein had come under Allied air attack and suffered minor shrapnel wounds. He seems to have endured several similar narrow escapes by early July, losing three command cars, a wireless truck, and two drivers.

On July 2, as the division prepared to transfer from the Tilly area to Villars-Bocage, British artillery zeroed in on divisional headquarters, smashing its transport and disrupting its communications, but personnel losses were negligible. After two hours, the staff scurried away during a lull in the attack, reaching Villers-Bocage safely by the third.

Casualty figures for the period from June 6 to 30 were listed as 490 dead, including 27 officers, 1,809 wounded (463 of them officers), 673 missing, and 435 on sick leave. Thus 3,407 of the division's 16,000 men were *hors de combat*, and material losses were much greater.

After a short ten days in reserve, the division was recommitted to the battle, for an attack on British positions before St. Jean de Daye, supported by a heavy panzer battalion of the 2nd SS Panzer Division. On July 11–12, with heavy losses, the Germans were unable to subdue the enemy, and in the succeeding days, U.S. counterattacks threw the division out of St. Hebert (July 14) and Les Mesnil-Dor (July 24–26). Then, on July 26–27, the Allied armor broke through near St. Lô and burst into open country, despite all the efforts of the hard-pressed German defenders. Massive aerial assaults, in which strategic bombers were used in a tactical role, had pulverized the German lines even before the armored and infantry attack had begun. Panzer Lehr headquarters was hustled out of Canisy just in the nick of time, relocating at Dangy.

Here, on the hot afternoon of July 26, with the front in turmoil, Lt. Col. Hans von Kluge, the son of the commander in chief of the Western Front, arrived from Army Group B headquarters with orders for the division: Panzer Lehr was to hold the St. Lô–Perieres line at whatever cost.

"With what?" Bayerlein claimed he asked.

"You fail to understand, General. These are hard and fast orders; not a man is to leave his place. The line is to be held!"

Bayerlein thereupon is supposed to have observed that of course no one would leave his post. Everyone was dead; consequently, they would hold the ground where they lay. Further conversation was made impossible when a fighter-bomber's cannon shells struck in the neighboring ammunition dump, which exploded with considerable fury, wrecking the farmhouse headquarters and forcing the various officers to beat a precipitate retreat. By noon the next day, Bayerlein was in another farmhouse in the little Soulle River with seven of his staff officers—Lieutenant Colonel Kauffmann, the Ia; Lieutenant Fischer, the Ic; Major Wrede, the IIb; Captain Huebner; Second Lieutenants Hesse and Heyden; and the general's aide, Major Hartdegen—as well as about fourteen surviving NCOs.

It is interesting to note—as the Panzer Lehr divisional historian carefully implied—that despite Bayerlein's claims that his division "had been annihilated," it was still a fairly potent force. Nor is this the last time the commanding general would report his unit's "annihilation."

But at Soulles Ford, American tanks began an attack on the new headquarters, forcing another wild scramble for safety, this time afoot, since all the headquarters vehicles had been destroyed. The Carell text now fatuously says, "At the Fuehrer's Headquarters a little flag was taken off the big situation map."[13] The divisional history, however, while mentioning the attack on the headquarters, continues to refer to the resistance the various fragmented units put up.

On July 29, in a series of sharp battles around Percy, Second Lieutenant Knebel of a panzer battalion shot up thirteen U.S. Sherman tanks. The "gallant commander" of the 902nd Panzer Grenadier Regiment, Lieutenant Colonel Welsch, was killed in the hard fighting, and Maj. Otto Kuhnow of the I Battalion assumed command. Nevertheless, there is no doubt whatsoever that at this point the division was far from being a viable entity. On August 2–3, Bayerlein was forced to create three battle groups of his survivors: *Kampfgruppe* Panzer Lehr 901, under Lt. Col. Baron Paul von Hausser; *Kampfgruppe* Gerhardt, the surviving tanks and recon units, sent to Alencon on detached service; and *Kampfgruppe* Grenadier Staff 902, under Major Kuhnow.

Ostensibly the general and his staff removed to Argentan, where they could maintain only loose control of the remnants of the division, and according to the divisional history, they considered that perhaps the remnant of the unit should be sent south to Fontainebleau under the 1st Army for a rest. But the dispersion of the unit on August 12 precluded this. It is certain that Bayerlein, roaming about the Habloville-Argentan area, was anxious for this to happen.

On August 13, the staff again came under fierce enemy fire, which scored minor wounds on almost everyone, but there is no official listing of any deaths, at least among the officers. Bayerlein now hurried back to the headquarters of Army Group B at La Roche Guyon, to secure a formal approval for the relief of the division. He obtained a conditional approval on August 17, but even this was to be frustrated—the next day, Field Marshal Kluge was removed from command by Field Marshal Model, who ran into Bayerlein outside the map room. The marshal dispelled his new general's hopes: "In the East our divisions take their rests in the front lines. And that is how things are going to be done here in the future. You and your formations will remain where they are!" ("*Im Osten werden die Divisionen an der Front aufgefrischt und so wirdes in zukinft ouch hier gehalten. Sie blieben mit Ihren Verbanden, so wie sind!*")

The reality of the situation, however, lay somewhere between Bayerlein's pessimism and Model's optimism. The Falaise pocket was at its worst, and the several battle groups, notably Major Kuhnow's grenadiers, were caught up in the desperate effort to break out. Bayerlein and his staff joined the remaining tanks of Colonel Gerhardt's group and escaped across the Laigle below Trun. Hausser's men broke out with the 116th Panzer, while Kuhnow drove with the remnants of SS Col. Kurt "Panzer" Meyer's 12th SS Panzer Division.

By August 20, the scattered units had passed through Soissons and Fontainebleau to the neighborhood of Senlis, where they finally reunited for the first time since July. They continued their retreat to Provins, which they reached on the twenty-fourth, but now under the acting command of Col. Rudolf Gerhardt. On the twenty-third, complaining of his several minor wounds and nervous exhaustion, Lieutenant General Bayerlein had gone on a period of leave, ostensibly to a hospital in Germany, but in reality he went to pick up the Swords to the Oak Leaves of his Knight's Cross, an award bestowed on him on July 20. This was the last gesture of Hitler's adjutant, Rudolf Schmundt, who was mortally wounded later that day by the assassins' bomb at Rastenberg.

Gerhardt and Kauffman, at Senlis, submitted the butchers' bill of the division over Bayerlein's signature. The survivors by unit were as follows:

901st Panzer Grenadier Regiment: 800 men with self-propelled guns, insufficiently equipped

902nd Panzer Grenadier Regiment: 300 men with softskin vehicles, insufficiently equipped

130th Panzer Lehr Regiment: 180 men, perhaps 20 PzKw IV and V tanks

130th Panzer Reconnaissance Battalion: 150 men, eight armored cars

130th Panzer *Jaeger* Battalion: perhaps five antitank guns

130th Panzer Artillery Regiment: six 105-millimeter howitzers, six 152-millimeter howitzers

130th Panzer Engineer Battalion: 150 men

311th Army Flak Battalion: reported as detached, status unknown, but in fact, the flak unit had been absent since before the invasion

The divisional personnel officer, Major Wrede, estimated a further 500 men as stragglers (who rejoined the headquarters by the twenty-eighth) and an additional 750 returning leave and wounded personnel, many of whom could be expected by September 1. Finally, late on the twenty-fourth, twenty-two new Panzer IVs were offloaded at Sezanne and taken over by the division's 5th Panzer Company, just up from Krampnitz.

Despite Hitler's orders that Paris should be held at all costs, the reality was that it fell to the French and Americans with very little fighting. Hotly pursued by the U.S. and British armored columns, the dispirited *Wehrmacht* continued its pell-mell flight toward the West Wall. Gerhardt allocated special battle groups of his understrength division to help delay the enemy at Oulchy and Rheims. On August 30, the gallant Maj. Helmut Ritgen's battle group inflicted a sharp setback on the U.S. 5th Infantry Division at Vouziers on the Aisne, thus allowing the rest of the division to escape across the Mans between Bezaney and Sedan.

Between September 1 and 7, despite a few hotly contested little fights, the Panzer Lehr was more or less safely drawn up along the West Wall, covering Bitburg. On September 8, Lieutenant General Bayerlein, sporting his newest honor, resumed command of the division and, within a very few days, began to act most arbitrarily with his officers.

First to go was the capable Major Werncke, the supply officer, who was supplanted by another general staff officer, Captain Heinrich. He did not suit Bayerlein either and was gone by mid-November. Rightly relying on the proven ability of his two chief regimental commanders, Rudolf Gerhardt and Paul von Hausser, the general took issue with the thoroughly capable Major Kuhnow, a longtime divisional veteran, and replaced him with a lieutenant colonel from the Home Army: Ritter Joachim von Poschinger.

Finally, the officers who had inherited the commands of the artillery regiment and the *Jaeger* battalion, Majors Zeisler and Barth, were removed for Majors Bartenwerfer and Bethcke. These officers were not ruined by this mass relief, however, and all subsequently found appropriate posts in other divisions. In fact, Major Kuhnow reverted to the command of his old II Battalion—a post his fellow officers were adamant on keeping for him.

During October, the division was rapidly rebuilt in rearward positions, and November 1, Kauffmann and Captain Heinrich were able to submit a readiness statement to the chief panzer maintenance officer, Gen. der Panzer Troops Horst Stumpff, listing an up-to-the-mark unit, including 14,200 officers and men. Bayerlein, however, sent in his own estimate:

> The morale of the soldiers is good and ready for action.
>
> However the assignment of replacements for missing personnel and equipment does not come up to proper standards to ready the division for the early resumption of battle none of us anticipate as being long delayed.
>
> Grade of mobility is 30%.
>
> Estimate of battle readiness: the division is for the time being unprepared for either attack or defense.

Pressure of events in Lorraine, however, put the division into action despite the protests of its commander. Southward, Patton's U.S. 3rd Army was dealing sledgehammer blows to a disorganized and understrength German Army Group G. On November 20, the Lehr was ordered to the area of Saargemuines to prepare a counterattack on three American divisions that had crossed the Marne-Rhine Canal and Saar River and were threatening to drive to the Rhine, thus cutting the army group in two by separating the 1st German Army from the 19th Army.

From Kastellaun to Saargemuines, the division traveled by road and railroad, arriving at its buildup area in driblets; two panzer grenadier battalions and two batteries of *Sturmgechutz* (assault guns) never even reached the area. The commander of the army group, the veteran panzer strategist Gen. of Panzer Troops Hermann Balck, was so shocked by the ill-prepared unit that he ordered a regiment of the 25th Panzer Grenadier Division from the southern sector to support the proposed Lehr attack. But this regiment arrived far too late to be of any help.

On the morning of November 22, the thirty Mark IV and thirty-five Panther tanks of the division's panzer regiment moved down to Saar Union, supported by the one intact grenadier regiment. Under the command of the veteran colonels Joachim von Poschinger and Baron Paul von Hausser, the attack was launched at 4 P.M. on November 23, traveling under the cover of darkness.

Early the next morning, they struck the weak flank of the U.S. 44th Infantry Division at Rauwiller and, in sharp fighting, drove the enemy back southwestward toward the Strasbourg highway. Around noon, advance units of the U.S. 4th Armored Division, which had crossed the Saar at Fenetrange a day before, struck the unprotected flank of the German troops.

Gerhardt swung one battalion of grenadiers, under Major Schoene, to hold off this dangerous enemy, while calling on Bayerlein, who was still at Saargemuines, to send up the available artillery. Lieutenant Berchtold with the 1st Company, 130th Panzer *Jaeger* Battalion, was the only force to arrive. Lieutenant Colonel Bartenwerfer of the artillery regiment was waiting for his two missing batteries, which were still en route from Bitberg to Saargemuines by rail. He refused to commit the four batteries on hand.

During the one-sided battle, which raged on November 25 and 26, Major Schoene was wounded and replaced by Captain Klein of the 10th Company. Poschinger with the 902nd Headquarters Company hastily came up to hold the flank. At the same time, Maj. Helmut Ritgen's tanks were coming under fire from an American armored battle group, and the whole effort hung perilously into the night of the twenty-fifth.

Meanwhile, Major General Mellenthin, Balck's chief of staff, had visited Bayerlein's battle headquarters at Domfessel and reluctantly agreed that the division, under heavy attack by infinitely superior U.S. forces, should retreat. OKW overruled this sensible suggestion, however, and only the arrival of the fresh regiment from the 25th Panzer Grenadier prevented the fighting Lehrs from being encircled.

During the twenty-seventh, Poschinger and Hausser fell back to their start line at Saar Union and consolidated a semblance of defense lines, which the rest of the 25th Panzer Grenadier occupied when it arrived that day. That night, Bayerlein began to withdraw his units northward. Nevertheless, units of the 902nd Panzer Grenadier Regiment continued on the defensive around Domfessel into December. On December 4, while disengaging to follow the rest of the division northward, the brave Major Kuhnow was seriously wounded, and almost 140 men of his battle group were taken prisoner. He was replaced by Reserve Captain Neumann of the V (*Versorgungstruppe*, or Supply) Company.

The Panzer Lehr had sustained serious losses in killed, wounded, and captured—not to mention in materiel. Though individually its officers had shown their customary bravery and skill, overall it had gone into action in ill-conceived and badly dispersed dispositions and consequently had accomplished virtually nothing. Now, however, it was to have a short—very short—period to regroup in its new cantonments along the Rohr River in preparation for the great Ardennes offensive, being planned by Hitler and his OKW cronies. Fritz Bayerlein set up his new divisional headquarters at Cochem, far back on the Moselle, on December 6. Between the tenth and twelfth, an additional 600 trained soldiers, plus a quantity of equipment—tanks, SP guns, and softskinned vehicles—poured into the area.

The unit was thus brought up to strength for the third time, with the report submitted to headquarters, XXXXVII Panzer Corps, on December 12, giving the following figures:

Establishment: 34 PzKw IVs; 34 Panthers; 21 assault guns; 13 PAK antitank guns; 13 light howitzers; 12 heavy howitzers

In Actual Possession: 34 PzKw IVs; 29 Panthers; 15 assault guns; 3 PAK antitank guns; 7 light howitzers; 12 heavy howitzers

Fit for Service: 30 PzKw IVs; 23 Panthers; 14 assault guns; 3 PAK antitank guns; 5 light howitzers; 9 heavy howitzers

Additional Reinforcement: 10 PzKw IVs; 10 Panthers; 4 assault guns; 6 PAK antitank guns, 0 howitzers

Out of Action: 2 assault guns; 4 PAK antitank guns; 5 light howitzers; 4 heavy howitzers

Over Establishment: 5 PzKw IVs, 10 Panthers.

This report is somewhat ambiguous. The figures for availability and out of action seem to imply that only the guns would not be reparable in time for action, yet there are minor discrepancies in both tank categories as well. Still, the report indicates that Panzer Lehr was a formidable combat force in the second week of December 1944.

General Bayerlein and his Ia, Lieutenant Colonel Kauffmann, were not let in on the secret of the offensive until the top-security meeting of corps and divisional officers held at Hitler's western headquarters on December 13, and the junior officers and men were made aware of what was to come only by the proclamation of Field Marshal Rundstedt, issued late on December 15. The attack began in the early hours of December 16, along a 100-kilometer (62-mile) front.

At the hastily held briefings during the night, Bayerlein had allowed his officers to deploy the divisional strength into three battle groups. The vanguard, under the overall command of the recon battalion CO, Maj. Gerd von Fallois, was composed of the 130th Panzer Reconnaissance Battalion; 8th Company, Panzer Lehr Regiment (fifteen PzKw IVs under Captain Falkenhayn); 3rd Company, 130th Panzer *Jaeger* Battalion (under Captain Wagner); 4th Battery, 130th Panzer Artillery Regiment (four light howitzers under Lieutenant Thiele); and the 2nd Company, 130th Panzer Engineer Battalion (under Captain Aidenbach), with some light bridging equipment.

The vanguard was supposed to cooperate with the neighboring 26th *Volksgrenadier* Division by bridging first the Our, then the Clerf River, and pushing for the road junction of Bastogne.

Kampfgruppe 901 was commanded by the gallant Col. Baron Paul von Hausser, the senior panzer grenadier officer, and comprised both battalions of the 901st Panzer Grenadier Regiment: I Battalion under Captain Hennecke and II Battalion under Captain Klein. In support were the 6th Company of the 130th Panzer Lehr Regiment, under Lieutenant Meyer with ten PzKw IVs, the understrength II Battalion of the 130th Panzer Artillery Regiment (5th and 6th Batteries) under Major Temming; and specially attached from the XXXXVII Panzer Corps, the 243rd Assault Brigade under Major Babich.

Kampfgruppe 902, under the command of Lt. Col. Ritter Joachim von Poschinger, consisted of both battalions of the 902nd Panzer Grenadier Regiment, plus the II Battalion of the Panzer Lehr Regiment (minus the 8th Company) under the recently promoted veteran Lt. Col. Helmut Ritgen. His 5th and 7th Companies were equipped with Panthers. Also attached were the I Battalion of the 130th Panzer Artillery Regiment, consisting of three batteries of heavy field howitzers under Major Sporkhorst, and the Supply Company.

As a reserve, Bayerlein kept the divisional guard (*Begleit*) company (under Lieutenant Regling), the twenty Panthers of the I Battalion, Panzer Lehr Regiment (under Captain Schulze), and the 1st and 3rd Companies of the 130th Panzer Engineer Battalion (under Captain Bethke). The whole reserve was under the command of the senior colonel, Rudolf Gerhardt. The rest of the Lehr Division's troops—two companies of the engineer battalion under Major Kunze—was attached to the 2nd Panzer Division for bridging the rivers, and the III Battalion and the siege battery of the artillery regiment (under Lieutenant Colonel Bartenwerfer) were attached to higher headquarters for the combined artillery barrage.

As originally conceived, *Kampfgruppe 901* would cross the Our at Gemund and drive to the west, while 902 would follow the 2nd Panzer across the river near Dasbourg, then diverge before reaching Clerf and rush via Murshauser and Drauffeldt to Eschweiler, where it would rendezvous with 901 and serve as a support to the 26th *Volksgrenadier* Division. In fact, the whole plan bogged down almost at once because of the terrible congestion on the roads of ingress. None of the three divisions of Luettwitz's XXXXVII Panzer Corps kept to their timetables. In spite of this problem, however, the U.S. resistance was weak and sporadic. The Germans had indeed fully achieved the element of surprise.

The many fine works focusing on the battles of the Ardennes, chiefly written by American and English historians, are unanimous in recording the weakness of the U.S. divisions resting in this supposed backwater of the war. It is probable that had the German units been those same magnificent divisions that had smashed into Belgium and France in May 1940, the victory envisioned by Hitler might well have been achieved. But this was 1944, and the veterans of the French campaign were long dead or burned out.

In spite of this, however, once across the Our and in less confined spaces, the battle groups of the Panzer Lehr performed creditably enough. By nightfall on Sunday, December 17, the Groups von Fallois and von Poschinger had made it across the Clerf and were racing westward. By Monday morning, the crossroads at Eschweiler had been captured. Group von Fallois swung left to capture the town of Wiltz, while Group von Poschinger, accompanied now by Bayerlein himself, headed on toward Bastogne.

With an advance guard of fifteen tanks and four companies of panzer grenadiers, Bayerlein pushed hurriedly toward Derenbach, while Poschinger followed at a slower pace and captured Erpelgange before also swinging northeast to try to rejoin Bayerlein on December 18 and throughout the night. After daybreak, the Germans secured both Ober and Niederwampach with some stiff fighting. At about this time, Bayerlein sent orders to Group von Fallois to leave the capture of Wiltz to the infantry of the 26th *Volksgrenadier* and hurry up along the stream of that name to help in the expected attack on Bastogne.

Bayerlein consulted with his officers over the maps in captured Niederwampach. A good road led southeast for about three and a half miles to the main road to Bastogne, another seven and a half miles—all told, eleven miles of good roads. Poschinger recommended it as being the safest bet. The general wasn't having any of this: Bastogne's capture was essential to the overall plan, and the maps also showed a rough track leading via Benonchamps to Mageret—just over a mile and a half distance—and from there to Bastogne was only three more miles.

But the dirt track became a cowpath, a sea of mud, and it took Bayerlein until midnight just to reach Benonchamps. A short time later, he and his men were engaged by an American blocking force on the outskirts of Mageret itself. In a sharp one-hour battle, the Germans secured the village, at a loss of three tanks. Here Bayerlein was alarmed when a purported pro-German civilian reported that just after nightfall, a great armored column of some fifty tanks and supporting infantry had rumbled through Mageret on its way to Bastogne. The man added that he had recognized an American major general as being in command.

In actuality, this column was a scratch force of the U.S. 10th Armored Division—thirty tanks in all plus a few trucks—and it was led by a captain. But Bayerlein's nerve failed. Without considering how unlikely it was that an American armored division could have gotten this far (there were, in fact, two U.S. armored divisions in the area, but they were widely scattered and understrength), the lieutenant general posted guards around Mageret and prepared to await sufficient reinforcements.

Poschinger's tanks and vehicles managed to get through the swamp that the dirt track had become. So noisy was their passage that, hearing it, Bayerlein was convinced it was the American "division" the civilian had reported. Meanwhile, Fallois's forces, coming up the Oberwampach road, ran into an American blocking force at Longvilly, which was now under attack by the 2nd Panzer Division from Clerf and Allerborn.

Now came another bizarre twist to the story. With the Panzer Lehr superimposed on the highway leading into Bastogne at Mageret, the Americans at Longvilly were actually cut off from their headquarters, and two senior U.S. commanders narrowly avoided being captured in their reconnaissance of the positions there. An American hospital convoy, making its way back to Bastogne was captured by the German forces, however. Neither Bayerlein nor the several U.S. officers involved seem to have been aware of the true situation until much later.

After sunrise on Monday, December 18, with the oppressive fog and low snow clouds still keeping the U.S. air forces in their airfields, the panzer general visited the improvised prison compound to speak to the American captives—and according to two completely separate reports, one American, one German, became intensely interested in a lovely blond American nurse. The unidentified German source maintained quite correctly that Bayerlein frittered away most of the day in a presumably futile effort at seduction; the U.S. historian also observed that Bayerlein wasted the day, from a military point of view, but implied that the German general was successful in his efforts.

One way or the other, the general lost much valuable time; in fact, a case could be made that the commander of the Panzer Lehr Division threw away the opportunity for the timely capture of Bastogne with his delays. Suffice it to say that from this evening on, the division was only tangentially involved in the continuing assault on Bastogne.

The capture of Bastogne was the responsibility of the XXXXVII Panzer Corps commander, Gen. Baron Heinrich von Luettwitz, who arrived in the advanced area late on the eighteenth and was appalled by the lack of initiative of the varied formations of his command. Under heavy pressure from the 5th Panzer Army commander, Gen. Hasso von Manteuffel, and Marshal Model, Luettwitz determined to leave Bastogne to the infantry and push his armored units on toward the crossing of the Meuse, the prime objective of the entire offensive and already far behind schedule.

Bayerlein smarted under the tongue-lashing he received and he seems to have retaliated later. In particular, he resented being deprived of his *Kampfgruppe 901* and some of his artillery, which were to continue in the now futile effort to reduce Bastogne. As a result, when Luettwitz returned to his headquarters across the Clerf, the Panzer Lehr continued to dally around Mageret, the recon battalion not setting off westward until midday on Tuesday, December 19, bypassing Wardin.

The divisional staff was still in this neighborhood on December 22. Bayerlein was again up with the vanguard nearing St. Hubert when Luettwitz unwisely sent in his summons for the enemy to surrender. First Lieutenant Henke, the Ic officer, who spoke some English, was chosen as one of the parliamentaries. The classic reply made by General McAuliffe, "Nuts," was roughly translated by Henke as *Quatsch*, meaning rubbish or nonsense.

The momentum of the German advance was stopped dead by now. Bayerlein managed to secure the town of St. Hubert on this same day. The panzer recon force under Fallois and *Kampfgruppe 902* under Poschinger converged on the road junction of Rochefort, where they fought a house-to-house battle from the evening of the twenty-second until noon on the twenty-third, until the American troops of the 335th Infantry Regiment were dislodged or captured.

A further advance on Humain and Buissonville, in cooperation now with units of the 2nd Panzer Division, took up Christmas Eve and most of Christmas Day. It required the arrival of advanced forces of the 9th Panzer Division under Major General Elverfeldt on December 26 to finally eject U.S. infantry and armor from their positions.

The way to Celles, the last barrier to the Meuse at Dinant, was now open, and three panzer divisions moved cautiously in that direction. A confused battle on the approaches to the important town began on December 27, but it was doomed to failure as British troops debouched out of Dinant to bolster the U.S. defenses. To make matters even worse, strong American forces, including armor, were now attacking the flanks and rear of the German spearhead at St. Hubert. The situation was growing critical.

Much of the initiative in the successes Panzer Lehr achieved during this period was furnished by the veteran battle group commanders. Maj. Gerd von Fallois of the recon battalion, however, had been severely wounded on December 24 at Humain, and his successor, First Lieutenant Werren, the senior surviving officer, did not have the necessary experience. Hence Captain of Reserve Neumann, of the II Battalion, 902nd Panzer Grenadier Regiment, was ordered to take over.

By January 1, 1945, losses had become critical. Lieutenant Colonel Kauffmann reported a death roster of 2,465, including 7 officers, and a sick and wounded list of another 1,475, of which another 8 were officers. In materiel, losses were equally heavy—the repair establishment reported some 75 percent of the division's rolling stock as more or less out of action at this time.

Early January saw the ferocity of the Anglo-American (particularly the latter) forces redoubled; simultaneously, as the skies cleared and the Allied air forces gained unlimited air control, smashing the German rear areas and disrupting the supply and reinforcement system. Elements of Patton's rampaging U.S. 3rd Army had relieved Bastogne, and the pressures were already forcing a slow German withdrawal.

During the first two weeks of January 1945, most of the captured territory was reoccupied by the Allied forces. St. Hubert was recaptured on the seventh, La Vacheres was lost after fierce fighting on the eleventh, and the Achouffe-Bonnerue-Mabompre line was broken between the fifteenth and seventeenth. The Allies also retook Houffalize on the seventeenth, and by the twentieth, Panzer Lehr was fighing on two fronts—near Wiltz on the west and Ettelbruck to the south.

At this juncture, Bayerlein, who was drifting from embattled unit to embattled unit in a complete daze, was notified by headquarters, OB West (Rundstedt), that he was to be relieved as soon as his replacement, the brave Col. Horst Niemack, could arrive from the Eastern Front, where he had commanded the crack *Grossdeutschland* Panzer Fusilier Regiment.[14] The situation in Germany by now was serious, as the Soviets had renewed their assaults in East Prussia, and Niemack was too heavily committed for immediate relief. On January 25, therefore, Bayerlein turned over the remnants of the division to Lieutenant Colonel Kauffmann, who also was being relieved as operations officer, and journeyed to the western headquarters for reassignment.

By now, the mutters of discontent with and criticism of the lieutenant general had registered even at these upper levels, and had there been any available officers with panzer experience, it is probable that Bayerlein would have been shunted into the Fuehrer Reserve. As it was, even officers with more dubious reputations than his were being recalled to duty, including Ernst Busch, a disgraced field marshal; Hans von Boineburg-Lensfeld; and Count Gerhard von Schwerin, under suspicion as being involved in the July 20 affair.

On February 1, Bayerlein was at the headquarters of the hard-pressed 7th Army as designated panzer officer, supposedly in command of whatever armored units were in the immediate area. It was not until the twelfth, however, that he actually established a staff and made the feeblest attempt to gather up the scattered panzer and panzer grenadiers, the staff being styled Panzer Corps Bayerlein.

In this case, as in the earlier phases of the European war, Bayerlein officiously ground out an extensive report on his operations in this capacity; a list of these reports appears in the notes section. The official U.S. Army History provides a much more forthright recapitulation, however. Never officially designated as a panzer corps, Bayerlein's ad hoc formation exercised loose control over numerous ragtag units in the desperate battles on the west bank of the Rhine until the complete collapse of German resistance took place in late February and necessitated a somewhat inglorious scramble to the safety of the east bank, during which the Remagen bridge was seized intact by the enterprising troops of the U.S. 9th Armored Division.

Walther Model, harried by angry orders from a vengeful Hitler, decided at once to unify the defensive forces under a single commander, and on March 8, the day after the capture of the bridge, he directed Bayerlein's staff to take over control of all units in the immediate vicinity: 300 men and fifteen tanks of Niemack's Panzer Lehr Division, 600 men and fifteen more tanks of Zollenkopf's 9th Panzer Division, a company-size remnant of the 106th Panzer Brigade with five tanks, some miscellaneous personnel grandiosely styled the 304th *Volksgrenadier* Division, an engineer battalion, and several *Volks* artillery units.

The corps headquarters was now designated as the LIII, a number with an unfortunate past: of its two most recent commanders, one had driven into an American unit and been captured, and the other, separated from his men and being blamed for the loss of the bridge, was wandering helplessly around the countryside, a wanted man. Bayerlein set up his new headquarters on March 9 and was immediately visited by Model. The marshal assured the lieutenant general that the understrength 11th Panzer Division (under Wietersheim, with 4,000 troops, twenty-five tanks, and fourteen assault guns) plus a class A infantry regiment (the 138th, from the Netherlands) would soon join him, giving him more than 10,000 men and upward of seventy tanks.

In his essay on the period, Bayerlein gratuitously blamed Model for his failure to launch a brisk counterattack, first on the afternoon of the ninth and later on the thirteenth. He was echoed by the U.S. Army historian, since Model did not live to defend himself. In actuality, the *Kampfgruppe* of the Panzer Lehr under Maj. Helmut Hudel arrived on the corps perimeter by noon on the ninth, ready to spearhead an attack, but according to the official history of the Lehr, Bayerlein neglected to give the unit orders.

As for the attack of the thirteenth, Wietersheim's 11th Panzer had been immobilized in and around Bonn from the eighth to the thirteenth because of a lack of fuel, as recorded in an account of the Remagen battles, and was unable to reach the front until early on March 14—although nonmotorized elements did recapture the hamlet of Honnef late on March 11. Notwithstanding this minor achievement, Bayerlein committed his armor, including the 16th when it finally arrived, directly into the defense lines. His sensible course of action should have been to keep his mobile forces in reserve to exploit any opportunities.

It seems as if the astute Bayerlein continually outmaneuvered Model, and even managed to deploy the up-to-strength and veteran 138th Infantry Regiment as an augmentation for his inadequate *Volks-grenadier* division, thus once again wasting a potential attack force. For all these reasons, the desperate field marshal now sought to somehow derail his subordinate. As the LXXIV Corps headquarters of Gen. Carl Puechler came into the line on the northern perimeter of the U.S. bridgehead, Model exchanged his staff for Bayerlein's LIII.[15] Thus, though much of the available armor remained as the LIII Corps' responsibility, the new headquarters could prosecute an attack with much more effect.

But it was now entirely too late. Not only Hodges's 1st but also strong elements of Patton's 3rd U.S. Army had pushed across the Rhine. The Germans had lost the chance to contain the Remagen bridgehead. Model, doubtless by now completely frustrated, issued new orders on the night of March 22–23, depriving Bayerlein and his corps staff of much of the armor, and the 11th Panzer, Panzer Lehr, and 9th Panzer Divisions were rushed to support Puechler's corps. Thus while the powerful U.S. offensive virtually destroyed the two southern corps in a five-day battle and pressed even deeper into Germany, Bayerlein's forces withdrew across the Sieg River voluntarily.

Though now technically under Gen. Gustav von Zangen's 15th Army, Bayerlein was by March 26 out of touch with army headquarters, as well as the two fleeing corps headquarters.[16] He therefore hurriedly advised Model that in his opinion, any further engagement with the oncoming Americans seemed "impossible and entirely hopeless." He also used his most familiar expletive: "insane!" In fact, the invincible advance of the U.S. forces had already virtually encircled the entire Army Group B (5th Panzer and 15th Armies) in the bomb- and shell-scarred Ruhr. Indeed, on April 1, the 1st and 9th U.S. Armies met at Lippstadt on the outer edge of the Ruhr, and the German forces were trapped. Map 5.2 shows the Allied encirclement of Army Group B and the Ruhr.

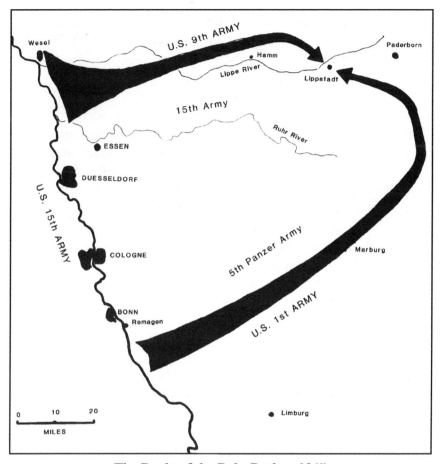

The Battle of the Ruhr Pocket, 1945

By this time, the surviving units of the army group were almost, but not quite, a disorganized and dispirited mob. Subjected to massive artillery bombardment and almost continous air strikes, the men hid in rubble-strewn basements or shell craters. The various headquarters took advantage of any protective covering available. Radio or telephone communication from unit to unit was desultory at best; Field Marshal Model generally had recourse only to runners to reach his generals.

Despite the apparent hopelessness of their position, the Germans could not consider surrender this early. Many senior officers were aware that their Fuehrer was assembling an 11th Army in the

Harz Mountains, which was preparing to launch a relieving counterattack. They did not know that Gen. of Infantry Otto Hitzfeld, the 11th's commander, had only a staff, a few makeshift battle groups, and nothing else.[17]

To make matters even worse, Model, who by now should have known better, resolved on none other than Fritz Bayerlein and his LIII Corps to lead the breakout from within. In a way, this choice is understandable. Model still believed that the general who had supposedly led the 3rd Panzer in the Kirovograd breakout a year before could do it again. This explains the continued reliance placed on the LIII Corps, when such panzer leaders as Col. Gen. Josef Harpe, Baron Heinrich von Luettwitz, and Horst Niemack were all available.[18]

Looking at these officers as Model must have done in this dire extremity, Harpe was now an army commander and as such not expendable, Luettwitz was under a slight cloud because of his strange performance at Bastogne, and Horst Niemack, not yet a major general, though a wearer of the Oak Leaves, was an unknown quantity. So once again, Bayerlein was the weak reed on whom the army group commander decided to lean.

Based on wooded hills around Winterberg, the remnants of the Panzer Lehr and 3rd Panzer Grenadier Divisions were to drive for the Eder-See, a large reservoir on the Weser and Lohne, where—it was hoped—they would meet up with the advance units of the 11th Army. Bayerlein indeed ordered the attack on April 1 but without awaiting the arrival of his infantry division, the veteran 176th, under Maj. Gen. Christian Landau.[19]

Niemack's Lehr forces were heavily engaged at once by superior U.S. armor and infantry. Promoted to major general on April 1, he was severely wounded in a second abortive attack the next day, and the gallant Colonel Hausser took over command. Similarly, Maj. Gen. Walter Denkert's heroic 3rd Panzer Grenadiers were involved in a furious hand-to-hand firefight lasting throughout the night.[20] The next morning, Landau committed his 176th into the fray, supported by a miscellaneous battle group made up of returning wounded, noncombat personnel, and some loyal *Volkssturm* volunteers, including a battalion of Russian scouts. It was all to no avail: the U.S. forces drove the Germans back by late evening.

Meanwhile, the circle around the Ruhr had been tightened, as more and more U.S. divisions carne into the battle. The order of battle of the trapped army group now was as follows:

Model's headquarters, with Maj. Gen. Carl Gustav Wagener as chief of staff

Headquarters, 15th Army (Gen. of Infantry Gustav von Zangen), with Major General Metzge as chief of staff

Headquarters, 5th Panzer Army (Col. Gen. Josef Harpe), with Maj. Gen. Wolf von Kahlden as chief of staff

XXXXVII Panzer Corps (General Luettwitz)

LXIII Corps (Gen. Erich Abraham)

LXXXI Corps (Gen. Friedrich Kochling)

LIII Corps (Lieutenant General Bayerlein)

LXXIV Corps (Gen. Karl Puechler)

LVIII Panzer Corps (Gen. Walther Krueger)

LXXX Corps (Gen. Dr. Franz Bayer)

Panzer Lehr Division (Col. Baron Paul von Hausser)

9th Panzer Division (Col. Helmut Zollenkopf)

116th Panzer Division (Maj. Gen. Siegfried von Waldenberg)

3rd Panzer Grenadier Division (Maj. Gen. Walter Denkert)

5th Parachute Division (Col. Ludwig Heilmann)

180th Infantry Division (Maj. Gen. Bernard Klosterkemper)

190th Infantry Division (Maj. Gen. Ernst Hammer)

176th *Volksgrenadier* Division (Maj. Gen. Christian Landau)

183rd *Volksgrenadier* Division (Col. Heinrich Warrelmann)

338th Infantry Division (Col. Rudolf von Oppen)

12th Infantry Division (Maj. Gen. Ernst Koenig)

166th Infantry Division (Lt. Gen. Eberhard von Fabrice)

59th Infantry Division (Lt. Gen. Walther Poppe)

62nd *Volksgrenadier* Division (Col. Arthur Juettner)

353rd Infantry Division (Col. Karl Koppenwaellner)

559th *Volksgrenadier* Division (Maj. Gen. Baron Kurt von Muehlen)

Elements, 560th *Volksgrenadier* Division (Col. Rudolf Langhaeuser)

719th Infantry Division (Maj. Gen. Heinz Gaede)

3rd Parachute Division (Lt. Gen. Rudolf Schimpf)

After the failure of the Winterberg attack, Bayerlein was moved up to another sector with his staff, taking over three units formerly under the XXXXVII Panzer Corps headquarters: the 116th Panzer and 180th and 190th Infantry Divisions. In exchange, Luettwitz took command of the Lehr, the 9th, and 176th Infantry Divisions, now falling back into the Ruhr under heavy U.S. pressure. Model had finally reached the conclusion that a more dynamic officer was needed at the hoped-for breakout area. Unfortunately for the Germans, he had come to this decision a week too late.

Under heavy artillery fire and round-the-clock air attack all around the perimeter, the understrength German troops—deprived of both supply and reinforcement by their isolation—gave ground after grim defenses, occasionally making sharp but generally hopeless spoiling attacks. As April ground along slowly, day by day the situation grew more hopeless.

Model was under ever-increasing pressure from his officers to capitulate, but his personal military philosophy forbade such a recourse. As the U.S. Arm's official history puts it, with reluctant admiration, "Model could not reconcile surrender with the demands he had put on his officers and troops through the years." Somewhat later, he told General Wagener: "Have we done everything to justify our actions in the light of history? What is there left to a commander in defeat? In ancient times, they took poison!"

Finally, however, this field marshal, who had once criticized Paulus at Stalingrad by saying, "A field marshal does not become a prisoner. Such a thing is just not possible," reached a compromise that salved his conscience. He would officially disband Army Group B, so that every single individual—officer, noncom, and soldier—could respond to his own set of standards.

The disbandment was to take place in three stages. From April 13, all youths and old men would be released from duty and allowed to make their way wherever they could. As of the fifteenth, the group would be dissolved down to its regimental levels, and from the seventeenth, all personnel would be free to try to escape singly or in groups, but without arms.

Bayerlein, in his postwar memoirs for the U.S. Army Historical Commission, ignored these three stages. He told of how on April 17, by which time all commanders would have been notified of Model's orders, he supposedly tricked Gen. Ernst Hammer and Gen. Berhard Klosterkemper, branded as ardent Nazis, into coming to his head-quarters while he sent staff officers to their divisional command posts to effectively surrender their men to the U.S. 7th Armored Division.[21]

In fact, between the fifteenth and seventeenth, all the various units gave themselves up in response to the orders from the field marshal, and Bayerlein, his staff, and his generals went into U.S. prisoner-of-war compounds. Oddly enough, Bayerlein's group seems to have been late, rather than early, in surrendering. Resist-ance as a whole, within the Ruhr pocket, collapsed with the issue of the April 15 order, though some few units may have continued to try to escape as late as the death of Model by his own hand on the twenty-first.

Bayerlein appears to have at once become very friendly with his captors, both American and British. A secret surveillance transcript by a British intelligence unit, dated on or after April 30, recounts somewhat angry reactions by other German officers imprisoned with the former LIII Corps commander. One of these, Bayerlein's old adversary in Africa, Maj. Gen. Gerhard Franz, was particularly resent-ful of the general's pretentious and self-serving attitude.

In the course of the year, the famous U.S. Brig. Gen. S. L. A. Mar-shall, involved in writing the first postwar history of the Bastogne bat-tle, had the chance to interview the three German generals chiefly involved in that battle. An outspoken Germanophobe, Marshall's comments are bitterly critical:

> Bayerlein is a short, solidly built man of fifty, sharp featured and keen of eye. All of his actions are vigorous and his aggres-siveness in and out of conversation reminds one of a terrier [Charles MacDonald and Hasso von Manteuffel also shared this last description]. His contempt for Luettwitz is obvious. When Luettwitz rambles in his conversation, Bayerlein waves a hand in his face and snarls: "Not important. Not impor-tant!" . . . the record indicates that Bayerlein's individual actions and estimates cost the corps some of its finest oppor-tunities. . . . When confronted with his own gross blunders, he puts his head back and laughs with abandon; it seems to be the one thing that thoroughly amuses him.

Subsequently, during 1946 and 1947, Bayerlein put his excellent grasp of the English language into the composition of a voluminous series of essays on the war in France—self-laudatory but quite readable accounts running to twenty-two separate items with 401 pages. Not only did he exhaustively discuss his own operations, but he also took it upon himself to describe the operations of the 26th *Volks-grenadier* Division during the Ardennes offensive and second-guess the late Field Marshal Model in the Ruhr.

Doctors by now had discovered that Bayerlein's service in Africa had left him with an irreversible kidney disease, and by 1948, when he was released to return to Wuerzburg, he was undergoing treatments to ameliorate the effects of his illness. His willingness to make observations on the war and the German conduct of it made him extremely popular with the many Anglo-American writers who were profilerating in these early postwar years. His earliest contribution was to Chester Wilmot during 1950 and 1951, for the author's exhaustive *Struggle for Europe*, but for some reason, possibly a deep-seated anti-Semitism, he refused to assist the equally capable Milton Shulman, whose 1955 *Defeat in the West* had to rely on the earlier U.S. 1st Army interrogations. During these years, he established a cordial relationship with the greatest of all the Western military historians, the late Basil H. Liddell Hart.

In 1954, at Hart's suggestion, he composed the chapter on El Alamein for Seymour Freiden and William Richardson's *Fatal Decisions*, published in 1955 in Great Britain and 1956 in the United States.[22] During the same period, he was collaborating on Liddell Hart's very valuable book, *The Other Side of the Hill*, published in Great Britain in 1957, and together with Liddell Hart and Manfred Rommel, he began the editing of *The Rommel Papers*, published in 1953.

In all of these contributions, Bayerlein was able to expand on his own exploits, so that most subsequent historians, using the "source materials," have perpetuated the legends of his great expertise as a military commander, his anti-Nazi sentiments, and all the rest of it. His most important collaborations, however, occurred in the later years of his life, this time with a fellow German, the reporter Paul Carl Schmidt, writing under the pseudonym Paul Carell.

Die Wustenfuchs was published in Germany in 1958, and it immediately sold out three printings before being secured by J.

MacDonalds in England in 1960. In his preface, Carell acknowledges the advice and help of the "gallant chief of staff of the Afrika Korps, Lieutenant General Bayerlein." Herein are a couple of the biggest distortions that worthy officer ever made.

First off, his account of witnessing Thoma's surrender at El Alamein on November 4, 1942, contains several inaccuracies over the years between his help of Desmond Young (*Rommel, The Desert Fox*) in 1950. Next, his report of the retreat of the Afrika Korps for the two middle weeks of November is carefully evasive. By now he was aware of the fact that other officers were telling a story closer to the truth, so after his high-flown account of Rommel giving him command, he allows the reader the impression that he was the hero of the hour—but carefully never lets Carell really say so.

In 1960 appeared Carell's excellent study in Normandy, *Sie Kommen*, which was published in Great Britain in 1962 and the United States in 1963. Here Bayerlein's accounts figure most prominently, particularly his insistence that the Panzer Lehr Division was annihilated. Oddly enough, however, the Panzer Lehr's own history describes its continued employment right through the Falaise pocket and even briefly as a battle group on the West Wall near Aachen.

Carell's last two books were both about events on the Russian Front: *Hitler Moves East*, the English translation published in 1965, and *Scorched Earth*, in 1966. The first work acknowledges some help from Bayerlein, but only from a staff officer position, as it also contains Guderian's own account, which would have kept his erstwhile Ia honest. The second volume, almost constantly in print in Germany since its publication, marked the end of the lives of both Carell, who died in 1968, and Bayerlein, who succumbed to his illness on January 30, 1970, at Wuerzburg. In this volume, the "legend" of the great breakout at Kirovograd during January 1944 and of Bayerlein's not being given command of Panzer Lehr until early May are set forth at great length.

So respected had Paul Carell become that even the most dedicated historians followed his versions of the campaign slavishly. "This author freely admits that he wrote a critical letter to the authors of an exceptional study of the Panzertruppe endeavoring to correct the assertion made therein that Bayerlein had been removed from the command of the 3rd Panzer Divison on January 5, 1944, and given command of the Panzer Lehr," Friedrich von Stauffenberg wrote in his papers in 1988.

Even the receipt of Bayerlein's personnel record from the National Archives did not convince me. It took reading the original sources to prove that, as Maj. Gen. Gerhard Franz succinctly put it, "not was all nonsense and boasting," but Bayerlein "took a great deal of trouble to see [he] wasn't forgotten."[23]

APPENDIX A

Table of Comparative Ranks

U.S. Army	German Army
General of the army	Field marshal (*Generalfeldmarschall*)
General	Colonel general (*Generaloberst*)
Lieutenant general	General of (infantry, panzer troops, and so on)
Major general	Lieutenant general (*Generalleutnant*)
Brigadier general*	Major general (*Generalmajor*)
Colonel	Colonel (*Oberst*)
Lieutenant colonel	Lieutenant colonel (*Oberstleutnant*)
Major	Major (*Major*)
Captain	Captain (*Hauptmann*)
First lieutenant	First lieutenant (*Oberleutnant*)
Second lieutenant	Second lieutenant (*Leutnant*)
None	Senior officer cadet or ensign (*Faehnrich*)
Officer candidate	Officer-Cadet (*Fahnenjunker*)

* Brigadier in the British Army

APPENDIX B

German Staff Positions in World War II

Chief of staff (Not present below the corps level)

Ia.	Chief of operations
Ib.	Quartermaster (chief supply officer)
Ic.	Staff officer, intelligence (subordinate to Ia)
IIa.	Chief personnel officer (adjutant)
IIb.	Second personnel officer (subordinate to IIa)
III.	Chief judge advocate (subordinate to IIa)
IVa.	Chief administrative officer (subordinate to Ib)
IVb.	Chief medical officer (subordinate to Ib)
IVc.	Chief veterinary officer (subordinate to Ib)
IVd.	Chaplain (subordinate to IIa)
V.	Motor transport officer (subordinate to Ib)
	National socialist guidance officer (added in 1944)
	Special staff officers: chief of artillery, chief of projectors (rocket launchers), and so on

APPENDIX C

Characteristics of Selected World War II Tanks

Model	Weight (in tons)	Speed (mph)	Range (miles)	Main Armament	Crew
BRITISH					
Mark IV Churchill	43.1	15	120	16-pounder	5
Mark VI Crusader	22.1	27	200	12-pounder	5
Mark VIII Cromwell	30.8	38	174	175mm	5
AMERICAN					
M3A1 Stuart	14.3	36	60	137mm	4
M4A3 Sherman	37.1	30	120	176mm	5
GERMAN					
PzKw I	6.0	25	100	2 MGs	2
PzKw II	9.3	25	118	120mm	3
PzKw III	24.5	25	160	150mm	5
PzKw IV	19.7	26	125	175mm	5
PzKw V Panther	49.3	25	125	175mm	5
PzKw VI Tiger	62.0	23	73	188mm	5
RUSSIAN					
T-34/Model 76	29.7	32	250	176mm	4
T-34/Model 85	34.4	32	250	185mm	5
KV 1	52	25	208	176.2mm	5
JSII Joseph Stalin	45.5	23	150	122mm	4

Notes

CHAPTER 1. BARON HANS VON FUNCK

1. The Treaty of Versailles, which ended World War I, limited the size of the German Army to 100,000 men, only 4,000 of which could be officers.

   The kaiser's Second Reich (1871–1918), also called Imperial Germany, was replaced by the Weimar Republic (1918–33) and then the Third Reich (1933–45). During the 1919–35 period, the German armed forces were called the *Reichswehr*. This was divided into two services: the *Reichsheer* (army) and *Reichsmarine* (navy).

2. The *Wehrkreis* (military district) exam was given once a year. Each officer with ten years' service was required to take it. The top 15 percent were eligible to attend the general staff course at the War Academy in Berlin. About one-third of those selected passed the three-year course and two-year probationary period and became general staff officers. Those who failed the *Wehrkreis* exam were allowed to take it again the following year. A second failure could cost a man his commission. Funck did not score in the upper 15 percent, but he nevertheless did very well.

   Erich von Tschischwitz was born in Kulm, West Prussia, in 1870. He was educated in various cadet schools and entered the service as a second lieutenant in the 6th Guards Regiment in 1889. He fought in World War I, during which he was promoted from major to colonel (1917) and earned the *Pour le Merite* with Oak Leaves. In the *Reichsheer*, he became commander of the 2nd Infantry Division on February 1, 1923, and assumed command of Group Command 1 (also transferred as Army Group 1) on February 1, 1927. He was promoted to general of infantry on November 1 of that year and retired in early 1929. He died in Berlin in 1958.

3. Edmund Wachenfeld (1878–1958), a native of Alsace, retired in 1932 as a general of artillery. He was recalled to active duty as a general of fliers in the *Luftwaffe* in 1935, where he set up *Luftgau III* (III Air District), a corps-level air district that was much like an army *Wehrkreis*. He returned to the army when World War II began on September 1, 1939, and was commander of *Wehrkreis VII* (Bavaria) from then until March 1, 1943, when he retired for a second and final time. See Wolf Keilig, *Die Generale des Heeres* (Friedberg, Germany: Podzun-Pallas-Verlag, 1983), 358–59.

4. Oswald Lutz was born in Bavaria in 1876. He joined the Bavarian Army as an engineer in 1896, and during World War I, he commanded the motorized troops in the 6th Army and was a general staff officer with railroad units. He later became the first general of mobile troops (1935) and the chief of army

motorization. He was forced into retirement by Adolf Hitler on February 4, 1938. Except for a brief period when he directed a special transitional staff at Frankfurt-Oder (1941–42), he was not employed during World War II. He died in Munich on February 26, 1944.

5. Baron Werner von Fritsch was born in Benrath in 1880 and joined the Imperial Army as a *Fahnenjunker* (officer-cadet) in 1898. Commissioned in 1900, he became a general staff officer in 1911. He fought on the Western Front in World War I, served in the *Reichsheer*, and commanded the 2nd Artillery Regiment (1928–30), 2nd Artillery Command (1930), 1st Cavalry Division (1931–32), and 3rd Infantry Division and *Wehrkreis III* in Berlin (1932–34). He became chief of the Army High Command and de facto commander in chief of the army on February 1, 1934.

   From 1919 to 1935, each *Wehrkreis* had one infantry division, which bore the same number as the military district. The *Wehrkreis* commander also commanded the infantry division.

6. When Hitler renounced the Treaty of Versailles on March 16, 1935, the Defense Ministry was renamed the War Ministry.

7. Hans-Karl von Scheele (1892–1955) entered the service as a *Fahnenjunker* in the infantry in 1911. Commissioned in 1912, he fought in World War I, served in the *Reichsheer*, and was promoted to colonel in 1938. During World War II, he rose to the rank of general of infantry, commanding the 191st Infantry Regiment (1939–41), 208th Infantry Division (1941–43), Corps Scheele (1943), LII Corps (1943), and II Field Jaeger Corps (1944). He ended the war as president of the Reich War Court (1945).

8. Wilhelm von Thoma was born in Dachau, Bavaria, on September 13, 1891. An incredibly brave man, he earned the Max Josef Order (along with the non-hereditary title of *Ritter*, or knight) during World War I. He was wounded fourteen times during his legendary career and survived more than 100 armored combats during the Spanish Civil War alone.

9. Wilhelm Faupel was born near Liepnitz in 1873 and joined the Imperial Army as an officer-cadet in the artillery in 1892. He fought in China during the Boxer Rebellion (1900–01) and against rebellious tribes in Southwest Africa (1904–07). He retired in 1911 but returned to active duty in 1914, when World War I broke out. He spent the war in general staff positions and in 1918 became chief of staff of the 9th Army. After the war, he commanded a large *Freikorps*. Still later, he served as military advisor to Argentina (1921–26) and a lieutenant general in the Peruvian Army (1926–30). Later he headed the Latin American Institute in Berlin. Named German ambassador to Spain in 1936, he was recalled in August 1937 because of conflicts with Gen. Hugo Sperrle, the commander of the Condor Legion. He retired in 1938 and received an honorary promotion to lieutenant general in 1939. He committed suicide in Berlin on May 1, 1945, as the Red Army overran the capital of the Reich.

10. Neither man was ever reemployed. Blomberg died in the witness wing of the Nuremberg prison in 1946. Fritsch was later acquitted of any dishonorable behavior and named honorary colonel of the 12th Artillery Regiment. He accompanied this unit to the field during the invasion of Poland in 1939. On September 22, he deliberately exposed himself to Polish machine-gun fire and was killed.

11. Walther von Brauchitsch was born in Berlin in 1881, the son of Gen. of Cavalry Bernhard von Brauchitsch. After being educated in various cadet schools, he

joined the army in 1900 and was a general of artillery commanding Army Group 4—Germany's panzer, motorized and light divisions—in early 1938. He was offered a promotion to colonel general, the post of commander in chief of the army, and a sizable bribe—to be paid as hush money to his wife, who agreed to divorce him quietly, without a public scandal—in exchange for helping Nazify the army, siding with Hitler against the senior generals and dismissing about three dozen senior commanders, including Gerd von Rundstedt, Lutz, and Ewald von Kleist. Brauchitsch took the deal. His older brother Adolf (1876–1935) retired as a major general in 1929. Walther's son Bernd was a colonel in the *Luftwaffe* and an aide to Hermann Goering.

12. Walther Warlimont (1894–1976) was an officer noted for his arrogance. He became deputy chief of operations of OKW and was promoted to general of artillery on April 1, 1944. On July 20, he was wounded in Col. Count Claus von Stauffenberg's attempt to assassinate Adolf Hitler. As a result of these wounds, he retired in September 1944. In 1949, he was sentenced to life imprisonment as a minor war criminal, but he was released in an amnesty in 1957. Although Hitler suspected him of having prior knowledge of the Stauffenberg conspiracy, he was in fact one of the most pro-Nazi generals. Warlimont had strained relations with Alfred Jodl, who rose to the rank of colonel general. Jodl was hanged as a war criminal at Nuremberg in 1946.

13. As chief of the powerful Army Personnel Office (HPA), Victor von Schwelder (1885–1954) was high on Hitler's list of officers that had to be replaced; however, because he was regarded as a non-Nazi (as opposed to being an anti-Nazi), Brauchitsch was allowed to transfer him rather than force him into retirement. One of Brauchitsch's first acts as commander in chief of the army was to promote Schwelder to general of infantry and transfer him to Dresden, where he assumed command of *Wehrkreis IV*. The active component of this military district went to the field as IV Corps in 1939, while the territorial component remained behind as *Wehrkreis IV*. Schwelder led the corps in Poland, France, and Russia until the early stages of the battle of Stalingrad. He fell ill in October 1942 and did not return to active duty until the following March, when he again assumed command of *Wehrkreis IV*. He held this post until January 31, 1945, when the bulk of the units of the Home Army were sent to the front. Schwelder surrendered to the Western Allies at the end of the war.

   Bodewin Keitel (1888–1953) was the younger brother of Hitler's notorious yes-man, Wilhelm Keitel, who was named commander in chief of the High Command of the Armed Forces on February 4, 1938. Bodewin replaced Schwelder and was promoted to major general on March 1, 1938. Promotions to lieutenant general and general of infantry followed. Wilhelm temporarily fell out of Hitler's favor in the fall of 1942, and Bodewin was sacked on September 30 of that same year. Bodewin was recalled to active duty on March 1, 1943, as commander of *Wehrkreis XX* (formerly Poland), a post that he held until late 1944. He surrendered to the Americans at the end of the war. The senior army officers unanimously considered Bodewin more intelligent than Wilhelm.

14. Hans-Joachim von Horn was born in Koenigsberg, East Prussia, in 1896. A former cavalry officer, he became chief of staff of the XII Corps when World War II began. He rose to the rank of lieutenant general, commanded the 198th Infantry Division on the Eastern Front (1943–44), and ended the war as military attaché to Switzerland (1944–45). He later joined the West German Army,

the Bundesheer, and in 1961, he retired as a lieutenant general, the equivalent of a U.S. three-star general in the new rank structure. He died in Wiesbaden in 1994.

15. Heinz Guderian, *Panzer Leader* (London: M. Joseph, 1952), 72.

16. Horst Stumpff was born in Giessen in 1887. He entered the service as a *Fahnenjunker* in 1907 and was commissioned in the 54t h Infantry Regiment in 1908. He fought in World War I, served in the *Reichsheer*, and was promoted to colonel 1935. Later he became a major general (1939), lieutenant general (1941), and general of panzer troops (November 9, 1944). He commanded the 3rd Panzer Brigade (1938–October 1939) and 3rd Panzer Division (1939–October 1941) before his health collapsed. He returned to active duty as inspector of the Koenigsberg recruiting area in April 1942. In 1944, he became inspector of army panzer replacement troops. He died in Hamburg in 1958.

17. Erich Hoepner was born in Frankfurt-Oder on September 14, 1886. He joined the army as an officer-cadet in the 13th Dragoon Regiment in 1905 and served as a general staff officer during World War I. He commanded the 1st Light/6th Panzer Division (1938), XVI Motorized Corps (1939–41), and 4th Panzer Group (later Army) (1941–42). He was an active member of the anti-Hitler conspiracy, and his chief supply officer was Claus von Stauffenberg. Hitler sacked him on January 8, 1942, for conducting an unauthorized retreat.

18. Horne, 316.

19. Ewald von Kleist (1881–1954) joined the army as an artillery *Fahnenjunker* in 1901 but spent most of his career in the cavalry. He commanded the 9th Infantry Regiment (1931–32), the 2nd Cavalry Division (1932–35), and *Wehrkreis VIII* (1935–38). Forced into retirement by Brauchitsch (i.e., Hitler) in February 1938, he returned to active duty in 1939 and commanded the XXII Corps (1939–40), Panzer Group von Kleist (1940), 1st Panzer Group (later Army) (1940–42), Army Group A (1942–43), and Army Group South Ukraine (1943–44). He was promoted to field marshal on February 1, 1943, and was retired by Hitler for a second and final time on March 31, 1944. He was handed over to the Soviets after the war and died in a Russian prison. Although a highly capable officer, in 1940 he was inexperienced in armored operations and was considered a much more conservative commander than Guderian.

20. Fedor von Bock was born in Kuestrin, Pomerania, in 1880. He was educated at cadet schools and was commissioned directly into the 5th Guards Regiment of Foot in 1898. A pure soldier and nothing else, Bock was an incredibly brave man who earned the *Pour le Merite* on the Western Front in World War I. Later he was deeply involved in arming the *Freikorps*. A major general by 1929, he commanded Army Groups 1 (1938–39), North (1939), B (1939–41), and Center (1941). He was promoted to field marshal on July 19, 1940. The battle of Moscow and the crisis on the central sector during the Soviet winter offensive of 1941–42 proved too much for him, however, and he was never the same after that. Relieved at his own request on December 12, 1941, he was given command of Army Group South on January 16, 1942, following the collapse of Field Marshal Reichenau. Bock was sacked by Hitler on July 13, 1942, for showing timidity in the attack—a charge that seems to have been justified. He and his daughter were killed in an Allied fighter-bomber attack on May 3 or 4, 1945.

21. Born on August 7, 1889, Fritz Kuehn entered the army as a *Fahnenjunker* in 1909. After serving in the infantry in World War I, he joined the 6th Motorized

Battalion as a company commander in 1925. He commanded the I/3rd Artillery Regiment from 1931 to 1935, before assuming command of the 4th Panzer Regiment (1935–38). After a tour as commander of the Panzer Troops School (1938–39), Kuehn led the 14th Panzer Brigade (1939–40), 3rd Panzer Brigade (1940), 3rd Panzer Division (acting commander, 1940), 15th Panzer Division (1940–41), and 14th Panzer Division (1941–42). He subsequently was chief of army motorization from June 30, 1942, until February 14, 1944, when he was killed in an air raid in Berlin.

22. It is unclear what positions these two general staff officers had with the 5th Light Division. Bernuth was chief of staff of the XV Panzer Corps, and Lorenz had commanded the 3rd Panzer Reconnaissance Battalion but had since been given command of an infantry battalion. Bernuth later became chief of staff of the 4th Panzer Army but was killed in an airplane crash on the Eastern Front on July 12, 1942. Lorenz was commander of the 376th Infantry Regiment on the northern sector of the Russian Front on December 27, 1942, when he was mortally wounded. He died in Demyansk on January 2, 1943. Apparently both men were on temporary duty with the staff of the 5th Light Division in late 1940.

23. Thoma had previously been the general of mobile troops at OKH from March 5, 1940. He was now given command of the 17th Rifle Brigade of the 17th Panzer Division. From July 18 to September 15, 1941, he served as acting commander of the division during the Russian campaign, following the wounding of Lt. Gen. Hans-Juergen von Armin and the death of Maj. Gen. Ritter Karl von Weber. Later he commanded the 20th Panzer Division on the Eastern Front (1941–42) before returning to OKH for a second tour as general of mobile troops.

24. Wilhelm Keitel (1882–1946) was known by the German officer corps as the "Nodding Ass" and "Hitler's Lacky." He wanted to be a farmer, but the family estate was too small to be divided, so he joined the army as an officer-cadet in 1901 and was commissioned in the artillery. He fought in World War I, served in the *Reichsheer*, and was chief of the organizational branch of the army when Hitler assumed power. He proved to be very efficient at this post. Later he served as artillery commander III and deputy commander of the 3rd Infantry Division (1933–34) and commander of the 26th Infantry Division (1934–35), before being transferred to Berlin as the head of Field Marshal Blomberg's Armed Forces Office in the Defense Ministry. Whether by design or stupidity, he betrayed Blomberg (whose daughter was engaged to Keitel's son) by handing incriminating evidence concerning the field marshal's second wife's shady past to Hermann Goering and thus indirectly to Hitler. In the ensuing scandal, Blomberg was forced to retire on February 2, 1938. Hitler recognized in Keitel an officer whom he could easily dominate, so he abolished the War Ministry and named Keitel commander in chief of the High Command of the Armed Forces (OKW) on February 4—in effect, Blomberg's successor. Keitel rose from colonel in 1934 to field marshal on July 19, 1940. He was hanged at Nuremberg on October 16, 1940.

25. A biography of General Streich is found in Samuel W. Mitcham, Jr., *Rommel's Desert Commanders* (Westport, CT: Greenwood, 2007).

26. Rommel went on to earn fame as the "Desert Fox," successively commanding the Afrika Korps, Panzer Group Afrika, Panzer Army Afrika and Army Group Afrika. He was promoted to field marshal in 1942 and commanded Army

Group B in the Normandy campaign of 1944. He was forced to commit suicide on October 14, 1944, because of his part in the anti-Hitler conspiracy.

27. Biographies of most of these men are found in Samuel W. Mitcham, Jr., *Rommel's Lieutenants* (Westport, CT: Greenwood, 2006).

28. Hans von Luck, one of the few officers who preferred serving under Rommel rather than Funck, left an excellent memoir, *Panzer Commander* (New York: Praeger, 1989), which was in print as a paperback in 2007.

29. Rudolf Schmidt was born in Berlin in 1886 and entered the Imperial Army as a *Fahnenjunker* in 1906. Commissioned in the infantry, he fought in World War I, served in the *Reichsheer*, and was named commander of the 1st Panzer Division in 1937. Later he commanded the XXXIX Panzer Corps (1940–41), 2nd Army (November–December 1941), and 2nd Panzer Army (1941–43). He was promoted to general of panzer troops in June 1940 and colonel general on January 1, 1942. He proved to be an excellent commander at all levels.

   Hermann Hoth was born in 1885, attended various cadet schools, and joined the army as a *Faehnrich* (a senior officer-cadet or ensign) in 1904. Commissioned in the 17th Infantry Regiment in 1905, he fought in World War I, served in the *Reichsheer*, and was named commander of the 17th Infantry Regiment in 1932. Later he served as commandant of Luebeck (1933–34), infantry commander III, and one of the two deputy commanders of the 3rd Infantry Division (1934–35), and commander of the 18th Infantry Division (1935), XV Motorized Corps (1938–40), 3rd Panzer Group (1940–41), 17th Army (1941–42), and 4th Panzer Army (1942–43). After being branded a defeatist by Hitler on November 30, 1943, he was relieved of his command and never reemployed. Captured by American forces in May 1945, he was tried as a minor war criminal and sentenced to fifteen years' imprisonment in 1948. Hoth was confined to Landsberg Prison (where Hitler was incarcerated in 1924) and was released in April 1954. He retired to Goslar in the Harz Mountains, where he died in early 1971. Hoth has not had the enthusiastic admirers such as those who have immortalized Guderian and Manstein, although he later wrote a book entitled *Panzer Operationen* (Heidelberg, Germany: K. Vowinckel, 1956). Unfortunately, no British or American publisher secured rights of translation to it—probably a mistake.

30. Hans Wilhelm Karl Zorn was born in Munich on October 27, 1891. He was educated in the cadet schools and entered the service as a *Faehnrich* in the 2nd Bavarian Infantry Regiment in 1911. After twenty-seven years of service, he was named commander of the 19th Infantry Regiment on May 1, 1938. He was chief of staff of the XXVII Corps in Poland and France (1939–40), before assuming command of the 20th Motorized Division on November 10, 1940. He led this unit until January 13, 1942, when he became acting commander of the XXXX Panzer Corps. He was either wounded or fell ill on February 16 of that year and did not return to active duty until June 10, when he became acting commander of the XXXII Corps in France. He had been promoted to general of infantry on June 1. He returned to the Eastern Front as commander of the XXXXVI Panzer Corps on October 1, 1942, and was killed by a Soviet fighter-bomber near Krassnaja-Roschtscha on August 2, 1943.

31. For a biography of Friedrich Fuerst, see Mitcham, *Rommel's Lieutenants*. Franz Landgraf was born in Munich in 1888 and attended cadet schools in Bavaria. He joined the 5th Bavarian Infantry Regiment as a *Faehnrich* in 1909, fought in

World War I with various Bavarian infantry and *Jaeger* units, and was selected for the *Reichsheer*. He became commander of the 7th Panzer Regiment in 1936. He commanded the 4th Panzer Brigade from late 1939 to 1940 and assumed command of the 6th Panzer Division on January 6, 1941. He was transferred back to Germany in the spring of 1942 and assumed command of the 155th Replacement Panzer Division on May 1. Landgraf's health failed and he gave up command of the division on October 1. He died in Stuttgart on April 19, 1944.

32. Eduard Hauser (1895–1961) joined the 17th Bavarian Infantry Regiment as a *Fahnenjunker* in 1914. Commissioned in 1915, he became a platoon leader until he was wounded and captured by the British in September 1916. He later served in the *Reichsheer* and was a lieutenant colonel on the staff of the XIX Motorized Corps when World War II began. He was on the staff of the 3rd Panzer Brigade and 7th Panzer Division (1939–41); commanded the 25th Panzer Regiment (1941–43), 13th Panzer Division (1943–44), and Battle Group Hauser (1944); served on the staff of *SS Reichsfuehrer* Heinrich Himmler (1944); was commandant of Loetzen and Angerburg (1944); and commanded the 605th Special Purposes Division on the Eastern Front (1944–45). He was promoted to major general in 1943 and lieutenant general on June 1, 1944. He was commander of Fortress Pillau in the spring of 1945 and escaped on the last boat April 25, apparently after being wounded. He was in the hospital at Bad Toelz when it was captured by the Americans on May 9, 1945. His older brother was Lt. Gen. Wolfgang Hauser (1893–1973).

33. Georg-Hans Reinhardt (1887–1963) joined the army as a *Fahnenjunker* in 1907. By 1937, he was a major general commanding the 1st Rifle Brigade. Later he led the 4th Panzer Division (1939–40), XXXXI Panzer Corps (1940–41), 3rd Panzer Group (later Army) (1941–44), and Army Group Center (1944–45). He was promoted to colonel general on January 1, 1942. He was relieved of his command by Adolf Hitler for ordering an unauthorized retreat in East Prussia in early 1945, but he was not aware of it; he had been struck in the head by a Soviet bullet and did not recover until months after the war ended.

34. Hasso von Manteuffel was born in Potsdam in 1897. Educated in various cadet schools, he joined the 3rd Hussars on the Eastern Front as a *Faehnrich* in early 1916. A course commandant at the Panzer Troops School from 1939 to 1940, he missed the Polish campaign and most of the battle of France. He then commanded the I Battalion/7th Rifle Regiment, 6th Rifle Regiment, and 7th Panzer Grenadier Brigade, all on the Eastern Front (1941–42). He commanded an ad hoc division in Tunisia (1943) and was wounded in action. After he recovered, he returned to the Eastern Front, where he led the 7th Panzer Division (1943–44) and the elite *Grossdeutschland* Panzer Grenadier Division (1944). On September 1, 1944, he was promoted to general of panzer troops and named commander of the 5th Panzer Army, although he had never commanded a corps. He led this army in the battle of the Bulge. He was transferred to the command of the 3rd Panzer Army on the Eastern Front in 1945 and managed to surrender most of it to the Western Allies at the end of the war. After a successful postwar business career, Manteuffel died on September 24, 1978.

35. Wolfgang Thomale was born in 1900 in Lissa, Posen, now part of the Poznan province of Poland. He was educated in cadet schools and joined the 5th Guards Grenadier Regiment as a *Faehnrich* in late March 1918—in time to see action in the last days of World War I. The next year, he was promoted to

second lieutenant. He joined the OKH staff as an inspector of panzer troops in 1938. In May 1941, he assumed command of the II/25th Panzer Regiment and led the 27th Panzer Regiment from August 5, 1941, until the spring of 1942. He then returned to OKH, where he was on the staff of the chief of army equipment and later was attached to the office of Munitions Minister Albert Speer. On March 1, 1943, he became chief of staff to the inspector of panzer troops, a post he held until the end of the war. He was promoted to colonel in 1942, major general in 1944, and lieutenant general on March 1, 1945. He died in 1978.

36. Adelbert "Panzer" Schulz was born in Berlin on December 26, 1903, and was too young to fight in World War I. He was a police lieutenant in Berlin in 1934 and was commissioned directly into the army as a first lieutenant. He was promoted to colonel on November 1, 1943. Only two months later, on January 1, 1944, he was promoted to major general and given command of the 7th Panzer Division. Twenty-eight days later, he was killed in the battle of Schepetowka. Except for his brief divisional command, Schulz spent his entire army career in the 25th Panzer Regiment, successively serving as a company, battalion, and regimental commander.

37. Born in Danzig in 1893, Hermann Balck joined the army as an infantry officer-cadet in 1913. By 1938, he was a lieutenant colonel on the staff of the Panzer Inspectorate and was one of Guderian's most promising disciples. He distinguished himself in the French campaign as the commander of the 1st Rifle Regiment. Later he commanded the 3rd Panzer Regiment (1940–41), 2nd Panzer Brigade (1941), 11th Panzer Division (1942–43), and *Grossdeutschland* Panzer Grenadier Division and briefly the XIV Panzer Corps in Italy (1943). He was severely injured when his reconnaissance airplane crashed in October 1943. After a brief recovery, he returned to the East, where he commanded the XXXX Panzer Corps, XXXXVIII Panzer Corps, and 4th Panzer Army (1943–44). A holder of the Knight's Cross with Oak Leaves, Swords, and Diamonds, he was promoted to general of panzer troops on November 1, 1943. On September 21, 1944, he became commander in chief of Army Group G but was relieved on December 23, 1944, because he could not work with Heinrich Himmler. Balck, however, was named commander of the 6th Army on the southern sector of the Eastern Front, which he led to the end of the war. He died in Erbenbach-Rockenau, near Ludwigsburg, on November 29, 1982, at the age of eighty-nine.

38. Johannes Friessner (1892–1971) later commanded Army Detachment Narva, Army Group North and Army Group South Ukraine (later South). He was promoted to colonel general on July 1, 1944, but Hitler fired him on December 22 of that year.

39. Nikolaus von Vormann was born in Neumark, West Prussia, on Christmas Eve, 1895. He attended cadet schools but joined the army as a war volunteer in August 1914. Commissioned in the infantry in 1915, he served in the *Reichsheer*, joined the general staff, and became operations officer (Ia) of *Wehrkreis X* in 1938. During World War II, he served as a special duties officer at Fuehrer Headquarters (1939), chief of staff of the III Corps (1939–40) and XXVIII Corps (1940–42), commander of the 23rd Panzer Division (1942–43) and XXXXVII Panzer Corps (1943–44), and acting commander of the 9th Army (1944). He was then named fortress commander of OB Southeast (1944–45) and Alps (1945). He was promoted rapidly—to lieutenant colonel (1938), colonel (1940), major general (1943), lieutenant general (1943), and general

of panzer troops (1944). After being released from the POW camps, he retired to Berchtesgaden, where he died on October 26, 1959.

40. Baron Leo Geyr von Schweppenburg, called von Geyr, was born in Potsdam in 1886. He joined the 26th Dragoons as a *Fahnenjunker* in 1904. In 1931, he assumed command of the 14th Cavalry Division, and from 1933 to 1937, he served as military attache to London, Brussels, and The Hague. Later he led the 3rd Panzer Division (1937–40), XXIV Panzer Corps (1940–42), XXXX Panzer Corps (1942), and LVIII Panzer Corps (1942–43). He assumed command of Panzer Group West on January 24, 1944. He was promoted to major general in 1935, lieutenant general in 1937, and general of panzer troops on April 1, 1940.

41. Gen. of Waffen-SS Sepp Dietrich temporarily assumed command of Panzer Group West until it could be withdrawn to the Paris area to reorganize and rebuilt.

42. Baron von Geyr was named inspector of panzer troops in August 1944, a post he held until the end of the war. An American prisoner until July 1947, he retired to Irschenhausen, Upper Bavaria, and died on January 27, 1974.

43. Guenther von Kluge was born in Posen in 1882. He was educated in the cadet schools and joined the army as a second lieutenant in the 46th Field Artillery Regiment in 1901. A captain in 1914, he spent most of World War I as a general staff officer, although he did command a battalion of infantry on the Western Front (1915–16). He was seriously wounded at Verdun in 1918. Recognized as an energetic and efficient general staff officer, he was selected for the *Reichsheer* and in 1928 became chief of staff of the 1st Cavalry Division at Frankfurt-Oder. He commanded the 2nd Artillery Regiment (1930–31) and Artillery Command III (1931–33) before becoming inspector of signals troops in 1933. Later he commanded the 6th Infantry Division (1934–35), *Wehrkreis VI* (1935–38), Army Group 6 (1938–39), 4th Army (1939–41), and Army Group Center (1941–43). He was severely injured in an automobile accident on an icy road in Russia on October 28, 1943, and did not return to active duty until late June 1944.

44. Hans Eberbach, "Panzer Group Eberbach and the Falaise Encirclement," *Foreign Military Studies* MS # A-922, Historical Division, U.S. Army, Europe.

45. Field Marshal Kluge had been ordered to report to Berlin and was sure that his peripheral involvement in the anti-Hitler conspiracy had been discovered by the Gestapo. He was, in fact, correct, so he took poison. Hitler ordered him buried secretly, with a military honor guard but without full military honors. His son was relieved the following month and taken off active duty. The field marshal's younger brother, Lt. Gen. Wolfgang von Kluge (1892–1976), the commander of the 226th Infantry Division and commandant of Dunkirk, was also relieved in September and was discharged from the service on December 31, 1944.

46. Gustav-Adolf von Nostitz-Wallwitz was born in Oschatz, Saxony, in 1898. He entered the Imperial Army as a *Fahnenjunker* in 1917 and was commissioned in the 12th Field Artillery Regiment in 1918. After fighting in the last year of World War I, he was accepted into the *Reichsheer*. A major when World War II broke out, he commanded battalions in the 216th Artillery Regiment (1939–40) and 12th Artillery Regiment (1940), the 117th Artillery Regiment (1940), and the 89th Panzer Artillery Regiment (1941–42). He was seriously wounded in the battle of Stalingrad on September 3, 1942, and did not recover for some time. After leaving the 9th Panzer Division, Nostitz-Wallwitz was

named commander of the 24th Panzer Division, which he led from August 1, 1944, to March 1945. He was promoted to major general on November 9, 1944. He ended the war as commandant of Eckernfoerde, a town near Kiel. Apparently wounded in the last days of the war, he died here on May 31, 1945. Keilig, *Die Generale des Heeres*, 244.

47. Walter Schroth was born in 1882 in Glumbowitz, Silesia, now part of Poland. He entered the service as an officer-cadet in 1902 and was commissioned into the 46th Infantry Regiment the following year. He was a colonel when Adolf Hitler assumed power in 1933. During the era of the Third Reich, Schroth commanded the Infantry School (1933–35), 1st Infantry Division (1935–38), *Wehrkreis XII* (1938–39), XII Corps (1939–42), *Wehrkreis IV* (1942–43), and *Wehrkreis XII* (1943–44). He fought in France (1940) and on the central sector of the Russian Front.

48. Kurt von Berg (1886–1952) had commanded the older-age 556th Infantry Division in the French campaign. He had held no other active commands during the war, but had served as head of Recruiting Area Koblenz (1939–40 and 1940–44) and commandant of prisoner-of-war camps in the XII Military District (1944–45). He was succeeded by Gen. of Artillery Herbert Osterkamp on November 1, 1944.

49. Adolf von Schell (1893–1967), a native of Magdeburg, had joined the army as a *Fahnenjunker* in 1914. A brilliant staff officer, he was invited to attend the U.S. Army's Infantry School at Fort Benning, Georgia, and to present a series of lectures, based on his experiences on the Eastern and Western Fronts in World War I, in 1930 and 1931. They were considered so good that, in 1933, the U.S. Army published them as a field manual titled *Battle Leadership*. During World War II, he was an office group chief at OKH; then he was attached to the Reich's Transportation Ministry, where he rose to the rank of undersecretary of state. Promoted to lieutenant general in 1942, he left the ministry on September 9 and assumed command of the 25th Panzer Division on the Eastern Front on January 1, 1943. He gave up command on November 15 of that year and returned to Germany. No doubt seeing the writing on the wall regarding Nazi Germany, he retired on December 31, 1944.

50. Walter Wenck was born in Wittenberg, Saxony, in 1900 and entered the service as an officer-cadet in *Freikorps von Oven* in 1919. He held many important general staff positions in World War II, including chief of operations of the 1st Panzer Division (1939–42) and chief of staff of the LVII Panzer Corps (1942), the 3rd Romanian Army after it was routed by the Soviets during the Stalingrad campaign (1942), Army Detachment Hollidt (later redesignated the 6th Army) (1942–43), 1st Panzer Army (1943–44), and Army Group South Ukraine (1944). He returned to Berlin in that year as chief of the operations branch at OKH, before becoming deputy chief of the general staff. He was promoted to general of panzer troops effective April 1, 1945, and was named commander of the 12th Army on April 10. For some reason, even though he told the Fuehrer the unvarnished truth, Adolf Hitler liked him. A successful industrialist after the war, Wenck reportedly was offered the post of commander in chief of the West German Armed Forces (*Bundeswehr*) in the 1950s. He was killed in an automobile accident in Austria on May 1, 1982.

51. Wilhelm Burgdorf was born in Fuerstenwalde on the Spree on February 15, 1895. He entered the service as a *Fahnenjunker* with the 12th Grenadier Regiment when

World War I broke out. A strong Nazi, he served as adjutant of *Wekrkreis IX* (1937–39), adjutant of the IX Corps (1939–40), and commander of the 529th Infantry Regiment (1940–42). He joined the Army Personnel Office as a branch chief on May 1, 1942, became deputy chief of the office later that year, and became acting chief of the HPA on July 20, 1944. On October 1, he became permanent chief when General Schmundt died of the wounds he had received on July 20. Burgdorf was promoted to colonel in 1940, major general on October 1, 1942; lieutenant general on October 1, 1943; and general of infantry on November 1, 1944. Known as the "Gravedigger of the Officer Corps," he helped force Field Marshal Rommel to commit suicide and, as Hitler's instrument, was partially responsible for the deaths or dismissals of many other officers. He committed suicide when Berlin fell to the Soviets, probably on May 1, 1945.

52. With Hoepner's full knowledge, the anti-Hitler conspirators had earmarked him to be named commander in chief of the Replacement Army after Hitler had been deposed. Hoepner showed up at the *Bendlerstrasse* on July 20, 1944, but when he realized the coup would fail, he berated Stauffenberg and his associates and stormed out of the building. He was arrested the next day, convicted of high treason on August 7, and hanged in the Berlin-Ploetzensee Prison on August 8, 1944.

53. Hitler thought very highly of Gen. of Panzer Troops Rudolf Schmidt, who rose to the command of the 2nd Panzer Army on the Eastern Front in late 1941, and promoted him to colonel general effective January 1, 1942. The feeling was not reciprocated. In 1943, the Gestapo arrested Schmidt's civilian brother and searched his house, uncovering several letters from the general that revealed his true opinion of Hitler and his intelligence level and of the Nazi regime. The SS (probably Himmler) showed the letters to the Fuehrer. Schmidt was immediately relieved of his command on July 10, 1943, during the middle of the battle of Kursk. He was discharged from the army that fall and was lucky he did not end up in a concentration camp. He died at Krefeld in 1957.

CHAPTER 2. BARON HARALD VON ELVERFELDT

1. Dermot Bradley, Karl-Friedrich Hildebrand and Marcus Roevekamp, *Die Generale des Heeres, 1921–1945* (Osnabrueck, Germany: Biblio, 1993–2004), 3: 329–30.

2. Wolfgang Fleck was born in Berlin on May 16, 1879. He was educated in the cadet schools and entered the Imperial Army as a second lieutenant in the 71st Infantry Regiment on March 13, 1897. In 1928, he became the commander of the elite 9th Infantry Regiment, referred to as "I.R. von 9" by the men of the *Reichsheer* because of its aristocratic officer corps. Fleck became infantry leader III—the leader of Infantry Command III and deputy commander of the 3rd Infantry Division in Berlin. He assumed command of Wehrkreis VI and the 6th Infantry Division on May 1, 1931. He was promoted to major general in 1929 and lieutenant general on February 1, 1930, and was officially retired as an honorary general of infantry on October 1, 1934, although apparently he had not held an appointment for more than a year. He was also named honorary colonel of the 9th Infantry Regiment. He died at Freiburg, Brunswick, on February 2, 1939.

3. Wilhelm Adam (1877–1949) later commanded the 7th Infantry Division (1933–35) and the short-lived *Wehrmacht* Academy (1935–36). In 1938, he

directed Army Group 2 on the West Wall, while the main German forces prepared to invade Czechoslovakia. In this post, he annoyed Hitler by making too
honest a report on the deficiencies of the West Wall. He was retired at the end
of 1938 with the honorary title of colonel general and was never reemployed.
He was, however, known as the "father" of the German mountain troops
branch.

Ludwig Beck was born in Bieberich in the Rhineland on June 29, 1880. He
joined the army as a *Fahnenjunker* in the 15th Artillery Regiment in 1898, was
commissioned in 1899, and became adjutant of the I Battalion in 1903. He
remained with his regiment until he was selected to attend the War Academy
for general staff training in 1911. After graduating in 1914, he spent World War
I as a general staff officer in the VI Reserve Corps (1914–15), 117th Infantry
Division (1915–16), and 13th Reserve Division (1916), and then served on the
staff of the crown prince (1916–18). He remained in general staff positions
until 1929, when he assumed command of the 5th Artillery Regiment. After
serving on the staff of Group Command 1 in Berlin (1931–32), Beck became
Artillery Leader IV (1932) and commander of the 1st Cavalry Division
(1932–33). He was chief of the General Staff from October 1, 1933, to August
27, 1938, when he resigned in protest of Hitler's aggressive foreign policy—the
only senior general to do so. He received an honorary promotion to colonel
general on November 1, 1938. Deeply involved in the anti-Hitler conspiracy,
Beck shot himself on the night of July 20, 1944, but succeeded only in critically
wounding himself. Col. Gen. Fritz Fromm, the commander in chief of the
Replacement Army, had a sergeant finish him off. Bradley et al., *Die Generale des
Heeres* 1: 251–52.

4. Franz Halder was born in Wuerzburg on June 30, 1884 and joined the Bavarian
Army as a *Fahnenjunker* in 1902. Commissioned in the Bavarian 3rd Field
Artillery Regiment in 1904, he attended the Bavarian War Academy (1911–14)
and was a general staff officer throughout World War I, serving on the staffs of
the III Corps, 6th Infantry Division, 2nd Army, and 4th Army. During the *Reichswehr* era, he served mainly as a tactics instructor and a training staff officer in
Bavaria. Promoted to colonel on December 1, 1931, he became chief of staff of
Wehrkreis VI in Muenster (Westphalia) and was named artillery commander VII
and deputy commander of the 7th Infantry Division in Munich on February 1,
1933. He assumed command of the 7th Infantry Division on October 1, 1935,
and became chief of the maneuver staff of the Troop Office on October 5,
1936. He then became chief of training (1937), chief of operations of the High
Command of the Army (1938), and chief of the general staff (1938). Halder
was promoted to major general (1934), lieutenant general (1936), general of
artillery (1938), and colonel general (1940). He was relieved of his duties by
Hitler on September 24, 1942, and forced into retirement. Halder had been an
anti-Hitler conspirator in 1938 but had disassociated himself from the plot the
next year. He was arrested by the Gestapo on July 21, 1944, and spent the rest of
the war in the Dachau and Flossenburg concentration camps. He was freed by
the Americans in the Austrian Tyrol on May 4, 1945, but spent the next two
years in Allied POW camps. Finally released, he spent the rest of his life as a
writer and an adviser to the U.S. Army Historical Division. His books include
Hitler as War Lord and *The Halder Diaries*. He died at Aschau im Chiemgau,
Bavaria, on April 2, 1972.

5. Adolf Kuntzen was born in Magdeburg in 1889. He was educated in cadet schools, entered the Imperial Army as a *Faehnrich* in 1909, and was commissioned in the 1st Hussar Regiment in 1910. He fought in World War I and served with the 7th Hussars until early 1917, when he underwent general staff training. He was on the general staff of the military governor of Metz in 1918 and ended the war as a general staff officer, 10th Replacement Division. He remained in the *Reichsheer* and in the 1920s served in general staff, cavalry, and Defense Ministry assignments. From 1929 to 1938, he was in the Army Personnel Office, rising to assistant chief. Turned out of his post as a result of the Hitler-Brauchitsch deal, he assumed command of the 3rd Light (later 8th Panzer) Division in 1938 and led it until February 1941. A month later, he became commander of the LVII Panzer Corps, and from April 1, 1942, to September 4, 1944, was commander of the XXXII Corps Command (subsequently LXXXI Corps). He was promoted to lieutenant colonel (1932), colonel (1934), major general (1938), lieutenant general (1940) and general of panzer troops (1941). He was sacked in the fall of 1944 because he could not keep Patton's U.S. 3rd Army from overrunning much of northern France and was never reemployed. Kuntzen had not done a particularly good job as corps commander either. He died in Hanover, Lower Saxony, in 1964.

6. Johann Joachim "Hajo" Stever was born in Berlin in 1889 and entered the service as a *Fahnenjunker* in 1908. Commissioned in the infantry the following year, he served in World War I and the *Reichsheer*. As a colonel, he became chief of staff of the XV Motorized Corps in 1938. Promoted to major general in 1939–40, he led the 4th Panzer Division in 1940, but was considered a mediocre panzer commander. He was sent back to the infantry late that year and led the 336th Infantry Division during its formational and training phases (1940–42), but did not accompany it to Russia in 1942. He was given a field administrative command later that year and in the fall of 1943 was a special purposes officer on the staff of Army Group Center. Despite a promotion to lieutenant general on June 1, 1941, he was not considered a particularly good commander (largely because of his questionable health) and was retired in the spring of 1944. He disappeared in May 1945, when the Soviets overran his town, and has not been heard from since.

7. Count Hans Theodor von Sponeck was born in Duesseldorf in 1888. Educated in various cadet schools, he entered the army as a second lieutenant in the 5th Grenadier Guards Regiment in 1908. After serving in World War I and the *Reichsheer*, he was given command of the 22nd Air Landing Division on October 1, 1938 and led it in the invasion of the Netherlands, where he was seriously wounded in May 1940. Meanwhile, he was promoted to major general (1938) and lieutenant general (1940). He was given command of the XXXXII Corps in the Crimea on October 10, 1941 and led it in a disastrous retreat in December. This led to his being relieved of his command and thrown in prison at the end of the year. He was held without trial until the July 20, 1944, assassination attempt on Hitler failed. Three days later, Sponeck was shot by the SS. His brother Theodor (1896–1992), who also rose to the rank of lieutenant general, commanded the 90th Light Division and was captured when Tunisia fell in May 1943.

8. Julius von Bernuth was born in 1897 in Metz, then part of Germany. He entered the service as a *Faehnrich* in 1914 and was commissioned in the 115th

Infantry Regiment later that year. He served in World War I and in the *Reichsheer* and became an instructor at the War Academy in 1937. He was operations officer (Ia) of Panzer *Verbaende* East Prussia in Poland in 1939. After leaving the XV Motorized Corps, he became chief of the Training Branch of OKH in October 1940. He was chief of staff of the 4th Army on January 10, 1942, and became chief of staff of the 4th Panzer Army three months later, on April 27. He was promoted to lieutenant colonel in 1939, colonel in 1940, and major general on April 1, 1942. An officer of great promise, he was killed in an airplane crash near Ssochkranaja, Russia, on July 27, 1942.

9. Considered by many to be the greatest general to emerge from World War II, Fritz Erich von Lewinski genannt von Manstein was born in Berlin on November 24, 1887, the tenth child of Gen. of Artillery Eduard von Lewinski (1829–1906). Frau Lewinski's sister was childless, however, so the Lewinskis allowed her to adopt him. His stepfather was Lt. Gen. Georg von Manstein, and his uncle was future Field Marshal Paul von Hindenburg. His brother, August Alfred Friedrich von Lewinski (1866–1957), retired as a major general in 1921. Young Manstein was educated in the cadet schools and entered the army as an officer-cadet in the 3rd Prussian Foot Guards Regiment in 1907. He attended the War Academy (1913–14) and fought in Belgium and East Prussia, where he was seriously wounded in November 1914. Returning to duty in mid-1915, he served successively as adjutant of the 12th Army, general staff officer with the 11th and 1st Armies on the Eastern and Western Fronts, Ia of the 4th Cavalry Division in Estonia and Courland, and general staff officer of the 213th Assault Infantry Division on the Western Front in 1918. During the *Reichswehr* era, Manstein served in various staff positions and as a company and battalion commander. During the Hitler era, he served as chief of staff of *Wehrkreis III* (1934–35); chief of operations of the general staff (1935–36); deputy chief of the general staff and *Oberquartiermeister I* (1936–38); commander of the 18th Infantry Division (1938–39); chief of staff of Army Group South (1939) and Army Group A (1939–40); commander of the XXXVIII Corps (1940–41), LVI Panzer Corps (1941), and 11th Army (1941–42); and commander in chief of Army Groups Don (1942–43) and South (1943–44). He was promoted rapidly, from colonel in 1933 to field marshal on July 1, 1942. Hitler—who feared him—sent him into forced retirement on March 31, 1944. He was never reemployed. He was sentenced to eighteen years' imprisonment in 1950 but was released for medical reasons in 1953. In retirement, he wrote his memoirs, *Lost Victories*, which were considered a classic. He died in Irschenhausen, Upper Bavaria, on June 12, 1973.

10. Erich Detleffsen was born in Kiel in 1904. He joined the *Reichsheer* as a *Fahnenjunker* in 1923 and was commissioned second lieutenant in the 8th Infantry Regiment in late 1927. He entered the clandestine general staff in the 1930s. During World War II, he served as Ia of the XXXV Corps Command (1939), on the general staff of OKH (1939–41), as Ia of the LVI Panzer Corps (1941–42) and the 330th Infantry Division (1942), as a tactics instructor at the War Academy (1942–43), and as chief of staff of the XXXIX Panzer Corps (1943–44) and 4th Army (1944–45). He was promoted to major (1940), lieutenant colonel (1942), colonel (1943), and major general (1944). He was chief of the Leadership Group at OKH for a month before becoming chief of staff of Army Group Vistula on April 29, 1945. A British POW until 1948, he died in Munich on July 4, 1980.

11. Erich von Manstein, *Lost Victories*, Anthony G. Powell, ed. and trans. (Novato, CA: Presidio, 1982), 190–92.

12. Ibid.

13. Wolfgang Fischer, who was born in Upper Silesia in 1888, entered the army as an infantry officer-cadet in 1910. He remained in the *Reichswehr* and was promoted to colonel in 1937. He led the 69th Infantry Regiment (1938–39), 10th Rifle Brigade (1939–41) and 10th Panzer Division (1941–43). Promoted to lieutenant general on November 1, 1942, he was mortally wounded in Tunisia on February 1, 1943, when his command car struck a mine and both his legs and his left arm were blown off. With iron self-control, he wrote a farewell letter to his wife as he bled to death. He was posthumously promoted to general of panzer troops.

14. Hans Krebs was born in Helmstedt, Lower Saxony, in 1889. He joined the army as an officer-cadet in the 78th Infantry Regiment when World War I broke out. He served in infantry and machine-gun units and was seriously wounded in mid-1915. Krebs was selected for the *Reichsheer* and remained in infantry units until 1929, when he began general staff training. During World War II, he served as chief of the Army Training Branch (1939) and chief of staff of the VII Corps (1939–42), 9th Army (early 1942–43), Army Group Center (1943–44), and Army Group B (1944–45). Promoted to lieutenant colonel in early 1939, he became a colonel (1940), major general (1942), lieutenant general (1943), and a general of infantry (1944). Krebs was named acting chief of the general staff on February 17, 1945. He was wounded in the U.S. Air Force's attack on Zossen on March 15, 1945 and committed suicide by shooting himself with a pistol in Berlin at 9:30 P.M. on May 1, 1945. Bradley et al., *Die Generale des Heeres* 7: 187–89.

15. Born in Freiberg, Burnswick, in 1889, Ferdinand Schaal joined the army as a *Fahnenjunker* in the dragoons in 1908. He was already a lieutenant general when World War II broke out. He commanded the 10th Panzer Division (1939–41), Afrika Korps (for two weeks in 1941), and LVI Panzer Corps (1941–43). After returning to Germany, he was named commander of *Wehrkreis* Bohemia and Moravia on September 1, 1943. He was involved in the anti-Hitler conspiracy and was arrested on July 21, 1944, the day after the Stauffenberg assassination attempt failed. Thrown into prison, he nevertheless survived the war and died in Konstanz on October 9, 1962.

16. Rudolf Schmundt was born in Metz on August 13, 1896. He joined the army as an officer-cadet in August 1914, when World War I began, and was commissioned in the 35th Infantry Regiment in 1915. He was a major in 1938 when he became chief adjutant to Adolf Hitler. Although not considered particularly bright, he was nevertheless thought to be a very effective personal officer. He was promoted rapidly after joining Hitler's staff—to lieutenant colonel (1938), colonel (1939), major general (1942) and lieutenant general (1943). On October 2, 1942, he added the post of chief of the Army Personnel Office to his duties. He was critically wounded and blinded during the July 20, 1944, assassination attempt. Hitler promoted him to general of infantry on September 1, but Schmundt died of his wounds on October 1, 1944.

17. Ritter Wolfdietrich von Xylander was born in Munich in 1903. He joined the *Reichsheer* as an officer-cadet in 1921 and was commissioned in the 19th Infantry Regiment in late 1924. By 1936, he had graduated from the War Academy and was a major on the general staff. In World War II, he served as chief intelligence

officer (Ic) of the 206th Infantry Division (1939–40), Ia of the 30th Infantry Division (1940–41), and chief of staff of the LI Corps (1941–43), 17th Army (1943–44), and Army Groups North Ukraine (1944), A (1944–45), and Center (1945). He was promoted to lieutenant colonel (1940), colonel (1943), major general (1944), and lieutenant general (1944). He fought in the Polish campaign, in France, and on the Eastern Front. Xylander was killed on the Eastern Front when his airplane crashed on February 15, 1945.

18. Gerhard Mueller was born in Breslau, Silesia, in 1896. He entered the Imperial Army as a *Fahnenjunker* in 1915 and was commissioned in the 154th Infantry Regiment the following year. He was not accepted into the *Reichsheer*, so he joined the police in 1920. When Hitler began his military expansion in 1935, Mueller reentered the service as a captain. In 1938, he was a major, commanding the 33rd Anti-Tank Battalion. He assumed command of the I Battalion/33rd Panzer Regiment on January 1, 1941, and led it for a week on the Russian Front. Here he lost an arm and was not able to return to active duty until February 1, 1942, when he assumed command of the 5th Panzer Regiment of the Afrika Korps. After distinguishing himself in Libya and Egypt, where he earned the Knight's Cross, Mueller served as a branch chief at OKH. Although still only a colonel, he served brief tours as acting commander of the 12th Infantry Division (1942) and the 116th Panzer Grenadier Division (1944). He was promoted to major general on September 1, 1944, the day he assumed command of the 9th Panzer Division. His leadership of the 116th Panzer Grenadier and the 9th Panzer, however, was considered unsatisfactory. He was relieved on September 16, his career ruined. He ended the war as deputy commandant of the city of Pilsen. He died in Landau in 1977.

19. Hugh M. Cole, *The Lorraine Campaign* (Washington, DC: Historical Division, Department of the Army, 1950), 212

20. Karl Rudolf Gerd von Rundstedt, the son of a Hussar officer, was born on December 12, 1875, at Aschersleben in the Harz Mountains. He attended cadet schools and graduated from Gross-Lichterfelde, the German equivalent of West Point, entering the Imperial Army in 1892 at the age of sixteen. Commissioned in the 83rd Royal Prussian Infantry Regiment the following year, Rundstedt became a member of the general staff in 1909. He spent most of World War I on the Eastern Front and joined the *Reichsheer* as a major. Promoted unusually rapidly in the Weimar era, he became commander of the 2nd Cavalry Division in 1928. In 1932, he served briefly as commander of the 3rd Infantry Division; later that year, he was given command of Army Group 1. He retired for the first time in 1938 but returned to active duty the following year and led Army Group South in the invasion of Poland. He later commanded Army Group B (later South) in the French campaign (1940) and on the Russian Front (1941). Hitler sacked him for the first time in December 1941 but recalled him to command OB West in March 1942.

21. Cole, *Lorraine Campaign*, 212.

22. Hans-Joachim Deckert was born in Tennrode, Thuringia, in 1904. He joined the *Reichsheer* in 1924 and earned his commission in the 4th Artillery Regiment in 1928. He commanded the 2nd Company, 4th Forward Observer Battalion (1936–39), in Poland; was an instructor in the forward observer course at the Artillery School at Jueterbog (1939–40); and was on the staff of the 302nd Higher Artillery Command during the Battle of France. Later, he commanded

the 35th Forward Observer Battalion (1940–42), returned to the Artillery School as an instructor (1942–43), and commanded the II/76th Panzer Artillery Regiment (1943) and then the regiment itself (1943–44). From October 10, 1944, to January 28, 1945, he was acting commander of the 15th Panzer Grenadier Division. He was promoted to major general on January 30 and on March 20 was named commander of the 19th Panzer Division on the Eastern Front. He was held in Soviet prisons from May 10, 1945, until October 1955. He died in Bielefeld in 1988.

23. Bodo Zimmermann was born in Metz in 1886. He attended the cadet schools, entered the service as a *Fahnenjunker* in 1904, and earned his commission in the infantry the following year. He fought in World War I but was discharged with the rank of major in 1920. Zimmermann rejoined the army around 1935 and served during World War II on the operations staff of the 1st Army (1939–40), as Ia of Army Group D in France (1940–43), and as Ic of OB West (1943–end). He was promoted to lieutenant colonel (1941), colonel (1942), major general (1944), and lieutenant general (1945). He retired to Bonn and died in 1963.

24. Meinrad von Lauchert was born in Potsdam on August 29, 1905. He joined the army as an officer-cadet in 1924 and was commissioned in the 5th Cavalry Regiment in 1931. By 1938, he was a company commander in the 35th Panzer Regiment in Bamberg. He led the I Battalion, 35th Panzer Regiment, in Poland, France, and on the Eastern Front (1939–43). In August 1943, he assumed command of the 15th Panzer Regiment, which he led until August 1, 1944. He apparently was wounded and did not return to active duty until December 15, 1944, when, to his amazement, he was given command of the 2nd Panzer Division— the day before the battle of the Bulge began. Despite his lack of familiarity with his unit, he distinguished himself during the Ardennes Offensive, and the 2nd Panzer gained more ground than any other German division. It also suffered appalling casualties when its spearhead was cut off and destroyed by the Allies. Lauchert was promoted to major general on March 1, 1945. On or about March 20, the division was pushed against the Rhine River without a crossing point in its rear. Lauchert ordered the division to break into small groups and escape any way it could. The major general swam across the Rhine, then deserted and walked to his home in Bamberg, apparently assuming that the Nazis would conclude that he had been either killed or captured and would not look for him. He was right. He lived in various locations after the war and died in Moehringen, a suburb of Stuttgart, on December 4, 1987, at the age of eighty-two.

25. Friedrich Wilhelm von Mellenthin, called "F. W.," was born in Breslau, Silesia (now Wroclaw, Poland), on August 30, 1904, the son of an old Prussian family. His father rose to the rank of lieutenant colonel before he was killed in action while directing artillery fire on the Western Front in 1918. Mellenthin was educated on the family estates and joined the army as an officer-cadet in the 7th Cavalry Regiment in 1924. He was an outstanding equestrian who won many gold trophies for horse racing, steeplechasing and dressage. Because of the slow rate of promotions in the *Reichsheer*, he was not commissioned until 1928. He remained with his regiment until 1935, when he began general staff training. In 1937, he was named Ic of *Wehrkreis III*. When the war began, this headquarters was divided, and Mellenthin went to Poland with the III Corps. After Warsaw fell, he was named Ia of the 197th Infantry Division, which played a minor role in the conquest of France. Following a brief period of occupation

duty in the Netherlands, he was named Ic of the 1st Army in France. In 1941 he held the same post in the 2nd Army, which saw action in the conquest of Yugoslavia. Mellenthin then became liaison officer to the Italian 2nd Army, before being sent to North Africa, where he became Ic of Panzer Group (later Army) Afrika. On June 1, 1942, he became Rommel's chief of operations, after the chief of staff and I-A were both wounded. He won the Knight's Cross in the first battle of El Alamein for personally repulsing a major Australian attack with a hastily assembled battle group. Shortly afterward, he contracted amoebic dysentery and was medically evacuated back to Germany. Following his partial recovery, he became chief of staff of the XXXXVIII Panzer Corps on the Eastern Front. He briefly served as acting commander of the 8th Panzer Division in July 1944 and was chief of staff of the 4th Panzer Army from August 15 to September 14 of that year. Then he became chief of staff of Army Group G on the Western Front.

Mellenthin had a dispute with General Guderian in late November 1944 and was sacked by the chief of the general staff. Ironically, his promotion to major general came through on December 1, 1944, while he was under house arrest. In late December he was allowed to return to the Western Front, where he commanded the 9th Panzer Division in the final stages of the battle of the Bulge. After working his way out of Guderian's doghouse, he was named chief of staff of the 5th Panzer Army. He escaped the Ruhr Pocket but was captured by the Americans on May 3, 1945. Mellenthin, now a homeless father of five, was released from the POW camps and started life over in the business world in 1948. He emigrated to South Africa in 1950, started his own airline, and died a millionaire at the age of ninety-two on June 28, 1997. He is the author of the World War II classic *Panzer Battles: A Study in the Employment of Armor in the Second World War* (Norman: University of Oklahoma Press, 1956), which was first published in 1956.

26. Mellenthin, *Panzer Battles*, 341.
27. Ibid., 341–42, 367.
28. Friedrich Koechling was a typical solid German corps commander. He was born in 1893 in Ahaus, in the North Rhine-Westphalia district, about 100 miles north of Cologne. He joined the army as an officer-cadet and was commissioned in the 159th Infantry Regiment in 1913. During World War I, he served as a company commander, machine-gun officer, and regimental adjutant, all with the 159th. He ended the war commanding the regiment's III Battalion—a high post indeed for a lieutenant. He was accepted into the *Reichsheer* in 1919 and spent the Weimar era in various infantry assignments. In late 1938, he was an office group chief in the Army Weapons Office. Promoted to colonel in 1939, he led the 287th Infantry Regiment (1939–42) in the Saar, in France, and on the Russian Front. He led the 254th Infantry Division on the northern sector of the Eastern Front until September 5, 1942, when he apparently was wounded. He did not returned to active duty until October 1943, when he became deputy *Wehrmacht* commander of the Crimea. On December 1, he became acting commander of the XXXXIV Corps on the southern sector of the Eastern Front. He returned to the Crimea as acting commander of the XXXXIX Mountain Corps in February 1944. He was promoted to major general (1942), lieutenant general (1943), and general of infantry (1944). General Koechling was unemployed (and possibly on leave) from March to June 1944, when he returned to the northern sector of the

Eastern Front as commander of the X Corps, but he was suddenly sent to the Western Front and, on September 9, assumed command of the LXXXI Corps, which he led for the rest of the war. He retired to Coesfeld-Legden (near his hometown of Ahaus) after the war and died there on June 6, 1970.

29. Cole, *Lorraine Campaign*, 233.
30. Keilig, *Die Generale des Heeres*, 80.

CHAPTER 3. ERWIN JOLLASSE

1. Erwin Jollasse, "9th Panzer Division (24 Jul–4 Sep 1944)," *Foreign Military Studies* MS # B-837, Historical Division, U.S. Army, Europe.

2. Hans Schreppfer was born in Brandenburg on April 1, 1893, and joined the army as a *Fahnenjunker* in 1911. He was commissioned in 1912 and fought in World War I but was not selected for the *Reichsheer*. He was in the police from 1920 to 1935, when he was allowed to join the *Luftwaffe* as a major during Hitler's initial military expansion. He transferred to the army as a lieutenant colonel in 1937 and was named commander of the I Battalion, 76th Infantry Regiment (1937–39). After the Polish campaign, he was given command of the 86th Rifle Regiment (1939–40) and was promoted to colonel on December 1, 1939. He later commanded the 101st Rifle Regiment (1941) and 18th Rifle Brigade (1941–42). His performance as a brigade commander apparently was less than satisfactory, for he was never given a division. After recovering from the injuries he suffered in an automobile accident on March 6, he was named Mobile Troops Commander VI (1942–44) and then directed the 675th Field Administrative Command from February 1944 until his retirement a year later. He received a belated promotion to major general on December 1, 1943. He settled in Koblenz after the war.

3. Johannes Schraepler was born in Wessnig-Torgau, on the Elbe River in Saxony, in 1896. He joined the army as an officer-cadet when World War I broke out and was commissioned in the 74th Field Artillery Regiment in 1915. He joined the *Reichswehr* in 1920 and, as a lieutenant colonel, assumed command of the 20th Observer Battalion in 1936. He led this unit until late 1939, when he joined the artillery staff of the 2nd Army. Promoted to colonel on January 1, 1940, he commanded the 88th Panzer Artillery Regiment from October 1 until late 1941. In early 1942, he became a course commander at the Artillery School at Jueterbog (1942–43), before taking charge of the 144th Artillery Command in late 1943. He led the 120th Artillery Command in France from July 3 to August 21, 1944, when he was captured by the Americans. He was promoted to major general on October 1, while still in captivity. He settled in Bad Godesberg after the war. I was unable to find a report indicating that Schraepler commanded the antitank battalion of the 20th Motorized Division as Stauffenberg states, but that does not mean he did not do so.

4. Max Sperling was born in Kulm on September 4, 1905. He joined the Prussian 4th Infantry Regiment at Neustettin in 1924 and was promoted to second lieutenant on February 1, 1928. He led the 11th Company of the 11th Infantry Regiment in the Polish campaign (1939) and was regimental adjutant of the 11th in France (1940). He assumed command of the III Battalion/101st Infantry (later Rifle) Regiment in September 1940 and took command of the 18th Motorcycle Battalion in March 1943, before leading the 88th Panzer

Reconnaissance Battalion (1941–43). In July 1943, he was given command of his old regiment, now designated the 11th Panzer Grenadier. Promoted to colonel on June 1, 1944, he became acting commander of the 9th Panzer Division on August 10 but led it for only three weeks. In September, he was so seriously wounded by an Allied fighter-bomber that he was placed in Fuehrer Reserve on October 1 and remained there for the rest of the war. He was in a hospital in Leipzig when the war ended. In 1956, Sperling returned to active duty with the West German Army, served in the new 5th Panzer Division, and later became deputy commander of the Panzer Troops School at Muenster. He retired in 1962 and died on June 6, 1984.

5. Max Fremerey was born in Cologne in 1889 and joined the Imperial Army as a *Fahnenjunker* in the 7th Dragoon Regiment. He was commissioned the following year. He remained in the cavalry during the war years, throughout the Weimar era and well into the Third Reich, commanding the 17th Cavalry Regiment (1934–39) and the 3rd Higher Cavalry Command (1939). He was given command of the 480th Infantry Regiment when World War II broke out. This unit, which was made up of reservists, was on the Western Front during the "Phony War" of 1939–40 and was only lightly engaged during the French campaign. It was nevertheless motorized in the fall of 1940. Fremerey, meanwhile, was given command, in October 1940, of the 18th Rifle Brigade, of which his former regiment was a part, was promoted to major general on June 1, 1941, and assumed command of the elite 29th Motorized Division on September 20 of that year. He led his division until September 28, 1942, when it was engaged in the early stages of the battle of Stalingrad. Fremerey, however, apparently fell ill; in any case, he was sent back to Germany and did not return to active duty until February 1, 1943, when he became commandant of Hanover. Promoted to lieutenant general on June 1, he did not see further field service but did command the 155th Reserve Panzer Division (1943–44) and the 233rd Reserve Panzer Division (1944–45). He was a POW until 1947 and then retired to Kruen, Upper Bavaria, where he died on September 20, 1968.

6. Count Hyazinth Strachwitz von Gross-Zauche und Camminetz was born on one of his family's estates in Upper Silesia in 1893. He joined the army as an officer-cadet in the summer of 1912, was commissioned in the cavalry in early 1914, and was captured in a raid behind French lines later that year. His application for an appointment in the *Reichsheer* was rejected, and he was discharged from the service in 1920, but he returned to the army as a *Rittmeister* (captain of cavalry) of reserves in the 7th Cavalry Regiment in 1935. During World War II, he was promoted rapidly, to major of reserves (1940), lieutenant colonel of reserves (1942), colonel of reserves (1943), major general of reserves (1944), and lieutenant general of reserves (1945). In the process, he gained an armywide reputation as a fearless man and a daring raider, earning the Knight's Cross with Oak Leaves, Swords, and Diamonds. He commanded a company and a battalion in the 2nd Panzer Regiment (1939–42), as well as the elite *Grossdeutschland* Panzer Regiment (1943), and served as higher panzer officer for Army Group North (1943–44) and Silesia (1945). After the war, he worked as a military and agricultural consultant for the government of Syria, until he was forced to flee following a military revolt. He died penniless in West Germany in 1951.

7. Walter Nehring was born in Stretzin, West Prussia (now Poland), in 1892, the son of a schoolteacher. He joined the army as an officer-cadet in the 152nd

Infantry Regiment in 1911 and fought in World War I, where he served on both the Eastern and Western Fronts and was seriously wounded three times. He also underwent flight training for a week but dropped out after the airplane in which he was riding as an observer crashed and he broke his jaw. He served as a platoon leader, battalion adjutant, and machine-gun company commander. After the war, he joined the *Freikorps* and fought against the Poles. He was accepted into the *Reichsheer* and began general staff training in 1923. After being admitted into the clandestine General Staff, he served in motorized and armored assignments thereafter. An early convert to mobile warfare, he was involved in the Spanish Civil War, commanded the 5th Panzer Regiment (1937–39), and was chief of staff of the XIX Motorized Corps (1939–40) and Panzer Group Guderian (1940). He commanded the 18th Panzer Division (1940–42) on the Eastern Front and led the Afrika Korps (1942) until he was seriously wounded at Alma Halfa Ridge. Before he had fully recovered, Nehring was given command of the ad hoc XC Corps and checked Eisenhower's advance on Tunis in late 1942. He was passed over for promotion to commander of the 5th Panzer Army in Tunisia because he informed Hitler that the country could not be held in the long run, leading Goebbels to brand him a defeatist. The fact that he was proven correct did not help Nehring. He was, however, considered too talented to simply sack, so he was given command of the XXIV Panzer Corps on the Eastern Front (1943–45). In the last weeks of the war, he commanded the 1st Panzer Army. He was a POW until 1947 and died in Duesseldorf on April 20, 1983. A general of panzer troops since July 1, 1942, he held the Knight's Cross with Oak Leaves, Swords, and Diamonds.

8. Baron Karl von Thuengen-Rossbach was born in Mainz in the Rhineland-Palatinate on March 26, 1893. He joined the Imperial Army as an officer-cadet in the 5th Dragoons in 1912 and was commissioned second lieutenant the following year. He fought in World War I, served in the *Reichsheer*, and was a colonel on the staff of OKH when World War II began. He was immediately given command of the 254th Replacement Regiment in Westphalia. In early 1940, he received a command more to his liking: the 22nd Cavalry Regiment, which he led in the conquest of the Netherlands. On May 22, 1940, he transferred to the mobile branch and assumed command of the 1st Rifle Brigade of the 1st Panzer Division, leading the brigade in the final conquest of France and on the Russian Front. Apparently he was wounded in August 1941, for he did not return to active duty until January 26, 1942, as commander of the 18th Panzer Division. He was promoted to major general on December 1, 1941, and to lieutenant general on January 1, 1943. He gave up command on April 1, 1943, and two months later became inspector of the Berlin Recruiting Area. Here he actively joined the anti-Hitler conspiracy. He was arrested for his part in the unsuccessful coup of July 20, 1944 and was hanged on October 24 of that year.

9. Walter Scheller was born in Hanover on January 27, 1892. He joined the army as an infantry *Fahnenjunker* in 1911, was commissioned the following year, fought in World War I, and as a colonel, he commanded the 66th Infantry Regiment (1938–39). When World War II began, he was named chief of staff of *Wehrkreis X* (1939–40), and on May 26, 1940 assumed command of the 8th Rifle Regiment, which he led during the final stages of the French campaign and the invasion of Russia. Promoted to major general on October 1, 1941, he assumed command of the 11th Panzer Division on October 20 and led it until June 16,

1943. On July 28, 1943, he assumed command of the 9th Panzer. Scheller was promoted to lieutenant general on January 1, 1943, but after he was wounded on July 22, he never received another mobile command. He returned to active duty on October 20 as commander of the 334th Infantry Division. He supervised its move from southern France to Italy but then returned to Russia. On November 27, he became commander of the 337th Infantry Division on the central sector of the Eastern Front. He took charge of the 399th Field Administrative Command in March 1944 and was named fortress commander of Brest-Litovsk in June. He was killed here in July. Sources differ as to the exact date of his death, but it was probably on the twenty-first or twenty-second.

10. Walter Gorn was born in 1898 in the Posen district of West Prussia, now Poznan, Poland. (This region was informally referred to as "southern Prussia.") He joined the army as a war volunteer in the 7th Guards Regiment in 1916 and emerged from World War I as a sergeant. Discharged in 1919, he joined the police in 1920 and officially rejoined the army in 1935, although he had in fact been commanding a company in the 3rd Motorcycle Battalion since June 1934. When World War II began, Gorn was commander of the Staff Company (i.e., Headquarters Company) of Guderian's XIX Motorized Corps (1939). He later commanded a company and a battalion in the 10th Rifle Regiment, as well as the replacement battalion of the 10th Rifle, before assuming command of the 59th Motorcycle Battalion (1942). On October 1, 1942, he took charge of the 10th Rifle Regiment, which he led until he was wounded on August 15, 1943. In March 1943, however, he attended the Regimental Commanders' Course at the Panzer Troops School in Germany. Gorn returned to active duty in October, as commandant of the tactics course at Panzer Troops School II. On January 1, 1944, he became commandant of the entire school. He returned to the field on July 21, when he assumed command of the 561st *Volksgrenadier* Division, which he led on the Eastern Front, fighting in Lithuania and East Prussia. He received several promotions: to major (1940), lieutenant colonel (1942), colonel (1943), and major general (1944). He was wounded again on March 1, 1945, near Koenigsberg. In April, he was discharged from the hospital, and on the fifteenth, he assumed command of the 710th Infantry Division in Austria, on the southern sector of the Eastern Front. After Hitler committed suicide, Gorn managed to disengage from the Russians and surrendered his division to the Americans on May 8. He was a POW until 1947, then lived in Papenburg in the 1950s but died in Rosenheim in 1968. A very brave man, he held the Knight's Cross with Oak Leaves and Swords.

11. As of 1943, the 408th Replacement Division consisted of the 332nd Grenadier Replacement Regiment, 518th Grenadier Replacement Regiment, 8th Reconnaissance Replacement Battalion, 8th Motorcycle Replacement Battalion, 18th Artillery Replacement Battalion, 300th Assault Gun Replacement and Training Battalion, 28th Engineer Replacement and Training Battalion, 213th Engineer Replacement Battalion, 518th Construction Engineer Battalion, 273rd Army Anti-Aircraft Artillery Replacement and Training Battalion, and 48th Fla (light antiaircraft) Replacement and Training Battalion. Andris J. Kursietis, *Wehrmacht at War: The Units and Commanders of the German Ground Forces during World War II* (Soesterberg, The Netherlands: Aspekt, 1999), 203; George F. Nafziger, *The German Order of Battle: Infantry in World War II* (London: Greenhill Books, 2000), 335; Georg Tessin, *Verbaende and Truppen der deutschen Wehrmacht und Waffen-SS*

im Zweiten Weltkrieg, 1939–1945 (Osnabrueck, Germany: Biblio-Verlag, 1973–80), 10: 107; U.S. Army Military Intelligence Division, "The German Replacement Army (Ersatzheer)," U.S. War Department (1945), 132.

12. Max Sachsenheimer was a native of Karlsruhe. Born in 1909, he joined the army as an enlisted man in the 14th Infantry Regiment in 1928 and did not receive his commission until 1934. Initially he was a signals officer in the 75th Infantry Regiment. He became a company commander in 1938, and on July 26, 1941, he assumed command of the II Battalion of the 75th Infantry on the Eastern Front. Three days later he was seriously wounded. He returned to the front in the fall and fought in the battle of the Demyansk Salient, until he fell ill in December 1942. He underwent an abbreviated general staff course in 1943–44 and served briefly as supply officer (Ib) of the 5th Jaeger Division (1943). On February 3, 1944, he became commander of his old regiment, which was now designated the 75th Jaeger. On September 1, he became commander of the 17th Infantry Division. Meanwhile, the highly decorated Sachsenheimer, who held the Knight's Cross with Oak Leaves and Swords, was promoted rapidly. A first lieutenant when the war began, he became a captain (1941), major (1942), lieutenant colonel (1944), colonel (1944), and major general (1944). After Hitler committed suicide on April 30, 1945, Sachsenheimer disengaged his division from the Red Army and surrendered it to the Americans. Discharged from the POW camps in 1947, he settled in Freiburg im Breisgau, where he died on June 2, 1973.

Hans Wagner was born in Saarbruecken in 1896. He joined the army as a war volunteer in August 1914 and received a reserve commission in the artillery in 1916. Discharged as a second lieutenant in 1920, he joined the police, then returned to active duty as a captain in 1935. He commanded the II/114th Artillery Regiment (1938–40), 5th Artillery Regiment (1940–43), and 411th Infantry Regiment (1943), and assumed command of the 269th Infantry Division on November 25, 1943. He led this division for the rest of the war and, like Sachsenheimer, managed to surrender it to the Americans in May 1945. General Wagner lived in Ulm after the war and died on May 13, 1967.

13. Rudolf Goltzsch was born in 1897 in Bautzen, a small city on the Spree River in eastern Saxony, in the extreme southeastern tip of today's Germany. He joined the army as an officer-cadet in 1916 and was commissioned in the infantry in 1917. He must have been an impressive second lieutenant, because he was selected for retention in the *Reichsheer*. He was a major and an instructor at the War School in Potsdam when World War II began. Later he commanded the I Battalion, 174th Infantry Regiment (1940), was a course commander at the Potsdam school (1941–42), and commanded the 324th Infantry Regiment on the Far North sector of the Russian Front (1942–43) and 41st Luftwaffe Field *Jaeger* Regiment on the Eastern Front (1943–44). He assumed command of the 21st Luftwaffe Field Division, of which the 41st Regiment was a part, on April 1, 1944, but led it for only eight days. Goltzsch then was used as a replacement division commander, so in rapid succession, he briefly commanded the 290th Infantry Division (beginning July 1, 1944), 719th Infantry Division (October 3), 344th *Volksgrenadier* Division (October 10), and 606th Special Purposes Division (November 7). He was promoted to major general on December 1, 1944. Apparently he briefly commanded the 344th again in March 1945, if Stauffenberg is correct on this point. He was named commander of the ad hoc Brigade

Goltzsch on the Ems River the next month, and surrendered to the Western Allies on May 1, 1945. A POW until late 1948, he was released and lived in Ratzeburg for a time. He died in Bad Heilburm in 1974.

CHAPTER 4. BARON HEINRICH VON LUETTWITZ

1. Smilo von Luettwitz was born in Stuttgart on December 23, 1895. He entered the service as an officer-cadet in the 24th Dragoon Regiment and spent most of World War I in the cavalry. Toward the end of the war, however, he gained admission to the general staff. (The normal three-year program had been reduced to three months because of the demands of the war.) Young Luettwitz was accepted into the *Reichswehr* in 1920. By 1938, he was a major and adjutant of the XV Motorized Corps (later 3rd Panzer Army) under General Hoth. On June 14, 1940, during the final days of the campaign in France, Luettwitz assumed command of the 12th Rifle Regiment. He led this unit until February 17, 1942, when he was struck by bomb splinters—the fifth wound of his career. When he returned to duty on March 1, he was given command of the 4th Rifle Brigade. He assumed command of the 26th Panzer Division on May 8, XXXXVI Panzer Corps on July 24, 1944, and 9th Army on September 1. He was relieved of his command on January 20, 1945, for ordering the evacuation of Warsaw without permission. He was nevertheless taken out of retirement on March 31 and given command of the LXXXV Corps on the Western Front. He surrendered to the Americans at the end of the war. He had been promoted to lieutenant colonel (1939), colonel (1941), major general (1942), lieutenant general (1943), and general of panzer troops (1944). He had also been highly decorated and held the Knight's Cross with Oak Leaves and Swords. In 1958, he returned to active duty as a lieutenant general (equivalent to a U.S. three-star general under the new rank structure) and commanded the III Corps. He retired again in 1961 and died at Koblenz on May 19, 1975.

2. Gustav Noske was born in Brandenburg on July 9, 1868. He joined the Social Democratic Party (SDP) and in 1892 became its chairman for Brandenburg. From 1897, he edited various SDP newspapers, and served in the German *Reichstag* (parliament) from 1906 to 1918. He was named defense minister in 1919. In this post, he put down Communist and leftist revolts throughout Germany, encouraged the right-wing paramilitary *Freikorps*, worked with the right-wing Officers' Corps, and did much to stabilize the Weimar Republic. In March 1920, however, he was unable to get the army to support the government against the right-wing Kapp Putsch. Shortly thereafter, he resigned. From 1920 to 1933, he was president of the province of Hanover, but he was deposed by the Nazis. He retired to Frankfurt-Main, but after the failure of the July 20, 1944, coup, he was arrested by the Gestapo and charged with suspicion of complicity in anti-Nazi activities. He was freed by the U.S. Army in 1945 and died in Hanover on November 30, 1946, at the age of seventy-eight.

3. Werner Kempf was born in Koenigsberg, East Prussia, in 1886. Educated in cadet schools, he entered the service as a second lieutenant in the 149th Infantry Regiment. He joined the mobile troops in 1922. An inspector of army motorization in 1936, he commanded the 4th Panzer Brigade (1937–39) and in Poland directed the ad hoc Division Kempf, which included mostly motorized SS formations. He was then given command of the 6th Panzer Division (1939–41), XXXXVIII Panzer Corps (1941–43), Army Detachment Kempf

(1943), and 8th Army (1943). Kempf was promoted to major general (1939), lieutenant general (1940), and general of panzer troops (1941). He was sacked by Hitler on August 18, 1943, and except for a brief tour as *Wehrmacht* commander *Ostland* (1944) was not reemployed. He died in Heidelburg in 1964.

4. Ritter Ludwig von Radlmeier was born in Freising on October 27, 1887. He entered the Bavarian Army as a *Fahnenjunker* in 1906 and was commissioned in the Bavarian 10th Infantry Regiment in 1908. An early advocate of motorization and armored warfare—even before Guderian—he commanded the handful of German tanks that fought in World War I. Somewhat frozen out of the Panzer Inspectorate by the Lutz-Guderian team, Radlmeier nevertheless commanded the 6th Panzer Brigade (1938–39), 5th Panzer Brigade (1939–40), and 4th Panzer Division (1940). Apparently relieved of his command, he directed the 5th Field Inspectorate (1940–41) before falling ill. He died on October 18, 1943, in a hospital on the Tegernsee, fifty miles south of Munich in Upper Bavaria.

5. Baron Anton von Hirschberg was born in Munich in 1878. Educated in cadet school, he joined the army as a *Faehnrich* in 1897. Commissioned in the Bavarian Life Guards Infantry Regiment, he transferred to the cavalry in 1906. By 1927, he was commander of the 17th Cavalry Regiment. After serving as commandant of Insterburg (1929–31), he became inspector of cavalry (1931–33). Promoted to major general in 1932 and lieutenant general in 1933, he retired later that year. He was recalled to active duty in 1939 and commanded the 441st Infantry Division (1939–40) and 554th Infantry Division (1940). He retired again in September 1940 and died in 1960.

6. Baron Wolfgang von Waldenfels was born in Hofgeismar in western Germany in 1889. He joined the army in 1906 as a *Fahnenjunker* in the 24th Dragoon Regiment. He was a colonel and higher cavalry officer on the staff of the Mobile Troops Command at OKH in late 1938. He was named commander of the 2nd Cavalry Brigade when the war began but died suddenly on February 1, 1940. For reasons not made clear by the records, he was posthumously promoted to major general four years later, on February 1, 1944.

7. Hans Kaellner was born in Kattowitz, Upper Silesia, in 1897. He joined the army as a war volunteer in 1915 and was promoted to private in 1916. He became a sergeant in the infantry in 1917 and earned a battlefield commission as a second lieutenant of reserves later that year. Discharged from the service in 1920, he joined the Potsdam police as a lieutenant. In 1935, he rejoined the army as a captain of cavalry. He commanded the II/4th Cavalry Regiment (1937–39), 11th Reconnaissance Battalion (1939–41), 73rd Panzer Grenadier Regiment (1941–42), 19th Panzer Grenadier Brigade (1942–43), 19th Panzer Division (1943), and XXIV Panzer Corps (1945). Highly decorated, he earned the Knight's Cross with Oak Leaves and Swords in 1944. He was also promoted from major in 1939 to lieutenant general on June 1, 1944. He was killed in action at Sokolnica (southeast of Brunn) on April 18, 1945.

8. Wilhelm Ulex was born in Bremerhaven in 1880. He joined the army as an officer-cadet in the 24th Field Artillery Regiment in 1899 and earned his commission in 1901. He fought in World War I, served in the *Reichsheer*, and commanded a battalion in the 6th Artillery Regiment. During the Nazi era, he was commander of the 2nd Artillery Regiment (1931–33), artillery commander VI at Muenster (1933–34), and briefly infantry commander II at Schwerin

(1935). He then commanded the 12th Infantry Division at Schwerin (1935–36) and *Wehrkreis XI* and the XI Corps at Hanover (1936–39), before retiring on March 31, 1939. He had been promoted many times: to first lieutenant (1909), captain (1913), major (1922), lieutenant colonel (1928), colonel (1931), major general (1933), lieutenant general (1935), and general of artillery (1936). Recalled to active duty when World War II began, Ulex commanded *Wehrkreis X* in Hamburg (1939), Frontier Guard Sector South in Poland (1939–40) and *Wehrkreis I* (1940–41). Together with Blaskowitz, 5th Army commander Curt Liebmann, and future field marshal Georg von Kuechler, Ulex protested against the SS atrocities in Poland from 1939 to 1940. He retired for the second and final time in 1941 and died in Bremen in 1959.

9. Friedrich Kirchner was born in Leipzig in 1885. Educated in the cadet schools, he entered the Imperial Army as a *Faehnrich* in the 107th Infantry Regiment in 1906 but transferred to the 17th Ulan Regiment in 1911. During World War I, he was a squadron leader, general staff officer, and battalion commander. He remained with the cavalry throughout the *Reichsheer* years and was commander of the 11th Cavalry Regiment (1933–34). Kirchner saw, however, that the future lay with the motorized forces and arranged to be given command of the 1st Rifle Regiment in late 1934. Later he commanded the 1st Rifle Brigade (1938–39), 1st Panzer Division (1939–1941), and LVII Panzer Corps (1941–45). Kirchner was promoted to major general (1938), lieutenant general (1940), and general of panzer troops (1942). He spent the entire 1941–45 period on the Eastern Front but surrendered to the Western Allies at the end of the conflict. He retired to Fulda in Hesse, where he died in 1960.

10. Franz Westhoven was born in Ludwigshafen in the Rhineland in 1894. He joined the army as a *Fahnenjunker* in 1913 and was commissioned in the infantry when World War I began. He remained in the *Reichsheer* and served a long tour in the powerful Army Personnel Office (1934–40), then commanded the 1st Rifle Regiment (1941–42) and 3rd Rifle (later Panzer Grenadier) Brigade (1942). Westhoven assumed command of the 3rd Panzer Division on October 1, 1942, but was wounded in action on October 20, 1943. He returned to active duty as a special adviser to General von Geyr, the commander of Panzer Group West, on February 1, 1944, and in August became the deputy inspector general of panzer troops, again under his friend Geyr. Westhoven was promoted to colonel (1939), major general (1942), and lieutenant general (1943). He ended the war as commander of panzer troops schools (1945). After a time in POW camps, he retired to Hamburg. He died in 1983 at age eighty-eight.

Hans Christoph von Heydebrand und der Lasa was born in Breslau, Silesia, in 1893. He joined the 1st Ulan Regiment as a *Fahnenjunker* in 1913 and was commissioned the following year. He remained in the *Reichsheer* and, on November 1, 1938, became commander of the 4th Cavalry Regiment. He commanded the 1st Cavalry Replacement Regiment (1939–1940), was adjutant of *Wehrkreis I* (1940), and led the 113th Rifle Regiment (1940–41). He assumed command of the 23rd Rifle Brigade on November 1, 1941, and was killed in action near Kharkov on May 15, 1942. He was posthumously promoted to major general that same month.

11. Baron Rudolf-Christoph von Gersdorff was born in Lueben, Silesia, in 1905. He joined the army as an officer-cadet in 1923 and was commissioned second lieutenant in the 7th Cavalry Regiment in late 1926. He began his general staff

training at the War Academy in 1938. An orderly officer with the 14th Army during the Polish campaign, he became I-C of the XII Corps (1939), Ia of the 86th Infantry Division (1940), Ic of Army Group Center (1941), chief of staff of the LXXXII Corps (1944), and chief of staff of the 7th Army (1944). He was promoted to lieutenant colonel (1942), colonel (1943), and major general (1945). He was a member of the anti-Hitler conspiracy and, after his wife died, even outfitted himself as a human bomb and pulled the timed detonator. But Hitler then suddenly left the room, and Gersdorff had to hurriedly find a restroom, where he defused the bomb and flushed part of it down the toilet. After the July 20, 1944, plot failed, Gersdorff was fortunate enough not to be identified by the Gestapo. He was, however, severely injured during the battle of the Falaise Pocket, where he escaped hails of American artillery fire and attacks by fighter-bombers, only to be struck by lightning. He surrendered to the Americans on May 9, 1945, and remained in the POW camps until November 1947. On August 16, 1967, he was injured in a horse-riding accident and was paralyzed for life. He died in Munich on January 26, 1980.

12. Baron Maximilian von Weichs (1881–1954) joined the Bavarian Army as a *Fahnenjunker* in 1900. He spent much of the pre-World War I, Great War, and *Reichsheer* eras in the cavalry, commanding the 18th Cavalry Regiment (1928–33) and 2nd Cavalry Division at Weimar (1933), before assuming command of the 1st Panzer Division in 1935. He took command of *Wehrkreis XIII* (and the XIII Corps) at Nuremberg in 1937. After the Polish campaign, he commanded the 2nd Army in France (1940), Yugoslavia (1941), and Russia (1941). He fell ill during the battle of Moscow but returned quickly to assume temporary command of Army Group South in mid-January 1942. From July 1942 to July 1943, he was commander in chief of Army Group B and played a part in the Stalingrad disaster. He nevertheless was promoted to field marshal on February 1, 1943. He was briefly placed in Fuehrer Reserve in the summer of 1943 but was reemployed in August as commander in chief, Southeast (OB Southeast) and Army Group F, in charge of the Balkans. He led the retreat from southeastern Europe in 1944–45 and did a brilliant job. Hitler nevertheless retired him on March 25, 1945, in part because he had always mistrusted Weichs's strong Catholic leanings. Almost alone of Hitler's surviving field marshals, Weichs was not tried as a war criminal.

13. Walter Duevert was born in Goerlitz in 1893. He joined the army as a *Fahnenjunker* in the 8th Foot Artillery Regiment in 1911. By 1937, he was a colonel commanding the 28th Artillery Regiment, and he was looked upon as a man who would rise to the highest levels of the German Army. He was, in fact, promoted to major general on January 1, 1941, and to lieutenant general exactly two years later. He was chief of staff of the VI Corps (1939–41) and commanded the 13th Panzer Division (1941–42). The strain of the Russian winter offensive of 1941/42 was too much for Duevert, however, who collapsed under the stress on February 16 and never really recovered. On July 1, he was given command of another panzer division, the 20th, but had to be relieved in October. This time he did not return to active duty for eight months; then he was given command of the 265th Infantry Division in occupied France. It was obvious, however, that General Duevert would never again be able to stand up to the strains of a combat command. After D-Day, he was relieved on July 27, 1944, and never reemployed. He retired at the end of November and died in Duesseldorf in 1972.

14. Mortimer von Kessel was born in Arnswalde, Pomerania, on May 25, 1893. He joined the Imperial Army in August 1914 as an officer-cadet and was commissioned in the 12th Hussars Regiment the following year. By the end of World War I, he was regimental adjutant. He spent the entire *Reichswehr* era in the 10th Cavalry Regiment (1920–1933). During the Nazi years, he was on the staff of the 13th Cavalry Regiment (1933–35), IIa (personnel officer) of the 3rd Cavalry Division (1935) and 1st Panzer Division (1935–37), and commander of the 9th Reconnaissance Battalion (1937–38), 8th Reconnaissance Battalion (1938–39), and 9th Reconnaissance Regiment (1939). Then he was a department chief of the Army Personnel Office (1939–43), commanded the 20th Panzer Division (1943–44), and ended the war as commander of the VII Panzer Corps (1944–45). He was promoted to colonel (1939), major general (1942), lieutenant general (1943), and general of panzer troops (1945). He died at Goslar in the Harz Mountains on January 8, 1981.

15. Kurt Zeitzler was born in Cossmar (Luckau) in Brandenburg on June 9, 1895, the son of a pastor. He joined the army as a *Fahnenjunker* on March 23, 1914, and was commissioned in the 72nd Infantry Regiment late that same year. By the end of World War I, he was a battalion commander. Promoted to colonel in 1939 and major general on February 1, 1942, he led the 60th Infantry Regiment (1939) and was chief of staff of the XXII Corps (1939–40), Panzer Group von Kleist (1940), 1st Panzer Group (later Army) (1940–42), and Army Group D (1942). He was Hitler's surprise choice to become chief of the general staff of OKH on September 24, 1942, when he was promoted to general of infantry, bypassing the rank of lieutenant general altogether. He was promoted to colonel general on January 30, 1944. He was relieved of his post the day after the July 20, 1944, assassination attempt failed, because Hitler thought he must have had advance knowledge of it. There seems to have been a considerable amount of truth to this view. Zeitzler's deputy, Gen. Adolf Heusinger, thought so and never forgave Zeitzler for it, because he left Heusinger in the room with Hitler (and the bomb), but Zeitzler himself was nowhere near the place. General Zeitzler was an extremely energetic officer who was considered harsh to his subordinates. He retired from the army on January 31, 1945, and was a British prisoner from 1945 to 1947. He died at Hohenashau-Chiemgau (Upper Bavaria) on September 25, 1963.

16. Vollrath Luebbe was born in Klein Lunow, Mecklenburg, on March 4, 1894. He graduated from the cadet school system and entered the service as an infantry *Faehnrich* in 1912. He spent virtually the entire period from 1912 to 1935 in the infantry, including ten years as a company commander in the elite 9th Infantry Regiment in Potsdam. Promoted to colonel in 1939, he commanded the 13th Cavalry Rifle Regiment (1938–41), 2nd Rifle Brigade (1941–42), and 2nd Panzer Division (1942–44). Later he led the 81st Infantry Division (1944) and 462nd Replacement (later *Volksgrenadier*) Division at Metz (1944), until he suffered a mild stroke in October. In late December 1944, he returned to active duty as commander of the 443rd Infantry Division. Captured by the Russians at the end of the war, he was released from the POW camps in 1955. He died at Bad Bramstadt in Schleswig-Holstein on April 25, 1969.

17. Gerhard Schmidhuber was born in Dresden, Saxony, on April 9, 1894. He joined the army as a volunteer in the spring of 1914 and earned a battlefield commission as a second lieutenant of reserves in 1915. Not selected for the

Reichswehr, he was discharged in 1920 and entered the private sector of the economy. He rejoined the service as a captain in 1935 and was a company commander in the 103rd Infantry Regiment in 1938. When the Second World War began, he was given command of the II Battalion of the 103rd and led it until May 1, 1942. After a tour at the Panzer Troops School, he assumed command of the 304th Panzer Grenadier Regiment on July 11, 1943. In February 1944, he returned to Germany to attend the Division Commanders' Course. He was named acting commander of the 7th Panzer Division on May 2 and became commander of the 13th Panzer Division on September 9. Meanwhile, he was promoted to lieutenant colonel (1941), colonel (1942), and major general (1944). He and his division were surrounded in Budapest in December 1944, along with the IX SS Mountain Corps. Schmidhuber spearheaded the breakout attempt on February 11, 1945, but the Red Army had already been informed that it was going to be launched. The 13th Panzer Division was cut to ribbons, and General Schmidhuber was killed at the head of his troops.

18. Hans Speidel was born in Metzingen, Wuerttemberg, on October 28, 1897. He joined the army as an infantry officer-cadet in late 1914. He fought in World War I, served in the *Reichsheer*, and was Ia of the 33rd Infantry Division (1937–39), IX Corps (1939–40), and Army Group B (1940). He then served as chief of staff to the military governor of France (1940–42), of the V Corps (1942–43), to the German general with the Italian 8th Army (1943), of the 8th Army (1943–44), and of Army Group B (1944). A lieutenant colonel when World War II began, he was promoted to colonel (1941), major general (1943), and lieutenant general (1944). During Rommel's absence on D-Day, Speidel performed poorly. Nevertheless, Rommel, Kluge, and Model retained him as chief of staff. Despite Field Marshal Model's efforts to protect him, Speidel was arrested on suspicion of being involved in the anti-Hitler conspiracy, but the Court of Honor did not expel him from the army; he therefore could not be executed, but he did spend the rest of the war in prison. In 1955, he became a lieutenant general (the equivalent of a three-star general in the U.S. Army under the new rank structure) in the West German Army and held high positions in NATO. Speidel retired on March 31, 1964, and died at Bad Honnef on November 28, 1984. See Hans Speidel, *Invasion, 1944: Rommel and the Normandy Campaign* (Chicago: Regnery, 1950).

19. These include "XLVII Panzer Corps—Ardennes," "The Assignment of the XLVII Panzer Corps in the Ardennes, 1944–45," and "XLVII Panzer Corps in the Ardennes Offensive," *Foreign Military Studies* MS #A-939, A-939, and A-940.

20. Alexander McKee, *Caen: Anvil of Victory* (New York: White Lion Publishers, 1976), 101.

21. John Keegan, *Six Armies in Normandy: From D-Day to the Liberation of Paris* (New York: Penguin Books, 1983), 155.

22. Dietrich Kraiss was born in Stuttgart on November 16, 1889. He was educated in the cadet school system and joined the army as a second lieutenant in the 126th Infantry Regiment in 1909. He fought in World War I as a platoon leader, machine-gun officer, and battalion commander, all in the 126th. He remained in the infantry except for the period from 1931 to 1934, when he was in the Defense Ministry. In 1937, he was promoted to colonel and named commander of the 90th Infantry Regiment. He led the 90th until March 1941, the month after he was promoted to major general. Later he led the 168th Infantry

Division (1941–43); the 355th Infantry Division (1943), and the 352nd Infantry Division (1943–44). His division bore the brunt of the Anglo-American attack on D-Day and almost destroyed the American attack on Omaha Beach. Promoted to lieutenant general on October 1, 1942, he was critically wounded on August 2, 1944, and died on four days later.

23. Erich Straube was born in Elsterwerda, Brandenburg, on December 11, 1887. He joined the army as an infantry officer-cadet in 1907 and received his commission in early 1909. By 1936, he was a colonel commanding the 82nd Infantry Regiment. He was named commandant of the War School at Munich in 1938, was promoted to major general on June 1, 1939, and assumed command of the 268th Infantry Division when World War II began. This unit did not see action in either the Polish or French campaign, but it was involved in the fighting on the Russian Front from the beginning. Straube, who had been promoted to lieutenant general on June 1, 1941, was given command of the XIII Corps on April 21, 1942, and was promoted to general of infantry on June 1. On August 1, 1943, he assumed command of the LXXIV Corps, and then led the LXXXVI Corps from December 17, 1944, until the end of the war. He retired to Osterode in the Harz Mountains and died on March 31, 1971.

24. Johannes Blaskowitz was born on July 10, 1883, in Peterswalde, East Prussia. He joined the army as a senior officer cadet in the 18th Infantry Regiment in 1901. He was already a major general when Hitler assumed power and was promoted to lieutenant general (1933), general of infantry (August 1, 1936), and colonel general (1939). He was commander of Army Group 3 prior to the start of World War II. During the war, he commanded the 8th Army (1939), 2nd Army (1939–40), 1st Army (1940–44), Army Group G (1944–45), and Army Group H (1945). He was also the OB Netherlands (supreme commander, the Netherlands, and commander of Fortress Holland) from April 7, 1945, until he surrendered it on May 5. He remained commander of German troops in the Netherlands under the 1st Canadian Army until June 6. A gentleman of the old school, he was never promoted to field marshal because Adolf Hitler despised him—and he had no use for Hitler or his party. He committed suicide during the war crimes trial in Nuremberg on February 5, 1948, by throwing himself off a balcony.

25. Hermann Balck was born in Danzig in 1893 and joined the Imperial Army as an infantry *Fahnenjunker* in 1913. He served in World War I and later in the *Reichsheer*. When World War II began, he was a lieutenant colonel and a staff officer on the Panzer Inspectorate (In 6). During the war, he commanded the 1st Rifle Regiment (1939–40), 3rd Panzer Regiment (1940–41), and 2nd Panzer Brigade (1941) in the early stages of the Russian campaign. After a tour of duty with the Office of Mobile Troops at OKH (1941–42), he led the 11th Panzer Division (1942–43), and was acting commander of the *Grossdeutschland* Panzer Grenadier Division (1943) and commander of the XIV Panzer Corps in Italy (1943). This last tour of duty was cut short when he was severely injured in an airplane crash. He returned to duty on November 15, 1943, as commander of the XXXXVIII Panzer Corps on the Eastern Front. Meanwhile, he was promoted to colonel (1940), major general (1942), lieutenant general (1943), and general of panzer troops (1943). He led the 4th Panzer Army from August 5 to September 21, 1944, when he was named commander in chief of Army Group G on the Western Front. Balck held this appointment until December 1944, when he was relieved as a result of one of Himmler's intrigues. He was,

however, given command of the 6th Army in Hungary and led it until the end of the war. He moved to Stuttgart after the war and died at Erbenbach-Rockenau on November 29, 1982, less than two weeks before he would have turned eighty-nine. He is buried at Asperg, near Ludwigsburg.

26. Heinrich-Walter Bronsart von Schellendorf was born in Neustrelitz, Mecklenburg, on September 21, 1906, and entered the service as a *Fahnenjunker* in the 6th Cavalry Regiment in 1924. Commissioned in 1928, he was a squadron leader in the 6th and captain of cavalry when the war broke out. In late 1939, he became commander of the 36th Reconnaissance Battalion, which he led until he was named commander of the 13th Panzer Grenadier Regiment in October 1942. He was promoted to major (1941), lieutenant colonel (1943), and colonel (1943). He apparently was wounded on February 2, 1944. Later that year, he became IIa of the 8th Army, before assuming command of the 111th Panzer Brigade in September 1944. On September 22, he was killed in action. He was posthumously promoted to major general.

27. Baron Kurt von Muehlen was born in Ulm on January 22, 1905, and joined the army as a *Fahnenjunker* in the engineers in 1923. Commissioned in the 13th Infantry Regiment in 1927, he was a company commander in the 75th Infantry Regiment when World War II began. By the following spring, he was a battalion commander. After the fall of France, he became adjutant of the 5th Infantry Division, and on October 1, 1941, he became commander of the 5th Machine Gun Battalion. He returned to the 75th Infantry as regimental commander in June 1942 and led it until June 1944, when he became commander of the 559th *Volksgrenadier* Division, which he led until the end of the war. He was promoted to colonel (1943), major general (1944), and lieutenant general (1945). As holder of the Oak Leaves, he died in Kressborn, Baden-Wuerttemberg on January 14, 1971.

28. Walter Krueger was born in 1892 in Zeitz, in Saxony-Anhalt in east-central Germany. He entered the service as an infantry officer-cadet in 1910 but transferred to the cavalry prior to the outbreak of World War I. He spent virtually the entire period from 1914 to 1939 in various cavalry units. In 1937, he was promoted to colonel and given command of the 10th Cavalry Regiment. He assumed command of the 171st Infantry Regiment when World War II began, but after the Polish campaign, he transferred to the mobile branch. On February 15, 1940, he assumed command of the 1st Rifle Brigade. Promoted to major general on April 1, 1941, he took command of the 1st Panzer Division on July 17 and led it very capably for two and a half years. He was promoted to lieutenant general on October 1, 1942, and assumed command of the LVIII Panzer Corps on January 1, 1944. A month later, he was promoted to general of panzer troops. Krueger directed the LVIII Panzer until March 25, 1945, when Hitler sacked him. The dictator held Krueger partially responsible for allowing the Americans to force the Rhine three days before. After the Fuehrer calmed down, Krueger was given command of *Wehrkreis IV* on April 10. He surrendered to elements of the U.S. 87th Infantry Division on the Czech border on May 6, 1945. He retired to Baden-Baden, where he died on July 11, 1973.

29. Guenther Blumentritt was born in Munich on February 10, 1892. He joined the army as a *Fahnenjunker* in 1911 and was commissioned in the 71st Infantry Regiment the following year. He fought in World War I, served in the *Reichsheer*, and was a colonel on the general staff of OKH in 1938. When World War II began,

he was Ia of Army Group South under Gerd von Rundstedt. He later served as Ia of Army Group A, also under Rundstedt (1939–40), chief of staff of the 4th Army (1940–42), chief of the operations staff of OKH (1942), and chief of staff of OB West, again under Rundstedt (1942–44). He was promoted to major general (1941), lieutenant general (1942), and general of infantry (1944). On October 1, 1944, he became acting commander of the LXXXVI Corps. He then assumed command the XII SS Corps (October 18, 1944), the 25th Army (January 29, 1945), the 1st Parachute Army (March 28, 1945) and the ad hoc Army Command Blumentritt (April 10, 1945). He surrendered to the British in Schleswig-Holstein on June 1, 1945. Released from the POW camps on New Year's Day 1948, he retired to Munich, where he wrote a biography of Field Marshal Rundstedt, whom he greatly admiredGuenther Blumentritt died in the city of his birth on October 12, 1967.

30. Henning Schoenfeld was born in Stettin in 1894. An officer-cadet in 1912, he was commissioned in the 7th Ulan Regiment in 1913. He served in the cavalry until he was discharged from the army in September 1918, apparently because of wounds suffered in World War I. He rejoined the army in 1934 and became commander of the 20th Reconnaissance Battalion (1938–40). A member of the staff of the general of mobile troops at OKH from 1940 to 1943, he led the 949th Infantry Regiment (1943–44) before assuming command of the 2nd Panzer Division on September 5, 1944. His appointment surprised and displeased Luettwitz. Schoenfeld owed his appointment to his friends at OKH and in the Panzer Inspectorate, rather than to any qualifications he had to command a tank division. He was promoted to major general on December 1, 1944, and was relieved of his command by Luettwitz fifteen days later. He was never reemployed. He died in Bad Canstatt, near Stuttgart, in 1958.

31. S. L. A. Marshall, *Bastogne: The Story of the First Eight Days* (Washington, DC: Infantry Journal Press, 1946), 58.

32. Carl Wagener was born in Stanowitz-Sriegau (Siliesia) in 1901. He entered the *Reichsheer* as an officer-cadet in 1921 and was commissioned second lieutenant in the 11th Cavalry Regiment in 1924. By 1938, he was a major on the general staff and Ia of the 4th Light (later 9th Panzer) Division. After the Polish campaign, Wagener became a tactical instructor at the War Academy, teaching future general staff officers. He was named Ia of the 10th Motorized Division in mid-June 1940, and thus participated in the very end of the French campaign. He was promoted to Ia of the 3rd Panzer Group (later Army) on February 1, 1941, and took part in the invasion of the Soviet Union. Next he served as chief of staff of the XXXX Panzer Corps (1942–43), 1st Panzer Army (1944), and 5th Panzer Army on the Western Front (1944–45). He was promoted to lieutenant colonel (1942), colonel (1943), and major general (1944). He was named chief of staff of Army Group B on February 16, 1945, and surrendered to the Americans in mid-April. He resided in Hanover after the war and died in 1988, at the age of eighty-six.

33. It was Stauffenberg's opinion that Manteuffel did not relieve Luettwitz because he thought even less highly of Bayerlein than Luettwitz. Personal communication, 1988.

34. Siegfried von Waldenburg was born in 1898 in Gross Leipe, near Breslau, Silesia. He joined the Imperial Army as an officer-cadet in July 1916. Commissioned in the 1st Guards Grenadier Regiment in August 1917, he performed

well in World War I and was retained in the *Reichsheer*. He was a major and Ia of the 6th Infantry Division when World War II began. Later he was chief of staff of the XII Corps (1940–41) and was appointed deputy military attaché to Rome in November 1941. He took command of the 26th Panzer Grenadier Regiment in April 1944 and was a colonel when he assumed command of the 116th Panzer Division on September 14. Many people did not expect him to be successful in this position, given the depleted state of the division and the fractious nature of its staff; however, Waldenburg proved more than equal to the task and was even singled out for special praise by the Fuehrer—a rare mark of distinction in the fifth year of the war. He was promoted to major general on December 1, 1944. After the war he moved to Hanover, where he died in 1973.

35. Ernst Hammer was born in 1884 in Falkenau-Eger in the Sudetenland, in what became Czechoslovakia after World War I. He joined the Austrian Army as a volunteer in the 3rd Foot Artillery Regiment in 1903, earned a reserve commission in 1905, and fought in the Great War. After the armistice, he was selected for retention in the *Bundesheer* (the postwar Austrian Army), where he earned an advanced engineering degree and became a member of the general staff. A major general when Hitler annexed the country in 1938, Hammer was promoted to lieutenant general on November 1, 1940. Meanwhile, he commanded the 75th Infantry Division from August 26, 1939, to October 10, 1942, fighting in the Saar, French and Russian campaigns. On November 10, he assumed command of the 190th Replacement (later Infantry) Division, which he led on the Western Front. He surrendered to the Americans on April 13, 1945, and remained in U.S. POW camps until the spring of 1947. Upon release, he returned to Vienna, where he died in 1957.

36. Albert Kesselring was born in Marktsheet, Bavaria, on November 20, 1885, the son of a local schoolteacher who saw to it that he received an excellent education at the Latin School in Bayreuth. Almost as soon as he graduated in 1904, he joined the Bavarian 2nd Foot Artillery Regiment as an officer-cadet. He was commissioned in 1906 and spent the next eight years with his regiment in the garrison town of Metz, where he became a trained balloon observer and adjutant of the balloon battalion. He fought in World War I as an artillery officer, and in 1917, he was appointed directly to the general staff without having to attend the War Academy—a rare mark of distinction indeed. He remained in the *Reichsheer*, and as a colonel in 1932, he was given command of the 4th Artillery Regiment in Dresden. Kesselring was transferred to the *Luftwaffe*—somewhat against his will—in October 1933. He was named chief of the general staff of the *Luftwaffe* in 1936-37 and was largely responsible for building the air force's ground establishment, but he could not work with Secretary of State for Aviation Erhard Milch, so he applied for retirement in 1937. Instead, Hermann Goering gave him command of the III Air District (*Luftgau III*). Later he commanded Air Group 1 (later 1st Air Fleet) (1938–39), 2nd Air Fleet (1940–43), and Army Group C/OB South (later Southwest) (1943–45). He was promoted to field marshal on July 19, 1940. He performed very well in the Italian campaign of 1943–45. On March 8, 1945, he replaced Rundstedt as OB West and surrendered to the Americans at the Berchtesgadener Hotel on May 15. He was convicted as a war criminal for the execution of 335 Italian civilians in the Ardentine catacombs on March 24, 1944, and was condemned to death. The sentence was commuted to life imprisonment in 1947, and after he developed

throat cancer in 1952, he was released as an act of clemency. He then wrote his memoirs, *Soldat bis zum letzten Tag*—literally, *A Soldier to the Final Day* but published as *Kesselring: A Soldier's Record* (Westport, CT: Greenwood Press, 1970). He became head of the *Stahlhelm*, an organization many considered to be neo-Nazi. Kesselring was the victim of an arranged marriage that was very unhappy, but he refused to divorce his wife on religious grounds. The couple had no children, although they did adopt a son. The field marshal's last years were plagued by ill health. He died of heart failure in Bad Nauheim on July 20, 1960, at age seventy-four. He is buried in a small cemetery at Bad Wiessee, near Munich. All that appears on his tombstone is his name and rank.

37. Erich Abraham was born in Marienburg, East Prussia, in 1895. He enlisted in the Imperial Army as a war volunteer in 1914 and earned a commission as a second lieutenant of reserves the following year. Discharged in 1920 as an honorary first lieutenant, he joined the police, but returned to the army in 1935 as a major. Promotions to lieutenant colonel (1938), colonel (1941), major general (1943), and lieutenant general (1944) followed, and he became a general of infantry on March 16, 1945. Meanwhile, he commanded the I Battalion, 105th Infantry Regiment (1936–39), II/266th Infantry Regiment (1939–40), 230th Infantry Regiment (1940–42), II Officers' Training School (1943), 76th Infantry Division (1943–44), and LXIII Corps (1944–45). Most of Abraham's service was on the Eastern Front. After being released from the POW camps in August 1947, he settled in Wiesbaden, where he died in 1971.

CHAPTER 5. FRITZ BAYERLEIN

1. Stauffenberg Papers.

2. Baron Kurt von Liebenstein was born in Jebenhausen, Wuerttemberg, on February 28, 1899, and joined the 26th Dragoon Regiment as a *Fahnenjunker* in 1916. He fought in World War I, served in the *Reichswehr*, and was a major on the staff of the German military attaché to Paris in 1937. Prior to the beginning of the war, Liebenstein was transferred to the staff of OKH (the High Command of the Army) and was promoted to lieutenant colonel on April 1, 1939. In early 1940, he became Ia of the 10th Panzer Division, and early the next year he was promoted to colonel and named chief of staff of Guderian's 2nd Panzer Group on the Eastern Front (1941–42). He assumed command of the 6th Panzer Regiment of the 3rd Panzer Division on June 20, 1942, and led it in the battles around Kharkov and the drive across the Don and into the Caucasus. He was named commander of the 3rd Panzer Grenadier Brigade of the 3rd Panzer Division in October 1942 but held the post only two weeks, as the brigade was dissolved on November 8. Now an excess officer, Liebenstein went on leave for several weeks and was then given command of the 164th Light Afrika. He took charge on December 29, 1942, and led the division in the final retreats from Libya and in the Tunisian battles, mostly against the British 8th Army. He was injured in an automobile accident on February 17, 1943, and was incapacitated, being forced to temporarily step down as divisional commander. He resumed command on March 13 and led the division until it surrendered on May 12, 1943. Liebenstein was released from the POW camps in 1947 or 1948 and returned to Germany. When the West German Army (*Bundesheer*) was created in 1956, he was appointed major general (equivalent to lieutenant general on

the old World War II scale) and was named commander of *Wehrkreis V*, which was headquartered in Stuttgart. He retired on September 30, 1960, but remained in Stuttgart until his death on August 3, 1975.

3. Siegfried Westphal was an officer noted for both his brilliance and his arrogance. He was born in Leipzig on March 18, 1902, the son of an army officer. He graduated from Berlin-Lichterfelde, the foremost cadet academy in Germany, and entered the service at age sixteen as a *Fahnenjunker* in the 12th Infantry Regiment on November 10, 1918. Germany signed the armistice the next day. Westphal remained in the service, however, and was commissioned second lieutenant in the 11th Cavalry Regiment in 1922. In 1932, he began clandestine general staff training. He graduated from the recently reopened War Academy in August 1935 and was assigned to the operations branch of the General Staff of the army. By 1938, he was a major, commanding a squadron in the 13th Cavalry Regiment at Lueneburg, *Wehrkreis X.* Just before World War II began, he was named Ia of the 58th Infantry Division. After serving in the Saar, Westphal was Ia of the XXVII Corps in the French campaign. He served on the French-German Armistice Commission (1940–41), before becoming Ia of Panzer Group Afrika on June 15, 1941. Westphal was wounded by British artillery during the battle of the Gazala Line on May 31, 1942, but returned to duty in October as chief of staff of Panzer Army Afrika (later the 1st Italian-German Army). From December 1 to 29, he was acting commander of the 164th Light Afrika Division. On February 1, 1943, he became Ia of OB South and on June 15 became its chief of staff. He collapsed as a result of stress and overwork on June 5, 1944, but returned to duty on September 9 as chief of staff of OB West. He received promotions to major general (1943), lieutenant general (1944), and general of cavalry (1945). Westphal surrendered in May 1945. After the war, he wrote *Defeat in the West* (1952). He died in Celle on July 2, 1982, at the age of 80.

4. Bayerlein in Erwin Rommel, *The Rommel Papers*, B. H. Liddell Hart, ed. (New York: Harcourt, Brace, 1953).

5. Ibid.

6. Desmond Young, *Rommel: Desert Fox* (London: Collins, 1950).

7. Gustav Fehn's biography is covered in Mitcham, *Rommel's Desert Commanders*. He gave up command of the Afrika Korps on January 15, 1943, when he was seriously wounded. He did not return to active duty until July 1. He later commanded the XV Mountain Corps and was murdered by Yugoslavian Communists on June 5, 1945, a month after he had surrendered.

8. Dietrich von Choltitz was born in Silesia in 1894. After being educated in cadet schools, he joined the Imperial Army in 1914 as a senior officer cadet. He fought in World War I, served in the *Reichsheer*, and was a lieutenant colonel in command of the II/16th Infantry Regiment when the war began. He advanced rapidly, to colonel (1941), major general (1942), lieutenant general (1943), and general of infantry (1944). He commanded the 16th Infantry Regiment (1940–42) and the 260th Infantry Division (1942), served on the general staff at OKH (1942), and was deputy commander of the XXXXVIII Panzer Corps (1942), acting commander of the XVII Corps (1942–43), and commander of the 11th Panzer Division (1943). He was again named deputy commander of the XXXXVIII Panzer Corps, a post he held until August 30, 1943, when he was wounded in action. He did not return to active duty until June 15, 1944, when he took command of the LXXXIV Corps in Normandy. After the Americans

broke the German line in Normandy in late July, 1944, Field Marshal Kluge—
who was looking for scapegoats, as usual—relieved Choltitz of his command.
Hitler, however, for once perceived the military situation correctly and realized
that Choltitz was in no way responsible for the disaster. He promoted Choltitz
to general of infantry and named him *Wehrmacht* commander of Greater Paris
on August 7. Despite Hitler's orders that Paris be razed, Choltitz surrendered it
intact on August 24. He was held in American POW camps until April 1947. He
retired to Baden-Baden, where he died on November 5, 1966.

9. August Schmidt was born in Fuerth in 1892. He entered the service as an officer-cadet in the infantry in 1911 and was commissioned in the Bavarian 21st
Infantry Regiment in 1913. He fought in World War I, served in the *Reichsheer,*
and as a colonel, assumed command of the 20th Infantry Regiment when
World War II started. Later he was promoted to major general (1941) and lieutenant general (1943). He commanded the 21st Infantry Regiment (1940–41),
the 51st Infantry Division (1942), and 10th Motorized (later Panzer Grenadier)
Division (1942–44). He was captured in Romania and not released until 1955.
He died in Munich in 1972.

Martin Unrein was born in Weimar on New Year's Day 1901, attended cadet
schools, and entered the service as a *Faehnrich* in the 71st Infantry Regiment in
March 1918. He remained in the *Reichswehr* and received his commission in the
9th Cavalry Regiment in 1922. He was a major and adjutant of the XI Corps
when the Second World War began. He commanded the 268th Reconnaissance
Battalion (1940), served on the staff of OKW (1940–41), and commanded the
6th Motorcycle Battalion (1941–42), 4th Panzer Grenadier Regiment
(1942–43), 14th Panzer Division (1943–45), and Panzer Division Clausewitz
(1945). He was, meanwhile, promoted to lieutenant colonel (1940), colonel
(1942), major general (1944), and lieutenant general (1944). Captured by the
Americans on April 21, 1945, he lived in Dachau, Bavaria after the war and died
in Munich in 1972.

Otto Schwarz was born in Baiersroederhof, Hesse, in 1897. He joined the
army as a war volunteer in the 9th Ulans in 1914 but transferred to the artillery
and was commissioned in the 27th Field Artillery Regiment the following year.
He was selected for the *Reichswehr* and was a lieutenant colonel and lecturer in
the War Academy in 1938. He served as Ia of the XXII Corps (1939), to the
military governor of the general gouvernement in Poland (1939–40), and to
the German Military Mission to Romania (1940–41). He then commanded the
134th and 370th Artillery Regiments on the Eastern Front (1941–42). He
returned to Germany in 1942 to teach at Artillery School I. Later he served on
the special Panther staff at Headquarters, Army Group Center. He assumed
command of the 376th Infantry Division on November 11, 1943, and led it for
the rest of the war. He was promoted to colonel (1940), major general (1944),
and lieutenant general (1944). He spent the first ten years after the war in
Soviet prison camps, and then lived in Bielefeld, North Rhine-Westphalia.

10. Oswin Grolig was born in Hamburg-Altona in 1894. He became a *Fahnenjunker*
in 1913 and was commissioned in the 11th Hussars in 1914. He fought in World
War I, served in the *Reichsheer,* and commanded the 8th Reconnaissance Battalion (1938–40), 33rd Rifle Regiment (1940–42), 1st Rifle Brigade (1942), and
Panzer Troop School II (1943). He briefly commanded the 21st Panzer Division (1944) and assumed command of the 25th Panzer Division on June 1,

1944. He was mortally wounded on the Eastern Front on August 18 and died a few days later in a hospital Litzmannstadt (now Lodz, Poland).

11. Historical Division, Headquarters, U.S. Army, Europe, *Guide to Foreign Military Studies, 1945–54* (1954).

12. Stauffenburg did not specify the name of the Panzer Lehr officer who was his source in his papers. He was presumably referring to Helmut Ritgen's *Die Geschichte der Panzer-Lehr-Division im Westen, 1944–1945* (Stuttgart, Germany: Motorbuch-Verlag, 1979), although it is possible that he is referring to Franz Kurowski's *Die Panzer Lehr Division* (Bad Nauheim, Germany: Podzun-Verlag, 1964).

13. Paul Carell, *Invasion: They're Coming* (London: Harrap, 1962).

14. Horst Niemack was born in Hanover in 1909. He entered the army as an officer aspirant in the 6th Motorized Battalion in 1927 and was commissioned second lieutenant in 1931, when he was a member of the 18th Cavalry Regiment. During World War II, he rose from captain to major general on April 1, 1945, and earned the Knight's Cross with Oak Leaves and Swords in the process. He led the 3rd Company, 5th Reconnaissance Battalion (1939–40), and 5th Reconnaissance Battalion (1940–41), and commanded a training group at Panzer Troop School II (1941–43). He returned to the front in the spring of 1943 as the commander of the 26th Panzer Grenadier Regiment, before taking over the Panzer Fusilier Regiment of the *Grossdeutschland* Panzer Grenadier Division on October 1, 1943. He led the Panzer Lehr Division from late January 1945 until the end of the war. After the war, he lived in Wahrendorf, near Celle in Lower Saxony. He was killed in an accident in Gross Hehlen, also near Celle, in 1992, at the age of eighty-three.

15. Carl Puechler was born in 1894 in Bad Warmbrunn, now Zdroj, Poland. He entered the service as a *Fahnenjunker* in the fall of 1913. He was commissioned in the 17th Engineer Battalion in 1914, fought in World War I, served in the *Reichswehr*, and was a lieutenant colonel commanding the II Battalion/34th Infantry Regiment on the West Wall when World War II began. He assumed command of the regiment and was promoted to colonel later that year. He then led the 228th Infantry Regiment (1940–42), 257th Infantry Division (1942–43), LXVII Corps (1944), LXXXVI Corps (1944), and LXXIV Corps (1944). Meanwhile, he was promoted to major general (1942), lieutenant general (1943) and general of infantry (1944). He surrendered on April 16, 1945. He settled in Heilbronn in northern Baden-Wuerttemberg after the war and died there in 1949.

16. Gustav-Adolf von Zangen was born in Darmstadt (Hesse) in 1892. He joined the army as an officer-cadet in the infantry in 1912. He fought in World War I but was not selected for the *Reichswehr*. Discharged in 1920, he had already joined the police. In 1935, he returned to the army as a lieutenant colonel and, in 1938, he was promoted to colonel and assumed command of the 88th Infantry Regiment. Promotions of major general (1942), lieutenant general (1943), and general of infantry (1943) followed. Meanwhile, he commanded the 17th Infantry Division on the Eastern Front (1941–43), LXXXIV Corps in France (1943), LXXXVII Corps in northern Italy (1943), Army Detachment von Zangen in northern Italy (1943–44) and 15th Army on the Western Front (1944–45). He surrendered on April 18, 1945. Zangen lived in Hanau-am-Main after the war and died in 1964.

17. Otto Hitzfeld was born in Blasiwald in the Black Forest in 1898. He joined the army as an infantry officer-cadet in 1915 and was commissioned the following year. He was chosen for the *Reichsheer* and was adjutant in 1938 at the War School at Wiener Neustadt, where his commander was Erwin Rommel. Hitzfeld assumed command of the III Battalion/158th Infantry Regiment when World War II began. He later commanded the 593rd Infantry Regiment (1940–41), 213th Infantry Regiment (1941–43), 102nd Infantry Division (1943), and Infantry School at Doeberitz (1943–44). He became deputy commander of the LXVII Corps in late 1944 and then led the corps itself (1944–45). He apparently was the commander of the 11th Army from April 2 to 19, 1945 (the exact dates are not made clear by the records), when he surrendered to the Americans. He was released from the POW camps in May 1947 and settled in Heidelburg. He died in nearby Dossenheim in 1990, at the age of ninety-two.

18. Joseph Harpe was born in Buer, Westphalia, in 1887. He joined the army as a *Fahnenjunker* in the infantry in 1911, fought in World War I, served in the *Reichswehr*, and was a lieutenant colonel commanding the 12th Cavalry Regiment in 1935. Seeing that the future lay in the armored branch, he managed to secure command of the 3rd Panzer Regiment later that year. This decision led to rapid advancements for Harpe: to colonel (1937), major general (1940), lieutenant general (1942), general of panzer troops (1942), and colonel general (1944). Meanwhile, he commanded the 1st Panzer Brigade (1939–40), Panzer Troop School (1940), 2nd Infantry (later 12th Panzer) Division (1940–42), XXXXI Panzer Corps (1942–43), 9th Army (1943–44), 4th Panzer Army (1944), and Army Group A (1944–45). Despite his pro-Nazi political convictions, Hitler sacked him on January 16, 1945, for a reversal on the Eastern Front. On March 9, however, after Hitler calmed down, he was given command of the 5th Panzer Army. Harpe surrendered on April 17 and remained in American POW camps until the spring of 1948. He lived in Nuremberg after the war and died in 1968.

19. Christian-Johannes Landau was born in Altona, near Hamburg, in 1897. He joined the army as a war volunteer in 1914 and earned a reserve commission in the artillery in 1917. Discharged in December 1918, he earned an advanced degree in agriculture from the technical high school in Bonn in 1923. He rejoined the army as a captain in 1934, and after commanding a battery in the 20th Artillery Regiment, he was on the staff of Frontier Guard Command Upper Rhine when World War II began. He was on the staff of the 14th Landwehr/205th Infantry Division before assuming command of the IV Battalion/205th Artillery Regiment in early 1940. He later served as adjutant of the 196th Infantry Division (1941–42) and commander of the 36th Artillery Regiment (1942–43), 248th Artillery Regiment (1943–44), and 176th Infantry Division (1944–45). He was promoted to major general on January 1, 1945, and surrendered to the Americans on May 9. Released in 1947, he died in Freiburg-Breisgau in 1952.

20. Walter Denkert was born in Kiel in 1897. He joined the Imperial Army as a war volunteer in August 1914 and in 1915 earned four promotions: to corporal, sergeant, staff sergeant, and second lieutenant of reserves. He went on to command an infantry platoon and a company before being wounded in March 1918. Discharged in 1919, he joined the Hamburg Police Department, but he reentered the army as a major in 1935. He successively commanded an infantry company, a machine-gun battalion, an infantry battalion (II/271st Infantry

Regiment, which he led on the Saar Front), and a supply and equipment regiment in *Wehrkreis X* in the winter of 1940–41. He briefly served on the staff of the general of infantry at OKH before assuming command of the 47th Infantry Regiment on the Eastern Front in July 1941. In September 1941, he became commander of the 8th Motorized Regiment of the 3rd Motorized (later Panzer Grenadier) Division. He led this regiment until September 28, 1942, when he apparently fell ill; there is no mention of his being wounded in his personnel record. In any case, he returned to active duty on March 13, 1944 as deputy commander of the 3rd Panzer Division. He also did a tour of duty as acting commander of the 19th Panzer Division from March 28 to May before returning to the 3rd Panzer Grenadier Division as its commander on October 3. The division surrendered to the Americans on April 16, 1945, but it is unclear when the general surrendered. Denkert, who had been promoted to major general on June 1, 1944, was promoted to lieutenant general on April 20, 1945. He was released from the POW camps in 1947 and died in his hometown in 1982. Bradley et al., *Die Generale des Heeres* 3: 77–79; Keilig, *Die Generale des Heeres*, 68.

21. Bernhard Klosterkemper was born in Coesfeld, North Rhine-Westphalia, in 1897. He joined the army as an officer-cadet in the infantry in 1916 and served as a platoon leader, company commander, and battalion adjutant. He was selected for the *Reichsheer* in 1920 and spent the next twenty-five years in staff positions or in infantry units. A major when the Second World War began, he rose to the rank of major general on December 1, 1944. He was on the staff of XXIII Corps (1939) and commanded the III Battalion/272nd Infantry Regiment (1939–41) and I Battalion/271st Infantry Regiment (1941), both in the 93rd Infantry Division. He was an officer on the staff of the XXIII Corps in 1942 and was named commander of the 920th Infantry Regiment in January 1944. During the Normandy campaign, he simultaneously led the 91st Air Landing Division and elements of the 243rd Infantry Division. On September 27, 1944, he assumed command of the 180th Infantry Division. After surrendering, he remained a POW until 1947. He settled in Breman, where he died in 1962.

22. Seymour Freiden and William Richardson, eds. *The Fatal Decisions* (New York: W. Sloan Associates, 1956).

23. British interrogation of Maj. Gen. Gerhard Franz, on file at the Air University Archives, Montgomery, Alabama.

Bibliography

Bradley, Dermot, Karl-Friedrich Hildebrand, and Marcus Roevekamp. *Die Generale des Heeres, 1921–1945*. Osnabrueck, Germany: Biblio, 1993–. 7 vols. to date.

Carell, Paul [Paul Carl Schmidt]. *The Foxes of the Desert*. Mervyn Savill, trans. London: Macdonald, 1960.

———. *Hitler Moves East*. Ewald Osers, trans. Boston: Little, Brown, 1964.

———. *Invasion: They're Coming*. Ewald Osers, trans. London: Harrap, 1962.

———. *Scorched Earth*. Ewald Osers, trans. London: Harrap, 1970.

Cole, Hugh M. *The Lorraine Campaign*. Washington, DC: Historical Division, Department of the Army, 1950.

Eberbach, Hans. "Panzer Group Eberbach and the Falaise Encirclement." *Foreign Military Studies* MS #A-922. Historical Division, U.S. Army, Europe.

Franz, Gerhard. British interrogation of Maj. Gen. Gerhard Franz. On file at the Air University Archives, Montgomery, Alabama.

Guderian, Heinz. *Panzer Leader*. London: M. Joseph, 1952.

Hart, B. H. Liddell. *The Other Side of the Hill*. London: Cassell, 1948.

Hoth, Hermann. *Panzer Operationen*. Heidelberg, Germany: K. Vowinckel, 1956.

Jollasse, Erwin. "9th Panzer Division (24 JULY–4 SEP 1944)." *Foreign Military Studies* MS #B-837. Historical Division, U.S. Army, Europe.

Keegan, John. *Six Armies in Normandy*. New York: Penguin Books, 1983.

Keilig, Wolf. *Die Generale des Heeres*. Friedberg, Germany: Podzun-Pallas-Verlag, 1983.

Kurowski, Franz. *Die Panzer Lehr Division*. Bad Nauheim, Germany: Podzun-Verlag, 1964.

Kursietis, Andris J. *Wehrmacht at War: The Units and Commanders of the German Ground Forces During World War II*. Soesterberg, The Netherlands: Aspekt, 1999.

Luck, Hans von. *Panzer Commander*. New York: Praeger, 1989.

Luettwitz, Heinrich. "XLVII Panzer Corps—Ardennes." *Foreign Military Studies* MS #A-938. Historical Division, U.S. Army, Europe.

———. "The Assignment of the XLVII Panzer Corps in the Ardennes, 1944–45." *Foreign Military Studies* MS #A-939. Historical Division, U.S. Army, Europe.

———. "XLVII Panzer Corps in the Ardennes Offensive," *Foreign Military Studies* MS #940. Historical Division, U.S. Army, Europe.

Manstein, Erich von. *Lost Victories*. Novato, CA: Presidio, 1982.

Marshall, S. L. A. *Bastogne: The First Eight Days*. Washington, DC: Infantry Journal Press, 1946.

McKee, Alexander. *Caen: Anvil of Victory*. London: Pan, 1966.

Mellenthin, F. W. *Panzer Battles: A Study in the Employment of Armor in the Second World War*. Anthony G. Powell, trans. Novato, CA: Presidio, 1982.

Mitcham, Samuel W., Jr. *Rommel's Lieutenants*. Westport, CT: Greenwood Press, 2006.

———. *Rommel's Desert Commanders*. Westport, CT: Greenwood Press, 2007.

Nafziger, George F. *The German Order of Battle: Infantry in World War II.* London: Greenhill Books, 2000.

Ritgen, Helmut. *Die Geschichte der Panzer-Lehr-Division im Westen, 1944–1945.* Stuttgart, Germany: Motorbuch-Verlag, 1979.

Rommel, Erwin. *The Rommel Papers.* B. H. Liddell Hart, ed. New York: Harcourt, Brace, 1953.

Shulman, Milton. *Defeat in the West.* London: Secker and Warburg, 1947.

Speidel, Hans. *Invasion 1944: Rommel and the Normandy Campaign.* Chicago: Regnery, 1950.

Stauffenberg, Friedrich von. Papers. Unpublished papers in possession of the author.

Tessin, Georg. *Verbaende and Truppen der deutschen Wehrmacht und Waffen-SS im Zweiten Weltkrieg, 1939–1945.* Osnabrueck, Germany: Biblio-Verlag, 1973–80.

U.S. Army Historical Division, U.S. Army, Europe. *Guide to Foreign Military Studies, 1945–54.* 1954.

U.S. Army Military Intelligence Division. "The German Replacement Army (Ersatzheer)." 1945. U.S. War Department.

Westphal, Siegfried. *German Army in the West.* London: Cassell, 1951.

Wilmot, Chester. *Struggle for Europe.* New York: Harper, 1952.

Young, Desmond. *Rommel: The Desert Fox.* London: Collins, 1950.

Index

Page numbers in italics indicate illustrations

African campaign
 Alam Halfa, battle of, 159
 Bayerlein at, 156–64
 Benghazi incident, 157
 El Alamein, first battle of, 158
 El Alamein, second battle of, 160–63,
 161
 El Duda incident, 157
 Funck at, 16–20
 theater of operations, *17*
 Tobruk, capture of, 158
Afrika Korps
 Bayerlein chief of staff of, 156
 withdrawal of, 163
Ardennes offensive, 75–78, 177–86
 battle plan, 179–80
 casualties, 183
Army Group B, disbandment of, 190
Aschen, Albrecht, 90
Aton contingency plan, 32

Baehr, Heinrich, 37
Balck, Hermann, 137, 176
Bartenwerfer, Lieutenant Colonel, 175,
 176
Battle Group Jollasse, 100
Bayerlein, Donat, 153
Bayerlein, Fritz, 41, 50, 78, *106*, 141,
 143, 144, 147, 153–94
 at African campaign, 156–64
 Afrika Korps chief of staff, 156
 ancestry, 153
 awards received by, 154, 157, 164, 174

on Bastogne battle, 191
blaming Model for failure to launch
 counterattack, 185
book collaborations of, 192–94
early military career, 153–54
on the Eastern Front, 155–56, 165–68
on estimate of battle readiness, 175
Franz on, 194
on Fuehrer Reserve, 156
German-Italian Panzer Army chief of
 staff, 164
Panzer Lehr Division commander,
 169
promotions of, 154, 164, 170
reports on operations at Western
 Front, 170–71
resentment of Stumme and Franz,
 160
Rommel relationship, 156
surrender of, 191
3rd Panzer Division commander, 165,
 166
on the Western Front, 169–71
Bayerlein, Luise, 153
Beck, Ludwig, 61
Berg, Elizabeth von, 60
Berg, Gustav von, 60
Berg, Kurt von, 52
Berger, Lothar, 20, 31
Bernuth, Julius von, 62, 63
Bismarck, Georg von, 159
Blaskowitz, Johannes, 137, 148, 150
Blomberg-Fritsch crisis, 6–7

Blumentritt, Gunther, 140
Bock, Fedor von, 13
Boineburg-Lensfeld, Hans von, 184
Boxberg, Albert von, 134, 142
Bradley, Omar N., 42
Brandenburger, Erich, 70, 148
Brauchitsch, Walther von, 85, 155
Breith, Hermann, 166
    Kursk offensive account, 33–34
Burgdorf, Wilhelm, 54, 69
Busch, Ernst, 184

Carell, Paul, 34, 166, 169, 171, 192–93
Choltitz, Dietrich von, 165
Cochenhausen, Ernst von, 135–36, 142
Cruewell, Ludwig, *103*, 156, 158

Decatur, Stephen, 129
Deckert, Hans-Joachim, 72, 139
Dehmel, Martin, 86
Denkert, Walter, 188
Detleffson, Erich, 63
Diesenhofer, Eduard, 42
Dietrich, Sepp, 45
Duvert, Walther, 123

Eastern Front
    Battles of Encirclement on, *26*
    Bayerlein on the, 155–56, 165–68
    Elverfeldt on the, 63–68
    Funck on the, 22–31, 32–34
    Jollasse on the, 84–93, 99–100
    Katyn Forest, 86
    Kiev, battle of, *88*
    Kirovograd, battles of, 166–68
    Klin, battle of, 30, 65
    Kursk, battle of, 125, *126*
    Kursk offensive, 33–34
    Luettwitz on the, 120–27
    map of, *24*
    Moscow, battle of, *66*
    Moscow Highway battle, 23
    Operation Barbarossa, 120–27, 155
    Operation Buffalo II, 67
    Operation Citadel, 33, 68, 92, 125
    Operation Kingfisher, 67
    Operation Robber Baron, 67
    Russian counterattack, 30
    Urgra, battle of, 91

Vyazma-Bryansk Encirclement, *28*
    Yefremov attack, 89
    Yelnia salient, 86
Eberbach, Hans, 39, *105*, 134
    on Avranches attack, 45–46
Eckesparre, Artur von, 46, 137,141
18th Panzer Division, 83
18th Panzer Regiment, 83–84
Elverfeldt, Ferdinand Johann Georg
    von, 59
Elverfeldt, Harald von, 59–79, *101*, 139,
    183
    ancestry, 59
    Ardennes offensive and, 75–78
    awards received by, 59, 62, 67, 79
    death of, 78–79
    early military career, 59–61
    on the Eastern Front, 63–68
    9th Panzer Division commander,
        69–70
    promotions of, 62, 67
    Siegfried Line campaign and, 71–75
    33rd Infantry Regiment commander,
        61
    Training School instructor, 69
    on the Western Front, 62–63
    wounding and hospitalization of, 77
Elverfeldt, Mechtilde Stephanie von, 60
Elverfeldt, Sigrid Maria von, 60
Engelmann, Jutta von, 115
Estor, Fritz, 84

Falaise
    "corridor of death" near, *109*
    destroyed convoy near, *107*
Fallois, Gerd von, 178, 183
Faupel, Wilhelm, 6
Fehn, Gustav, 163
5th Light Division, 14–15
    Funck commander of, 16
5th Panzer Regiment, Funck com-
    mander of, 8–9
52nd Infantry, Jollasse commander of,
    83
52nd Rifle Regiment, 83
    on the Eastern Front, 84–93
59th Rifle Regiment
    on the Eastern Front, 120–27
    Luettwitz commander of, 120

1st Reconnaissance Battalion, Luettwitz
  commander of, 119
Fischer, Wolfgang, 65
Fleck, Emil, 60–61
4th Cavalry Regiment, Luettwitz com-
  mander of, 118
47th Panzer Corps, Funck relinquishes
  command of, 50–52
408th Replacement Division
  on the Eastern Front, 99–100
  Jollassee commander of, 99
Franke, Hermann, 84
Franz, Gerhard, 159, 164, 191
  on Bayerlein, 194
  security violation incident, 160
Freiden, Seymour, 192
Fremerey, Max, 84
Friedel, Wilhelm, 70, 93
Friessner, Johannes, 35
Fritsch, Werner von, 4, *103*
Froehlich, Gottfried, 27, 31
  awards received by, 32
Froehlich, Richwein, 37, 137
Fuehrer Begleit Brigade, 147
Funck, Albrecht von, 1
Funck, Burkhard von, 9, 57
Funck, Carl von, 1
Funck, Hans Joachim von, 9, 35, 57
Funck, Hans von, 1–57, *106*, 129, 134,
  136, 170
  African campaign and, 16–20
  ancestry, 1
  awards received by, 12, 23, 31, 34–35
  Blomberg-Fritsch crisis and, 6–7
  capture of, 55
  death of, 57
  early military career, 1–8
  on the Eastern Front, 22–31, 32–34
  5th Light Division commander, 16
  5th Panzer Regiment commander,
    8–9
  on Fuehrer Reserve, 34–35
  imprisonment of, 56
  incidents involving soldiers and,
    21–22
  promotions of, 6, 16, 31, 36
  reasons for retirement of, 54–55
  relinquishes command of 47th Panzer
    Corps, 50–52

Reserve Panzer Headquarters XII
  commander, 53
  Rommel meeting, 36
  7th Panzer Division commander, 20
  3rd Panzer Brigade commander, 14
  on the Western Front, 36–50
  wounding of, 34
Funck, Irmgard von, 7

Gabler, Adolf, 13, 14
Gause, Alfred, 156, 158, 159
Gerhardt, Rudolf, 173, 175, 176, 179
German Army
  staff positions, 197
  U.S. Army comparative ranks, 195
German-Italian Panzer Army, Bayerlein
  chief of staff of, 164
Gersdorff, Rudolf von, 120
Glaesemer, Wolfgang, 32
Goering, Hermann, 160
Gorn, Walter, 92
Grolig, Oswin, 169
Guderian, Heinz, 3, 33, 53, 55, 89, *104*,
  117, 120, 124, 153, 155, 156, 169
Gultlingen, Lonnie von, 1

Halder, Franz, 61, 155
Hammer, Ernst, 150, 191
Hannut, battle of, 10–11
Harlessen, Ingeborg von, 82
Harpe, Josef, 188
Hart, Basil H. Liddell, 192
Hartlieb, Max von, 62
Hauser, Eduard, 31, 84
Hausser, Paul von, 41, *110*, 134, 172,
  175, 176, 179
Hausser, Wolf, 14
Henke, Willi, 146, 182
Heppendorf, Hermann von, 59
Herschel, Lieutenant Colonel, 37
  death of, 46
Heydebrand, Hans Christoph von, 120
Hirschberg, Anton von, 117
Hitler, Adolf, 41, *108*, 117, 136, 137,
  147, 155
  conspiracy to overthrow, 129
  great winter offensive, 141
  reactions to Funck report, 18–19
  suicide of, 100

Hitzfeld, Otto, 188
Hoepner, Erich, 120, 121
Holland campaign, 83
Horn, Hans-Joachim von, 8
Hossbach, Friedrich, 68
Hoth, Hermann, 62, 63, *112*
  in Fuehrer Reserve, 69
Hoyningen-Huehne, Oswald von, 8
Hube, Hans Valentin, 165
Hudel, Helmut, 185

Jodl, Alfred, 7
Jollasse, Brigitte, 82
Jollasse, Erwin, 81–100, *101*
  ancestry, 81
  awards received by, 82, 83, 85, 87, 88,
    89, 93
  Battle Group Jollasse commander, 100
  death of, 100
  early military career, 81–83
  on the Eastern Front, 84–93, 99–100
  52nd Infantry commander, 83
  408th Replacement Division
    commander, 99
  Inspectorate of Panzer Troops
    position, 99
  on 9th Panzer Division operations,
    93–99
  promotions of, 84, 92
  344th Volksgrenadier Division
    commander, 100
  on the Western Front, 93–99
  wounding of, 82, 91–92, 99
Jollasse, Harald, 82
Jollasse, Johannes, 81
Jollasse, Martilla, 81

Kauffmann, Lieutenant Colonel, 141,
  169, 183, 184
Keegan, John, 131
Keitel, Bodewin, 7, 16, *106*
Keitel, Wilhelm, 16, *108*
Keltsch, Rudolf, 84
  death of, 91
Kempf, Werner, 116
Kessel, Guido von, 63
Kessel, Mortimer von, 124
Kesselring, Albert, 150
Kleemann, Ulrich, 159

Klein, Captain, 177, 179
Kleinschmidt, Albrecht, 139, 141
Kleinschmidt, Eugen, 63
Kleist, Ewald von, 12–13
Klosterkemper, Berhard, 191
Kluge, Guenther von, 39, 40, 67, 134,
  137, 139, 171, 173
  suicide of, 47
Knobelsdorf, Otto von, 137
Koechling, Friedrich, 78
Kohler, Hello, 63
Kokott, Heinz, 141, 143, 144
Kraiss, Dietrich, 133
Kraus, Ewald, 71, 93
Krebs, Hans, 67
Krueger, Walther, 139
Kuehn, Friedrich "Fritz," 13, 14
Kuhnow, Otto, 172, 173, 175, 177
Kuntzen, Adolf, 61, 69, 79, 121
Kurowski, Eberhard von, 67

Lammerding, Heinz, 42
Landau, Christian, 188
Lang, Rudolph, 166, 168
Lauchert, Meinrad von, 76, 142, 143,
  144
Leeb, Wilhelm von, 120
Lemcke, Max, 32
Lemelsen, Joachim, 84
Liebenstein, Kurt von, *105*, 155
Lucht, Walther, 55
Luck, Hans von, 20, 21
Ludendorff, Erich, 114
Luebbe, Vollrath, 127
Luettwitz, Christa von, 116
Luettwitz, Ernst von, 113
Luettwitz, Hans von, 115, 137
Luettwitz, Hans-Jurgen von, 117
Luettwitz, Heinrich von, 40, 49, *101*,
  113–51, 182, 188, 189
  ancestry, 113
  awards received by, 114, 119, 121, 122,
    123, 136
  death of, 151
  early military career, 113–18
  on the Eastern Front, 120–27
  59th Rifle Regiment commander, 120
  1st Reconnaissance Battalion
    commander, 119

4th Cavalry Regiment commander,
118
imprisonment of, 150–51
101st Motorized Infantry Regiment
commander, 119
promotions of, 117, 118, 119, 121,
124, 125, 140
summons to surrender, 145–46
surrender of, 150
20th Rifle Brigade commander, 123
on the Western Front, 127–50
wounding of, 114, 119, 123, 136
Luettwitz, Karl von, 113
Luettwitz, Smilo von, *101*, 113
Luetzow, Marie von, 1
Lungershausen, Gunther, 27
Lutz, Oswald, 3

McAuliffe, Anthony C., 145, 146
McKee, Alexander, 131
Manstein, Fritz Erich von, 63, 64, 165
on his staff, 63–64
Manstein Plan, 9–13
map of, *10*
Manteuffel, Hasso von, 27, 29, 31, 34,
103, *110*, 138, 140, 142, 145, 146,
147, 182
Marshall, S. L. A.
on Luettwitz, 143
writing on Bastogne battle, 191
Marwitz, Georg von der, 46
Mauck, Wolfgang, 148
Mellenthin, Friedrich Wilhelm von, 77,
177
Merdorp, battle of, 10–11
Messe, Giovanni, 164
Meyer, Kurt "Panzer," 173
Mickle, Johannes, 20
Mieth, Friedrich, 88
Miracle of Dunkirk, 12
Mirbach, Maria von, 7–8, 9
Model, Walther, 49, 67, 68, 69, 71, 79,
103, 139, 146, 150, 173, 182, 185,
187, 188
disbandment of Army Group Border,
190
suicide of, 191
Monschau, Rudolph, 142
Montgomery, Bernard, 73, 148, 160

Mortain, battle of, 42–45
capture of German Landser in, *104*
map of, *43*
Muehlen, Kurt von, 138
Mueller, Gerhard, 50, 70, 81

Nehring, Walther, 83, 88, 91, 119, 154,
155, 156, 158, 159
Niemack, Horst, 184, 188
Niemann, Horst, 63
9th Panzer Division, 81
Ardennes offensive and, 75–78
Elverfeldt commander of, 69
employment on Normandy invasion
front, 94–98
Siegfried Line campaign and, 71–75
on the Western Front, 93–99
Normandy invasion, 93–99
Caen, *111*
troops, *110*, *111*, *112*
Nostitz, Eberhard von, 136
Nostitz-Wallwitz, Gustav von, 50

Ohrloff, Horst, 30
101st Motorized Infantry Regiment,
Luettwitz commander of, 119
111th Panzer Brigade, 138

Panzer Group Eberbach, strength
roster, 135
Panzer Lehr Division
Bayerlein commander of, 169
casualties, 177
order of battle, 189
orders for, 172
survivors of, 174
troops involved in Ardennes
offensive, 178–79
on the Western Front, 169–91
Panzer Troops School, Wunsdorf, *102*
Patton, George S., 138, 147
Poschinger, Joachim von, 175, 176, 177,
179
Puechler, Carl, 186

Radlmeier, Ludwig von, 117
Randow, Heinz von, 159
Reich, Johannes, 72
Reinhardt, Georg-Hans, 29

Reinhardt, Walther, 37, 46
Reisch, Johannes, 93
Rendulic, Lothar, 88
Reserve Panzer Headquarters XII,
   Funck commander of, 53
Richardson, William, 192
Ritgen, Helmut, 174–75, 177, 179
Rittberg, Jurgen von, 37
Roetiger, Hans, 67
Rommel, Erwin, 19, 20–21, 62, *105*, 129,
   153, 156, 160, 162, 163, 165
   Bayerlein relationship, 156
   Funck meeting, 36
   health of, 159
   at Hitler's headquarters in East
      Prussia, 163–64
   wounding of, 39
Rose, Maurice, 78
Rundstedt, Gerd von, 71

Sachsenheimer, Max, 99
Schaal, Ferdinand, 64, 65, 68, 79
   arrest of, 69
Schaffhausen, Stephanie, 60
Schell, Adolf von, 52, 54
Schellendorff, Heinrich Karl Bronsart
   von, 138
Scheller, Walter, 92
Schmidhuber, Gerhard, 127, 130
Schmidt, August, 167, 168
Schmidt, Paul Carl, *see* Carell, Paul
Schmidt, Rudolf, 61, 89–90
Schmundt, Rudolf, 68, 127, 165, 169, 174
   mortal wounding of, 69
Schoene, Major, 176, 177
Schoenfeld, Henning, 141, 142
Schraepler, Johannes, 84
Schroth, Walther, death of, 52
Schultz, Johannes, 92
Schulz, Adalbert, 32
Schwarz, Otto, 167
Schweppenburg, Leo Geyr von, 36, 37,
   38, *106*, 129
Schwerin, Gerhard von, 39, 40, 50, 184
2nd Panzer Division, 127
   order of battle, 130
7th Panzer Division
   on the Eastern Front, 32–34
   Funck commander of, 20
   journey to France, 31–32

order of battle, 20
   unit commendation received by, 27
Seydlitz, Friedrich von, 87, 90, 91
Shulman, Milton, 192
Siegfried Line campaign, 71–75
Sigler, Erich, 77
Speer, Albert, 125
Speidel, Hans, 129
Sperling, Max, 46, 49, 81, 84, 92, 93, 99
Sponeck, Karl Theodor von, 62
Stauffenberg, Claus von, ix
Stauffenberg, Franz Wilhelm, ix
Stauffenberg, Friedrich von, 194, ix–xi
   on Bayerlein, 153
Stefeldt, Wolf, 158, 159
Stein, Hans von, 115
Stein, Jutta von, 116
Steinkeller, Friedrich von, 20, 27, 31
Stever, Johann Joachim "Hajo," 62
Stohrer, Eberhard von, 7
Straube, Erich, 136
Streich, Johannes, 14, 19, 85
Stumme, Georg, 159, 160–61
   security violation incident, 160
Stumpff, Horst, 9, 120, 121, 175
Stunzner, Georg von, 90

tanks
   American, 199
   British, 199
   Ferdinand, 125
   German, 199
   Panther, *107, 108*, 125
   Russian, 199
   Sdkfz 234, *108*
   Skoda, 134
   T-34, 85
   Tiger, *109*
3rd Panzer Brigade, Funck commander
   of, 14
3rd Panzer Division
   Bayerlein commander of, 165, 166
   change of command in, 168–69
   reorganization of, 14
33rd Infantry Regiment, Elverfeldt com-
   mander of, 61
Thoma, Wilhelm von, 15, *105*, 121, 123,
   159
   capture of, 162
Thomale, Wolfgang, 31, 33, 55, 99

304th Panzer Grenadier Regiment, 135–36
344th Volksgrenadier Division, Jollasse commander of, 100
Thuengen-Rossbach, Karl von, 91
Treptow, Hans, 91
20th Rifle Brigade, Luettwitz commander of, 123
21st Army Group, 148

Ulex, Wilhelm, 120
U.S. Army, German Army comparative ranks, 195
Unrein, Martin, 167
Unruh, Klara von, 113

Vaerst, Gustav von, 159
vehicles, experimental half-track, *102*
Vormann, Nikolaus von, 35
Voss, Wilhelm, 166–67

Wachenfeld, Edmund, 3
Wagener, Carl Gustav, 147
Wagner, Hans, 99, 178
Waldenburg, Siegfried von, 148
Waldenfels, Wolfgang von, 118
Warlimont, Walther, 7
weapons, 88-millimeter antiaircraft, *112*
Weichs, Maximilian von, 123
Weiz, Rudiger, 134, 141
  Panzer Group Eberbach strength roster, 135
Wellmann, Ernst, 165, 166, 167
Wenck, Walter, 53, 54, 55
Western Front
  Allied drive to the Seine, *51*
  Ardennes, battle of, *149*

Ardennes offensive, 75–78, 177–86
Army Group B Area of Operations, *38*
Avranches attack, 45–46
Bastogne battle, 191
Bayerlein on the, 169–91
  casualties, 171
Elverfeldt on the, 62–63
Falaise Pocket, 47–49, *48*, 173
Falaise Sector, *44*
French campaign, 62–63
Funck on the, 36–50
hidden infantry squad on, *109*
Luettwitz on the, 127–50
map of, *128*
Mortain, battle of, 42–45
Normandy Front, 40
Normandy invasion, 93–99
Ruhr Pocket, battle of the, *187*, 187–91
Saar Union, battle at, 176–77
Siegfried Line campaign, 71–75
Villers-Bocage, battle of, 131–32, *132*
Westhoven, Franz, 120, 165, 166
Westphal, Siegfried, 158, 160, 161
Wilmot, Chester, 192
Wisch, Theodor, 41
Wolter, Hans, 90

Xylander, Wolfdietrich Ritter von, 68

Young, Desmond, 193

Zangen, Gustav on, 186
Zeitzler, Kurt, 124
Zimmermann, Bodo, 73
Zugehor, Gunther, 37
Zydow, Georg von, 14, 31, 37, 56, 57

Stackpole Military History Series

Real battles. Real soldiers. Real stories.

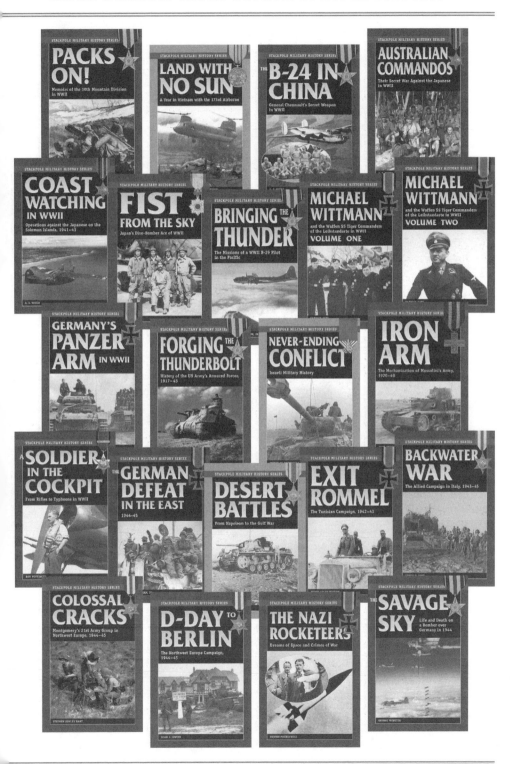

Stackpole Military History Series

Real battles. Real soldiers. Real stories.

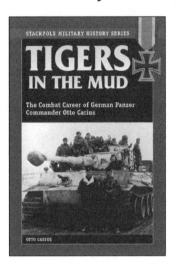

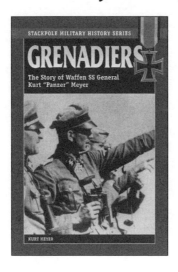

Stackpole Military History Series

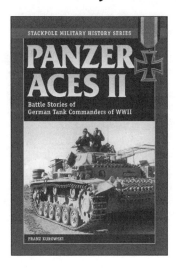

PANZER ACES II

BATTLE STORIES OF
GERMAN TANK COMMANDERS OF WORLD WAR II

Franz Kurowski,
translated by David Johnston

With the same drama and excitement of the first book,
Franz Kurowski relates the combat careers of six more
tank officers. These gripping accounts follow Panzer
crews into some of World War II's bloodiest engagements—with Rommel in North Africa, up and down
the Eastern Front, and in the hedgerows of the West.
Master tacticians and gutsy leaders, these soldiers
changed the face of war forever.

$19.95 • Paperback • 6 x 9 • 496 pages • 71 b/w photos

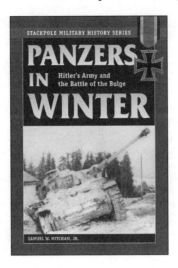

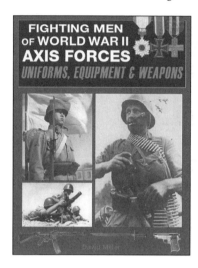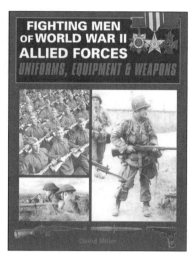